Italian Verbs For Dummies

MW01011942

Personal Pronouns

Subject Pronoun Classification	Singular	Plural
First Person	io (*I*)	noi (*we*)
Second Person	tu (*you*, familiar)	voi (*you*, familiar)
Third Person	lui (*he*), lei (*she*), Lei (*you*, formal)	loro (*they*), Loro (*you*, formal)

Conjugating the Seven Simple Tenses of Regular Verbs

To form these verb tenses, first determine which stem you need; then add the verb endings that I list in the table. Check out Chapters 1 and 2 for more information on forming verb stems.* Note that some **-ire** verbs require that you add an **-isc** to the stem before adding the verb ending. Check out Chapter 2 and Appendix A for more on **-isc** verbs.

Regular -are Verb Endings

Tense	io	tu	lui/lei/Lei	noi	voi	loro
Present	-o	-i	-a	-iamo	-ate	-ano
Imperfect	-avo	-avi	-ava	-avamo	-avate	-avano
Absolute Past	-ai	-asti	-ò	-ammo	-aste	-arono
Subjunctive	-i	-i	-i	-iamo	-iate	-ino
Future	-ò	-ai	-à	-emo	-ete	-anno
Conditional	-ei	-esti	-ebbe	-emmo	-este	-ebbero
Imperfect Subjunctive	-assi	-assi	-asse	-assimo	-aste	-assero

Regular -ere Verb Endings

Tense	io	tu	lui/lei/Lei	noi	voi	loro
Present	-o	-i	-e	-iamo	-ete	-ono
Imperfect	-evo	-evi	-eva	-evamo	-evate	-evano
Absolute Past	-ei	-esti	-è	-emmo	-este	-erono
Subjunctive	-a	-a	-a	-iamo	-iate	-ano
Future	-ò	-ai	-à	-emo	-ete	-anno
Conditional	-ei	-esti	-ebbe	-emmo	-este	-ebbero
Imperfect Subjunctive	-essi	-essi	-esse	-essimo	-este	-essero

Regular -ire Verb Endings

Tense	io	tu	lui/lei/Lei	noi	voi	loro
Present	-o	-i	-e	-iamo	-ite	-ono
Imperfect	-ivo	-ivi	-iva	-ivamo	-ivate	-ivano
Absolute Past	-ii	-isti	-ì	-immo	-iste	-irono
Subjunctive	-a	-a	-a	-iamo	-iate	-ano
Future	-ò	-ai	-à	-emo	-ete	-anno
Conditional	-ei	-esti	-ebbe	-emmo	-este	-ebbero
Imperfect Subjunctive	-issi	-issi	-isse	-issimo	-iste	-issero

*Future and conditional stems differ from the other tenses. See Chapters 10 and 11.

For Dummies: Bestselling Book Series for Beginners

Italian Verbs For Dummies®

Conjugating Six Compound Tenses of Regular Verbs

In Italian compound tenses, *transitive verbs* take the auxiliary verb **avere,** and *intransitive verbs* take the auxiliary verb **essere.** These auxiliary verbs accompany the past participle of the verb in question. In the tables below, I've used the past participles of **parlare** and **arrivare.** You can substitute the past participle of other transitive and intransitive verbs, respectively. See Chapter 14 and Appendix A for more information on forming past participles and transitive and intransitive verbs.

Regular Transitive Verbs (Parlare)

Tense	io	tu	lui/lei/Lei	noi	voi	loro
Present Perfect	ho parlato	hai parlato	ha parlato	abbiamo parlato	avete parlato	hanno parlato
Past Perfect	avevo parlato	avevi parlato	aveva parlato	avevamo parlato	avevate parlato	avevano parlato
Past Subjunctive	abbia parlato	abbia parlato	abbia parlato	abbiamo parlato	abbiate parlato	abbiano parlato
Past Perfect Subjunctive	avessi parlato	avessi parlato	avesse parlato	avessimo parlato	aveste parlato	avessero parlato
Future Perfect	avrò parlato	avrai parlato	avrà parlato	avremo parlato	avrete parlato	avranno parlato
Conditional Perfect	avrei parlato	avresti parlato	avrebbe parlato	avremmo parlato	avreste parlato	avrebberro parlato

Regular Intransitive Verbs (Arrivare)

Tense	io	tu	lui/lei/Lei	noi	voi	loro
Present Perfect	sono arrivato/a	sei arrivato/a	è arrivato/a	siamo arrivati/e	siete arrivati/e	sono arrivati/e
Past Perfect	ero arrivato/a	eri arrivato/a	era arrivato/a	eravamo arrivati/e	eravate arrivati/e	erano arrivati/e
Past Subjunctive	sia arrivato/a	sia arrivato/a	sia arrivato/a	siamo arrivati/e	siate arrivati/e	siano arrivati/e
Past Perfect Subjunctive	fossi arrivato/a	fossi arrivato/a	fosse arrivato/a	fossimo arrivati/e	foste arrivati/e	fossero arrivati/e
Future Perfect	sarò arrivato/a	sarai arrivato/a	sarà arrivato/a	saremo arrivati/e	sarete arrivati/e	saranno arrivati/e
Conditional Perfect	sarei arrivato/a	saresti arrivato/a	sarebbe arrivato/a	saremmo arrivati/e	sareste arrivati/e	sarebbero arrivati/e

Imperative Forms of Regular Verbs

Subject	Parlare (-are Verbs)	Prendere (-ere Verbs)	Partire (-ire Verbs)	Finire (-ire -isc Verbs)	Divertirsi (Reflexive Verbs)
tu	Parla!	Prendi!	Parti!	Finisci!	Divertiti!
noi	Parliamo!	Prendiamo!	Partiamo!	Finiamo!	Divertiamoci!
voi	Parlate!	Prendete!	Partite!	Finite!	Divertitevi!
Lei	Parli!	Prenda!	Parta!	Finisca!	Si diverta!
Loro	Parlino!	Prendano!	Partano!	Finiscano!	Si divertano!

For Dummies: Bestselling Book Series for Beginners

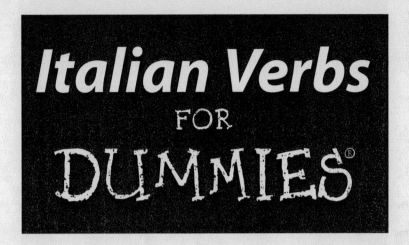

Italian Verbs
FOR
DUMMIES®

by Teresa L. Picarazzi, PhD

WILEY

Wiley Publishing, Inc.

Italian Verbs For Dummies®

Published by
Wiley Publishing, Inc.
111 River St.
Hoboken, NJ 07030-5774
www.wiley.com

For general information on our other products and services, please contact our Customer Care Department within the U.S. at 800-762-2974, outside the U.S. at 317-572-3993, or fax 317-572-4002.

For technical support, please visit www.wiley.com/techsupport.

Wiley also publishes its books in a variety of electronic formats. Some content that appears in print may not be available in electronic books.

Library of Congress Control Number: 2006925886

ISBN-13: 978-0-471-77389-4

ISBN-10: 0-471-77389-1

Manufactured in the United States of America

10 9 8 7 6 5 4 3 2 1

1B/RV/QY/QW/IN

WILEY

About the Author

Teresa L. Picarazzi has taught Italian language, literature, and cinema for over 20 years at a number of universities, including Dartmouth College, The University of Arizona, and Wesleyan University. She currently teaches Italian at The Hopkins School in New Haven. She has lived, studied, conducted research, and directed study-abroad programs in Florence, Siena, Urbino, Cortona, and Ravenna. She has two edited volumes and several articles in the area of contemporary Italian political theater and cultural studies. She is also the author of a feminist psychoanalytic book, entitled *Maternal Desire: Natalia Ginzburg's Mothers, Daughters, and Sisters,* on one of Italy's foremost twentieth-century authors. She lives in Connecticut with her husband, Giancarlo, their daughter Emilia, and their dog, Toby, during the school year and in Ravenna during the summer.

Dedication

I dedicate this book to all of my students, present and past. Without them I would never have written it. I also dedicate this book to my father, Domenico Picarazzi, for instilling in me a strong work ethic, love of Italian, and the importance of family.

Acknowledgments

I would like to first thank the two most industrious and creative editors one could ever imagine working worth: Josh Dials and Mike Baker from Wiley Publishing. Secondly, I need to credit my nephew, Giancarlo Marotti, for helping me to assemble Appendix B. Finally, I must thank my daughter, Emilia, and husband, Giancarlo, for putting up with me while I was writing this book — for their patience, understanding, support, and help.

Publisher's Acknowledgments

We're proud of this book; please send us your comments through our Dummies online registration form located at www.dummies.com/register/.

Some of the people who helped bring this book to market include the following:

Acquisitions, Editorial, and Media Development

Project Editor: Mike Baker

Acquisitions Editor: Tracy Boggier

Copy Editor: Josh Dials

Editorial Program Coordinator: Hanna K. Scott

Technical Reviewer: Elisa Lucchi-Riester

Editorial Manager: Christine Meloy Beck

Editorial Assistants: Erin Calligan, David Lutton

Cartoons: Rich Tennant (www.the5thwave.com)

Composition Services

Project Coordinator: Tera Knapp

Layout and Graphics: Andrea Dahl, Stephanie D. Jumper, Barry Offringa, Heather Ryan, Rashell Smith, Julie Trippetti

Proofreaders: Betty Kish, Jessica Kramer, Susan Moritz

Indexer: Kevin Broccoli

Publishing and Editorial for Consumer Dummies

Diane Graves Steele, Vice President and Publisher, Consumer Dummies

Joyce Pepple, Acquisitions Director, Consumer Dummies

Kristin A. Cocks, Product Development Director, Consumer Dummies

Michael Spring, Vice President and Publisher, Travel

Kelly Regan, Editorial Director, Travel

Publishing for Technology Dummies

Andy Cummings, Vice President and Publisher, Dummies Technology/General User

Composition Services

Gerry Fahey, Vice President of Production Services

Debbie Stailey, Director of Composition Services

Contents at a Glance

Table of Contents

Introduction

So, you love Italy and want to be able to read the classics of Italian literature, travel to small, out-of-the-way towns where people don't speak English, understand exotic singers' lyrics (such as Andrea Bocelli and Josh Groban), and carry on a conversation in an Italian train. Or, a bit less exciting but just as important, you're looking for extra information and practice so you can pass your next Italian test. Either way, welcome to *Italian Verbs For Dummies,* your fun and easy guide to all the tenses and conjugations of Italian verbs.

You can't get around using verbs in Italian. Most sentences in Italian require verbs in order to be complete sentences, just like in English. Italian verbs vary in tense (depending on whether you're talking about the present, the past, or the future); in mood (indicative and subjunctive); and in voice (active and passive) and person (depending on who or what does the action). Speaking in only infinitives would be nice and easy, but that type of talk won't get you very far — not when Italian has over 16 different tenses from which to choose (plus many irregular verbs, with their uncommon conjugation patterns to memorize)!

When speaking and writing in your native language, you unconsciously choose the correct tense without asking yourself if you need, for example, a verb in the conditional tense. But when you speak and write in Italian, you need to know what tenses to use, when to use them, and how to navigate them down the slippery path of constructing meaning. Italian verbs, with all their irregularities, exceptions, and situation-specific uses, can drive any earnest scholar crazy, which is precisely what *Italian Verbs For Dummies* is here for. No, not to drive you crazy — to help you overcome the confusion generated by the different tenses, moods, and voices. I've filled each of the chapters in this book with verb conjugations, varying uses of the different tenses, and plenty of practical exercises that allow you to conjugate the verbs in some type of context. Verbs don't exist in a vacuum, *vero?* They connect ideas and subjects to objects, and they allow you to ask questions, narrate, and communicate over a wide range of topics — from the every day to the sublime.

About This Book

Italian Verbs For Dummies is a review, a reference, and a workbook with exercises all wrapped into one package. In each chapter, I address a tense or a particularly unique verb that can span the tenses (like **piacere,** which means *to like*). I show you how to conjugate the verbs, and I provide you with examples in context. After I've said my piece, you get the chance to check your comprehension by applying your knowledge of the verbs in the practice exercises. (You can always check your answers in the Answer Key, too!)

In some exercises, all you have to do is conjugate the verbs I provide for you; in others, I ask you to translate what work you've just done. I also ask you some pretty open-ended questions that require you to bring together the different points of the chapter. Often, I ask you to travel with me to Italy and describe the things you're doing and seeing there so you can cast your verbs into some type of meaningful context, which is the best way to learn them. Yes, you can gain some benefit through drilling and repetition, especially for the purpose of memorizing forms, but nothing compares to actually creating the language when using it.

Conventions Used in This Book

I've adopted several conventions in this book for the sake of consistency. As you work through the text, you'll become familiar with the following:

✔ **Conjugation boxes:** I've created clear-cut conjugation boxes throughout the book to present many conjugations of verbs. The following figure shows a typical conjugation box. You see the Italian verb, its English translation, the three singular persons, the three plural persons, and an example sentence. I bold the verb ending for each person, and if the particular conjugation is irregular, I bold the whole verb.

parlare (*to speak*)	
io parl**o**	noi parl**iamo**
tu parl**i**	voi parl**ate**
lui, lei, Lei parl**a**	loro parl**ano**
Parli italiano? (*Do you speak Italian?*)	

✔ **Verb and vocabulary tables:** I often provide you with a different kind of table that illustrates a series of verbs or vocabulary terms that prove useful for one of the tasks in your chapter. In these tables, I provide you with the word in Italian and its translation. With some verbs or expressions, I also provide examples in context and their translations.

✔ **Instructions and examples for practice activities:** I include short, simple instructions for each exercise, and I precede the exercises with helpful examples. Both are designed to allow you to jump easily into the exercise.

✔ **Answer Keys:** At the end of a chapter, I create an Answer Key that provides the correct answers to the practice questions. At times, I give you a couple possible responses. With open-ended questions, I insert my subjective responses — all you have to do is check your verb form (and sentence structure) against mine to verify that you've answered yours correctly. Finally, I also include translations so that you can check your comprehension.

✔ **Abbreviations:** You quickly get used to the following abbreviations:

• sing. (singular)
• pl. (plural)
• masc. (masculine)
• fem. (feminine)
• fam. (familiar)
• form. (formal)

Foolish Assumptions

In the writing of this book, I've made some assumptions I hope are not too foolish!

✔ You already have some experience studying Italian, and you either need a different perspective and additional practice on a particular tense or you want to review and add to what you know about all the Italian verb tenses. (If you're a true novice, you may want to start with *Italian For Dummies* [Wiley], by Francesca Romana Onofri and Karen Antje Moller, and come back to see me a bit later.)

✔ You can pronounce everything you read in this book.

✔ You want to help your son, daughter, or grandchild with Italian homework, and you haven't spoken Italian for years.

✔ You're planning a trip to Italy and want to brush up on your Italian.

✔ You love Italian and Italy (just like me!).

How This Book Is Organized

You can approach this book in any way that will be beneficial to you. You can work on the chapters progressively, from start to finish, which makes sense from a practical point of view. Or you can jump around and work on the chapters that are most relevant to you and your situation: You don't have to master Chapters 2 through 7 to do Chapter 8, for example. I try to provide ample cross-references to point you to information from different chapters that will help illustrate a point in the chapter you happen to be working on. So, feel free to climb aboard at any of the following six parts of the book.

Part 1: Speaking of the Present

There's no time like the present to gather your ideas and base knowledge of verbs and their meanings. The present is your springboard to move into the future or hark back to the past. This part delineates the present indicative conjugations of regular and irregular verbs and reflexive verbs. You also find information on commands here because you generally speak commands in the present tense.

Part II: Looking to the Past and the Future

Part II covers a lot of territory: the future, the past, and even a different mood — the subjective subjunctive! This part should be the most challenging, but think of how proud you'll be when you master it! Here, I cover two of the main past tenses: the imperfect and the past absolute (preterit). You also start talking about the future with the future tense and conditionally with the conditional tense. I introduce the subjunctive mood as well, through the scope of the present and imperfect subjunctive tenses.

Part III: Building Compound Tenses

In Part III, you find the eight compound tenses that use **avere** (*to have*) and **essere** (*to be*) as auxiliary verbs. The tenses range from the present perfect, to the future perfect, to the past subjunctive. (Don't worry, the other five tenses are waiting for you, too.) You also discover how to determine which of the two helping verbs to use and how to form past participles (without which no compound tense in Italian is complete).

Part IV: Reviewing a Few Underappreciated Tenses and Forms

Part IV is the place where I bring together some of the most commonly used, yet underappreciated tenses and forms in Italian. Here, you discover hypothetical constructions throughout most of the tenses, with which you can form an "if" or "as if" clause. Similarly, I walk you through the impersonal si, which appears in all the tenses I've thus far presented. Finally, I present the gerunds and the progressive forms that you use with the gerunds. With the present progressive, you come full circle back to the present. How? Open this book and see!

Part V: The Part of Tens

In Part V, you find two Part of Tens, or lists that provide tips, warnings, and fun information. Specifically, you get the ten most frequently used Italian verbs and the ten Italian verbs most frequently mixed up.

Part VI: Appendixes

I put a few verb appendixes at the back of the book for easy and quick reference. One appendix provides a list of all the Italian/English verbs I use in this book (plus more); another provides an English/Italian list; and a third takes the top-ten greatest hits of irregular verbs and conjugates them in all their irregular forms.

Icons Used in This Book

This icon serves as a reminder to make certain you don't forget an essential piece of information.

Sometimes I throw in a tip that can save you time or provide added insight to getting a handle on the subject at hand.

I often use this icon when I'm done talking about something and am ready to show you exactly what I mean. If you get stuck on a particular practice exercise, looking back at the text that this icon accompanies can help.

This icon points out the directions for every practice set I include in this book.

Where to Go from Here

All *For Dummies* books are organized in self-contained modular parts so you can organize your approach in the way that best suits you. This, being a *For Dummies* book, is no different. You may want to work through one whole part and then move on to another part, trying a chapter here and there. Or maybe you want to turn straight to the chapter that reviews the particular verb tense you're currently working on in school or the tense with which you want to begin your review of Italian verbs. Although I provide many easy-to-understand chapters at the beginning of the book, I make sure that no single chapter is inherently any more difficult than another.

Part I
Speaking of the Present

The 5th Wave   By Rich Tennant

"Here's something. It's a language school that will teach you to speak Italian for $500, or for $200 they'll just give you an accent."

In this part . . .

The present is your springboard to move into the future or hark back to the past. This part delineates the present indicative conjugations of regular and irregular verbs and reflexive verbs. You also find information on commands here because you generally speak commands in the here and now.

Chapter 1

Jumping into Action with Italian Verbs

In This Chapter
▶ Running through the breakdown of Italian verbs
▶ Factoring pronouns into the verb picture
▶ Classifying verb categories by tense and mood

*W*elcome to the world of Italian verbs! I recently noticed, while reading an Italian children's story to my young daughter, that we expose young people at a very early age to *all* the verbs and tenses of a language. Evidently, when we learn a language naturally, from a young age, we don't learn to speak and master one tense and then move to another and another and so on; rather, we learn all the tenses together. Alas, you, the reader, are probably not a youngster. Therefore, I generally throw one tense at a time at you, but you should note that in authentic language construction, you may very well have several tenses going on at the same time.

One of the goals of this book is to help you feel at ease in all the tenses and constructions (individually and collectively) so that you can pass easily from one to the other without getting bogged down in wondering about conjugation and meaning. But every book has a beginning, and you've found a good place to start here. In this chapter, I break down the types of Italian verbs you'll see in this book. I let you in on how pronouns fit in. And I conclude with an introduction to the tenses and moods at work in the Italian language.

Breaking Down Italian Verbs

In Italian, just like in English, every verb has an *infinitive* (or infinito) form — the *infinitive* is the form of the verb you'd find if you looked it up in the dictionary. English often couples infinitives with the word *to*, as in *to eat* or *to drink*. In Italian, you can identify infinitive verb forms because they all end in **-are, -ere,** or **-ire**, as in **mangiare** (*to eat*), **leggere** (*to read*), and **dormire** (*to sleep*).

Infinitives are amazing bridges when learning Italian! Many nouns and adjectives are derived from verbs, so when you learn a verb, you often learn a noun and an adjective at the same time! For example, the noun "lavoro," which means *a job,* derives from the verb **lavorare,** which means *to work.* In Appendix A, you can find over 500 common Italian infinitives. Start familiarizing yourself with them right away and go back to the Appendix whenever you come upon a verb that you don't recognize.

All infinitives in Italian fall under three main verb types, also known as *conjugations.* I usually just call them **-are, -ere,** and **-ire** verbs:

> ✔ **First Conjugation** verbs have infinitives that end in **-are.** Some common examples of **-are** verbs include **parlare** (*to speak*), **giocare** (*to play*), and **telefonare** (*to call, to telephone*).

> ✓ **Second Conjugation** verbs have infinitives that end in **-ere**. Some common examples include **prendere** (*to take, to have*), **ripetere** (*to repeat*), and **mettere** (*to put*).

> ✓ **Third Conjugation** verbs have infinitives that end in **-ire**. Some common examples are **partire** (*to depart*), **capire** (*to understand*), and **aprire** (*to open*).

In addition to the infinitive form, each verb also has its own stem (or *root*). The *stem* of the infinitive is what you have left after you take the **-are**, **-ere**, or **-ire** ending off of it. For example:

> ✓ With First Conjugation verbs like **parlare** (*to speak*), the stem is **parl-**.

> ✓ With Second Conjugation verbs like **prendere** (*to take, to have*), the stem is **prend-**.

> ✓ With Third Conjugation verbs like **capire** (*to understand*), the stem is **cap-**.

Most stems follow this pattern and are regular. When you come upon an irregular stem in this book, though, I'll let you know that it doesn't follow this simple pattern. Stems are essential because they are the structures to which you attach the different verb endings of the different tenses. And most tenses use these stems (with the exception of the future and conditional tenses, which we get to in Chapters 10 and 11).

You can classify Italian verbs into these four broad categories:

> ✓ **Regular:** Regular verbs follow the standard verb conjugations for **-are**, **-ere**, and **-ire** verbs. (Check out Chapter 2 for a further introduction to regular verbs.)

> ✓ **Irregular:** The Italian language contains many challenging irregular verbs that don't follow a pattern of standard endings. Therefore, you need to memorize them (see Chapters 3 and 4).

> ✓ **Stem-changing:** Some verbs require a spelling modification or a stem adjustment, and I point these out to you throughout the book. You can find many of these verbs in Chapters 2 and 3.

> ✓ **Reflexive:** Reflexive verbs are conjugated just like **-are**, **-ere**, and **-ire** verbs — in all of the tenses. The one caveat is that reflexive verbs require their own set of reflexive pronouns. (I cover reflexive verbs in detail in Chapter 5.)

Here's your chance to review some verb infinitives before you jump into conjugations. Flip to Appendix A (if you don't know the verb already) and provide the translation of the following 15 verbs. Here's an example to get you started:

0. eleggere

A. *to elect*

1. dedurre *deduce*

2. trascinare *drag*

3. spingere *push*

4. bere *drink*

5. avvertire *to warn, inform*

6. sopportare *stand, bear, support*

7. concedere *concede*

8. accontentarsi di *to be satisfied with*

9. litigare *fight, argue*

10. sentire *hear, taste, feel*

11. dimagrire *lose weight*

12. appartenere *belong*

13. ricordare *remember*

14. opporsi *oppose*

15. fermarsi *to stop oneself*

Meeting the Personal Pronouns Face to Face

Italian verb conjugations feature three singular persons and three plural persons. Each verb, when conjugated, must correspond to a person. Additionally, a personal pronoun can substitute as the subject of a sentence. One of your main jobs is to know what personal pronoun to use and what person to conjugate your verb into; therefore, getting the pronouns down should be one of your first steps. Table 1-1 presents the pronouns that correspond to the three singular persons and the three plural persons.

Table 1-1	Classifying Subject Pronouns	
Subject Pronoun Classification	*Singular Subject Pronouns*	*Plural Subject Pronouns*
First Person	io *(I)*	noi *(we)*
Second Person	tu *(you,* familiar)	voi *(you,* familiar)
Third Person	lui *(he)*, lei *(she)*, Lei *(you,* formal)	loro *(they)*, Loro *(you,* formal)

Because you conjugate verbs according to the subjects that accompany them in Italian, the personal pronouns are redundant. So, after you master the personal pronouns, you don't really need to include them anymore, except in cases of emphasis. For example: "Mio marito **preferisce restare** a Ravenna tutta l'estate; io **preferisco viaggiare.**" (*My husband prefers to stay in Ravenna all summer; I prefer to travel.*) In this example, the "io" adds emphasis and contrasts what the husband prefers with what the speaker prefers; the "io" really means *I, on the other hand . . .*

Many students often get confused between the tu and Lei and the voi and Loro (because they all translate into *you* in English). Distinguishing between these constructions isn't as difficult as it first appears. Here are a few ways you can keep things straight:

- ✔ You use tu when speaking directly to one person with whom you're familiar (friends, children, and relatives, for example).

  "Tina, (tu) **mangi** a casa sabato?" (*Tina, are you eating at home on Saturday?*) **Note:** The tu isn't necessary in this sentence; I just add it to drive home the point that when you're on a first-name basis with someone, you use the tu form of the verb.

- ✔ You use Lei when speaking with someone whom you don't know very well or whom you may be meeting for the first time (anyone in a restaurant, hotel, post office, or shop, for example, or with professors and older people).

  "Professore, (Lei) **può ripetere** per favore?" (*Professor, would you please repeat?*) In this example, you're speaking to a professor, so you must use the Lei person.

- ✔ You use voi when speaking directly to more than one person.

  "Mamma e papà, (voi) dove **andate?**" (*Mom and Dad, where are you going?*) In this example, the subject is *you plural,* or voi (you're speaking to your Mom and Dad), so the verb has to be in the voi person as well.

- ✔ You use Loro very rarely. In fact, I include it in only a couple of exercises throughout the book. You hear the Loro person under formal circumstances, such as when you check into a hotel, and in the Loro command form (see Chapter 5).

  "Mi scusino!" (*Excuse me!*) Here you are speaking formally to more than one person.

In any exercise in this book, when you see a person's name followed by a comma, a lightbulb should go off in your head! This construction is your cue that the sentence is in direct discourse, which means you need to use the tu person, the Lei person, or the voi person verb form, according to the context. (You don't have to worry about the Loro person for the most part.)

In this exercise, identify what pronouns you'd use to speak *about* the following people. Here's an example:

Q. your doctor _____

A. lui

16. your daughter _____   21. you and your family _____

17. your students _____   22. your children _____

18. yourself _____   23. your girlfriend _____

19. your son _____   24. you and your wife _____

20. my mom and me _____   25. your husband _____

For this exercise, identify what pronoun you'd use to speak *to* the following people. Here's an example:

Q. your doctor _____

A. Lei

26. your sister _____   29. hotel concierge _____

27. your students _____   30. your grandmother _____

28. your best friends _____

Other Ways to Classify Verbs and Amaze Your Friends

You can use the contents of this section to amaze your friends (if they're really into Italian, I guess)! Okay, now that I have your attention, I'm going to cover some other pigeonholes and categories that people place various Italian verbs into. I use the terms I cover here throughout the book, so you can always turn back to this section if you get tripped up.

Tenses are verb inflections, or conjugations, that denote specific time distinctions, like the the present, the past, and future, for example. However, there are two over-arching types of tenses:

✔ **Simple:** A simple tense is made up of one verb only.

✔ **Compound:** A compound tense is made up of two verbs. The most common construction for compound tenses in Italian uses the auxiliary verb **avere** or **essere** (in whatever tense you need it) + a past participle.

All verbs are either transitive or intransitive (see Chapter 14 for the full story on distinguishing between transitive and intransitive verbs):

- ✔ **Transitive:** Transitive verbs may be accompanied by direct objects. They take the auxiliary verb **avere** (*to have*) when conjugated in a compound tense.

- ✔ **Intransitive:** Intransitive verbs take the auxiliary verb **essere** (*to be*) when conjugated in a compound tense.

Moods provide you with another way of distinguishing how to conjugate the verb. Each mood has its own set of tenses:

- ✔ **Indicative:** Verb tenses in the indicative mood express a fact or a certainty. The following tenses can be grouped under the indicative mood:

  - **Present** (*Il presente*). Simple tense. Includes reflexive verbs. See Chapters 2 through 5.

  - **Present perfect** (*Il passato prossimo*). Compound tense. Includes reflexive verbs. See Chapters 14 and 15.

  - **Imperfect** (*L'imperfetto*). Simple tense. See Chapter 8.

  - **Past perfect** (*Trapassato prossimo*). Compound tense. See Chapter 18.

  - **Past absolute** (*Il passato remoto*). Simple tense. See Chapter 9.

  - **Past anterior** (*Il trapassato remoto*). Compound tense.

  - **Future** (*Il futuro*). Simple tense. See Chapter 10.

  - **Future perfect** (*Il futuro anteriore*). Simple tense. See Chapter 16.

  - **Present progressive** (*Il presente progressivo*). Formed with **stare** + gerund, so, in a way, a compound tense. See Chapter 23.

  - **Imperfect progressive** (*L'imperfetto progressivo*). Formed with **stare** + gerund, so, in a way, a compound tense. See Chapter 23.

- ✔ **Subjunctive:** Verb tenses in the subjunctive mood express doubt or uncertainty:

  - **Present subjunctive** (*Il congiuntivo presente*). Simple tense. See Chapter 12.

  - **Past subjunctive** (*Il congiuntivo passato*). Compound tense. See Chapter 19.

  - **Imperfect subjunctive** (*Il congiuntivo imperfetto*). Simple tense. See Chapter 13.

  - **Past perfect subjunctive** (*Il trapassato congiuntivo*). Compound tense. See Chapter 20.

- ✔ **Imperative:** The imperative is the command form. I cover it in Chapter 6.

- ✔ **Conditional:** Verbs in conditional forms imply a condition or a supposition; in English, the conditional corresponds to the word *would* + a verb:

  - **Conditional** (*Il condizionale*). Simple tense. See Chapter 11.

  - **Past conditional** (*Il condizionale passato*). Compound tense. See Chapter 17.

You can find a wealth of information about Italian at your fingertips through the Internet. Just search for topics that interest you (newspapers, literature, music, summer attractions in specific towns [most towns have official Web sites], museums, cooking schools, and so on). You can hunker down with some Italian films in the evening. You can also find yourself an Italian pen pal to help you practice your Italian in concrete terms.

Answer Key

1	**dedurre** *to deduce*	*16*	lei
2	**trascinare** *to drag*	*17*	loro
3	**spingere** *to push*	*18*	io
4	**bere** *to drink*	*19*	lui
5	**avvertire** *to inform, to warn*	*20*	noi
6	**sopportare** *to be able, to stand*	*21*	voi
7	**concedere** *to concede, to allow*	*22*	loro
8	**accontentarsi di** *to be satisfied with*	*23*	lei
9	**litigare** *to argue*	*24*	noi
10	**sentire** *to hear, to feel, to smell, to listen to*	*25*	lui
		26	tu
11	**dimagrire** *to lose weight*	*27*	voi
12	**appartenere** *to belong*	*28*	voi
13	**ricordare** *to remember*	*29*	Lei
14	**opporsi** *to oppose*	*30*	tu
15	**fermarsi** *to stop*		

Chapter 2

Talking in the Present Tense

- -

- -

If you're going to learn one tense in Italian, it should be the present tense. The present tense is essential to speaking Italian, and you can use it in a number of situations, from asking directions, to describing your health, to simply chatting with the person next to you on the train. Italians love it when non-heritage speakers communicate with them in Italian, and there's no place to start like the present!

This chapter gets you started in Italian, because, as you'll see, the present tense can take you pretty far. Here, I present the regular present tense verb conjugations — **-are, -ere,** and **-ire** verbs. These groups of verbs are also known as *first conjugation, second conjugation,* and *third conjugation verbs,* respectively.

Making Use of the Present Tense

You use the present to talk about events or situations going on in the present (**studio;** *I'm studying*), habitual actions (**frequento** l'università; *I'm in college* and **parlo** italiano; *I speak Italian*), conditions (**sono** scapolo; *I'm a bachelor*), and states of beings (**sono** triste; *I'm sad*).

The present tense has different meanings depending on the context in which you use it. For example, "Io **mangio** la carne" can mean *I eat meat, I do eat meat, I'm eating the meat* (right now), or *I'm eating meat* (maybe later on, or for dinner).

But you may also use the present tense to talk about events or actions happening in the future, whether that future is later on, tomorrow, or next year! This is a very common practice, especially in spoken Italian. (See Chapter 10 for a discussion of the uses of the future tense.) Here are a couple examples:

- ✔ Domani **vado** in palestra. (*Tomorrow I'm going to the gym.*)
- ✔ La prossima estate, **studio** a Perugia. (*Next summer, I'll be studying in Perugia.*)

Conjugating -are Verbs

You can easily conjugate a present tense verb after you distinguish between the stem and the ending of the infinitive. (I cover the infinitives and the verb types in Chapter 1.) The *stem* is what you have left when you take the ending off, and with verbs ending in **-are,** that ending is **-are.** Here's an example:

parlare (*to speak*): The stem is **parl-,** and the ending is **-are.**

To conjugate present tense **-are** verbs, simply add the appropriate ending according to the subject onto the verb stem. In other words, the verb ending has to agree with the person (first-, second-, or third-person singular or first-, second-, or third-person plural). The following table shows you the present tense **-are** endings.

Present Tense **-are** Endings	
io — **o**	noi — **iamo**
tu — **i**	voi — **ate**
lui, lei, Lei — **a**	loro — **ano**

The following table presents an example of a regular **-are** verb conjugated in the present tense.

parlare (*to speak*)	
io parl**o**	noi parl**iamo**
tu parl**i**	voi parl**ate**
lui, lei, Lei parl**a**	loro parl**ano**
Lei **parla** italiano. (*She speaks Italian.*)	

Table 2-1 shows a list of common **-are** verbs that have the same endings as **parlare**. You can find many other common **-are** verbs in Appendix A.

Table 2-1   Common -are Verbs

Infinitive	Translation	Infinitive	Translation
abitare	to live	imparare	to learn
amare	to love	inquinare	to pollute
ascoltare	to listen to	insegnare	to teach
aspettare	to wait for	lavorare	to work
cantare	to sing	mandare	to send
camminare	to walk	pensare	to think
cercare	to look for	portare	to take, to bring
comprare	to buy	preparare	to prepare
contare	to count	provare	to try, to try on, to feel
continuare	to continue	ricordare	to remember
desiderare	to wish or desire	ritornare	to return
diventare	to become	suonare	to play an instrument
guardare	to watch, to look at	volare	to fly

Conjugate the following **-are** verbs in parentheses. Try this example first:

Q. Noi _____ Ravenna! (amare)

A. Noi **amiamo** Ravenna! (*We love Ravenna.*)

1. _____ gli occhiali? (portare [tu])

2. Noi _____ a casa dopo il film. (ritornare)

3. Massimo _____ di portare i libri a lezione. (ricordare)

4. Io _____ un po' di musica mentre _____. (ascoltare, lavorare)

5. Molte persone _____ il mondo ogni giorno. (inquinare)

6. Voi _____ la mamma? (aspettare)

7. AnnaMaria ed io _____ la cena di Natale. (preparare)

8. Quale strumento musicale _____? (suonare [tu])

9. Mia madre _____ sempre a tutto! (pensare)

10. _____ noi l'italiano? (imparare)

You need to pay attention to some spelling exceptions, though, for verbs ending in **-care, -gare,** and **-iare.** The following sections outline these exceptions.

Verbs ending in -care and -gare

With verbs like **pagare** and **dimenticare,** you need to add an **h** to the stem of the second-person singular (tu) and the first-person plural (noi) forms before adding the standard **-are** ending. You do this to maintain the hard "c" (as in the word "car") and hard "g" (as in the word "go") sounds throughout the verb conjugation. Check out some of the most common **-care** and **-gare** verbs in Table 2-2.

Table 2-2	Common Verbs Ending in -care and -gare		
Infinitive	*Translation*	*Infinitive*	*Translation*
dimenticare	*to forget*	**pagare**	*to pay*
giocare	*to play a sport, a game, or cards*	**sporcare**	*to dirty*
litigare	*to fight or argue*	**staccare**	*to take off, to detach, to unplug*
nevicare	*to snow*	**stancare**	*to tire*

You conjugate all verbs that end in **-gare** just like the verb **pagare** in the following table.

pagare (*to pay*)	
io pag**o**	noi pag**hiamo**
tu pag**hi**	voi pag**ate**
lui, lei, Lei pag**a**	loro pag**ano**
Noi **paghiamo** la cena. (*We're paying for dinner.*)	

You conjugate all verbs that end in **-care** just like I conjugate **dimenticare** in the table that follows.

dimenticare (*to forget*)	
io dimentic**o**	noi dimentic**hiamo**
tu dimentic**hi**	voi dimentic**ate**
lui, lei, Lei dimentic**a**	loro dimentic**ano**
Tu **dimentichi** sempre tutto! (*You always forget everything!*)	

Provide the proper subject pronouns for the following sentences. Here's an example:

Q. _____ pago.

A. **Io** pago. (*I am paying.*)

11. _____ pagate

12. _____ cerchi

13. _____ giochiamo

14. _____ dimentichiamo

15. _____ stacco

Now conjugate the following verbs in parentheses. Follow the example:

Q. Gix _____ la spina. (staccare)

A. Gix **stacca** la spina. (*Gix unplugs the plug.*)

16. _____ sempre i libri! (dimenticare [tu])

17. Emilia _____ il cane! (stancare)

18. _____ domani? (nevicare)

19. Noi _____ a calcio domenica. (giocare)

20. Mio marito ed io _____ poco. (litigare)

Verbs ending in -iare

Verbs ending in **-iare**, like **studiare**, **mangiare**, **viaggiare**, and **cominciare**, don't double up on the **i** in the second-person singular (tu) and the first-person plural (noi). You include only one **i** throughout these verbs' conjugations. The **i** in the stem, therefore, is dropped. Table 2-3 contains a number of common verbs ending in **-iare**.

Table 2-3	Common Verbs Ending in -iare
Infinitive	*Translation*
cominciare	*to begin*
mangiare	*to eat*
ringraziare	*to thank*
studiare	*to study*
viaggiare	*to travel*

The following verb table illustrates how to conjugate verbs ending in **-iare**.

mangiare (*to eat*)	
io mang**io**	noi mang**iamo**
tu mang**i**	voi mang**iate**
lui, lei, Lei mang**ia**	loro mang**iano**
Dove **mangi** stasera? (*Where are you eating tonight?*)	

In the following exercises, conjugate the verbs in parentheses. Here's an example:

Q. Con chi _____ domani? (mangiare [noi])

A. Con chi **mangiamo** domani? (*With whom are we eating tomorrow?*)

21. Dove _____ tu? (mangiare)

22. A che ora _____ la partita? (cominciare)

23. Noi _____ in Italia in autunno. (viaggiare)

24. _____ meglio di notte o di giorno? (studiare [voi])

25. Io _____ mia madre per la sua gentilezza. (ringraziare)

This exercise gives you the opportunity to mix it up with **-are** present-tense conjugations. Conjugate the following verbs in parentheses. Here's an example:

Q. Teresa _____ una lettera a Laura. (mandare)

A. Teresa **manda** una lettera a Laura. (*Teresa sends a letter to Laura.*)

26. Maria _____ la mamma. (cercare)

27. Marinella e Gianni _____ una casa. (comprare)

28. Mio padre _____ bene. (cantare)

29. Giancarlo ed io _____ a Ravenna. (abitare)

30. Tu _____ italiano? (parlare)

31. Tu e Emilia _____ a casa questa sera? (mangiare)

32. Loro _____ visitare l'Italia quest'estate. (desiderare)

33. Io non _____ mai la televisione. (guardare)

34. Mamma, _____ con la carta di credito? (pagare)

35. Noi _____ sempre i libri! (dimenticare)

Conjugating -ere Verbs

To conjugate **-ere** verbs in the present tense, you simply cut the **-ere** endings off of the infinitive verbs, and then you add the appropriate **-ere** present-tense endings, depending on the personal pronouns you're dealing with. The following table shows the endings of all regular **-ere** verbs. After you learn these endings, you will be able to conjugate any regular **-ere** verb.

Present Tense -ere Endings	
io — **o**	noi — **iamo**
tu — **i**	voi — **ete**
lui, lei, Lei — **e**	loro — **ono**

The following table presents a regular present-tense **-ere** verb, **correre**. In this case, **corr-** is the stem, and **-ere** is the ending.

correre (to run)	
io corr**o**	noi corr**iamo**
tu corr**i**	voi corr**ete**
lui, lei, Lei corr**e**	loro corr**ono**
Voi **correte** bene! (You (pl.) run well!)	

The verbs in Table 2-4 are conjugated just like **correre:** You keep the stems and add the endings. (You can find more **-ere** verbs in Appendix A.)

Table 2-4		Common -ere Verbs	
Infinitive	*Translation*	*Infinitive*	*Translation*
accendere	*to ignite, to light*	**perdere**	*to lose*
cadere	*to fall*	**piangere**	*to cry*

Infinitive	Translation	Infinitive	Translation
chiedere	*to ask, to ask for*	**prendere**	*to have* (like in a restaurant or bar), *to take*
chiudere	*to close*	**ricevere**	*to receive*
credere	*to believe*	**ripetere**	*to repeat*
crescere	*to grow, to raise*	**rispondere**	*to answer*
discutere	*to argue, to discuss*	**scendere**	*to descend/to go down* (the stairs), *to get off*
distruggere	*to destroy*	**scrivere**	*to write*
esistere	*to exist*	**smettere**	*to quit*
esprimere	*to express*	**spendere**	*to spend*
godere	*to enjoy*	**vedere**	*to see*
leggere	*to read*	**vincere**	*to win*
mettere	*to put, to place*	**vivere**	*to live*

Gianna is spending the summer studying in Urbino, a Renaissance city in Italy. Help Gianna write an e-mail to her mother to describe what's going on in her daily life by conjugating the verbs in parentheses.

Cara mamma,

Io ti ³⁶_____ (scrivere) dalla Fortezza a Urbino sul mio laptop: il panorama è stupendo! Ogni mattina ³⁷_____ (prendere) 0 un cappuccino e una pasta al Bar del Colle. Il Bar del Colle ³⁸_____ (ricevere) le paste fresche ogni giorno. Ogni giorno in classe la professoressa ³⁹_____ (scrivere) le nuove parole alla lavagna e noi studenti ⁴⁰_____ (ripetere). Poi tutti gli studenti ⁴¹_____ (leggere) ad alta voce il giornale. Noi ⁴²_____ (vivere) nel dormitorio dell'Università di Urbino, ma la mia amica Rachele ⁴³_____ (perdere) sempre la chiave, e ⁴⁴_____ (correre) molto! Mamma, perchè non ⁴⁵_____ (rispondere) a questa mia e-mail con il babbo?

Ciao, ti bacio!

Gianna

Conjugating -ire Verbs

In Italian, you come across two types of **-ire** verbs:

- Verbs that take **-isc** in some of the persons — you add an **-isc** to the stem for all the persons except for noi (first-person plural) and voi (second-person plural) before adding the standard ending
- Verbs that don't take **-isc** in any of the persons

The best way to learn the differences between these two verbs is by memorizing one or both of the tables that follow (Tables 2-5 and 2-6). ***Here's a hint:*** There are fewer **-ire** verbs that don't take the **-isc** in any of the persons, so you may want to memorize those. At the same time, it's easy to remember that a verb like **capire** (*to understand*) takes an **-isc** ending, because most folks have heard the word **Capisci?** (*Understand?*), at least in a movie; even Mr. Bubble says it on *Lilo and Stitch*.

The good news is that the endings are the same for both. The following table shows you the endings for all **-ire** verbs.

Present Tense -ire Endings	
io — **o**	noi — **iamo**
tu — **i**	voi — **ite**
lui, lei, Lei — **e**	loro — **ono**

-ire verbs that don't take an -isc ending

You can conjugate the verbs in Table 2-5 (those that don't take an **-isc**) like I conjugate **offrire** in the verb table that follows.

offrire (*to offer or to treat someone to something*)	
io offr**o**	noi offr**iamo**
tu offr**i**	voi offr**ite**
lui, lei, Lei offr**e**	loro offr**ono**
Offri tu i biglietti? (*Are you treating for the tickets?*)	

Table 2-5		Verbs That Don't Take an -isc Ending	
Infinitive	*Translation*	*Infinitive*	*Translation*
aprire	*to open*	**partire**	*to leave or depart*
dormire	*to sleep*	**seguire**	*to follow, to take a class*
fuggire	*to flee or escape*	**sentire**	*to feel, hear, touch, smell*
offrire	*to offer*	**servire**	*to serve, to be useful*

Conjugate the following **-ire** verbs from Table 2-5. Here's an example:

Q. Tu _____ quel buon profumo? (sentire)

A. Tu **senti** quel buon profumo? (*Do you smell that nice scent?*)

46. Io _____ la cena! (offrire)

47. A che ora _____ tu? (partire)

48. Emilia _____ bene! (dormire)

49. Io _____ uno strano rumore. (sentire)

50. Loro _____ la cena alle otto. (servire)

-ire verbs that take -isc

The following table shows the conjugation for the verb **capire**. In the first three singular persons (io, tu, lei) and in the third-person plural (loro), you must insert **-isc** between the stem and the **-ire** ending. The first-person singular (io **capisco**) and the third-person plural (**capiscono**) have hard "c" sounds. The second-person (tu **capisci**) and third-person (lei **capisce**) singular have soft "sh" sounds. And you conjugate the noi and voi persons just like you do the **-ire** verbs that don't take the **-isc** ending.

capire (*to understand*)	
io cap**isco**	noi cap**iamo**
tu cap**isci**	voi cap**ite**
lui, lei, Lei cap**isce**	loro cap**iscono**
Tu **mi capisci?** (*Do you understand me?*)	

You can conjugate the verbs in Table 2-6 (those that take an **-isc** ending in some persons) like I do for **capire** in the previous table.

Table 2-6	-ire Verbs That Take an -isc Ending		
Infinitive	*Translation*	*Infinitive*	*Translation*
arrossire	*to blush*	**impazzire**	*to go crazy*
capire	*to understand*	**impedire**	*to prevent*
costruire	*to build, to construct*	**preferire**	*to prefer*
finire	*to finish*	**pulire**	*to clean*
gradire	*to wish*	**restituire**	*to give back, to return*
guarire	*to heal*	**sparire**	*to disappear*

restituo

Now you can practice with full sentences. Conjugate the following verbs as I do the following example:

Q. Jodi _____ la carne. (preferire)

A. Jodi **preferisce** la carne. (*Jodi prefers the meat.*)

51. Noi _____ sempre il compito. (finire)

52. Gli studenti _____ bene l'italiano! (capire)

53. Il babbo _____ la casa? (pulire)

54. Voi _____ tutto? (restituire)

55. Tu _____ questi stivali? (preferire)

Putting It All Together

For this set of exercises, insert the correct form of the regular present tense into the brief dialogues. Follow my lead:

Q. Lui: _____ quella musica? (sentire)

Lei: No, non _____ niente! (sentire)

A. Lui: **Senti** quella muscia? (*Do you hear that music?*)

Lei: No, non **sento** niente! (*No, I don't hear anything.*)

56. Sandro: Abi, _____ per l'esame d'italiano questa sera? (studiare)

Abi: No, _____ dormire! (preferire [io])

57. Nina: Mamma, cosa _____ stasera? (mangiare [noi])

Mamma: _____ un po' di pollo. (preparare [io])

58. Anna Maria: Daniel, Giancarlo, e Maria, perchè non _____ le vostre camere oggi? (pulire)

Daniel, Giancarlo, Maria: Perchè _____ a calcio tutto il giorno. (giocare)

59. Nicole: L'anno prossimo _____ il primo anno dell'università. (frequentare [io])

Maria Paola: _____ di guidare all'università? (pensare [tu])

Nicole: No, Mamma, _____ il treno o l'autobus, o mi _____ tu! (prendere [io], portare)

60. Laurie: _____ queste scarpe nere. (comprare [io])

John: Come _____, in contanti o con la carta di credito? (pagare [tu])

Answer Key

1. **Porti** gli occhiali? (*Do you wear glasses?*)

2. Noi **ritorniamo** a casa dopo il film. (*We're going back home after the film.*)

3. Massimo **ricorda** di portare i libri a lezione. (*Massimo remembers to bring his books to class.*)

4. Io **ascolto** un po' di musica mentre **lavoro.** (*I listen to a little music while I work.*)

5. Molte persone **inquinano** il mondo ogni giorno. (*Many people pollute the world every day.*)

6. Voi **aspettate** la mamma? (*Are you (pl.) waiting for mom?*)

7. AnnaMaria ed io **prepariamo** la cena di Natale. (*AnnaMaria and I are preparing Christmas dinner.*)

8. Quale strumento musicale **suoni?** (*What musical instrument do you play?*)

9. Mia madre **pensa** sempre a tutto! (*My mom always thinks of everything!*)

10. **Impariamo** noi l'italiano? (*Are we learning Italian?*)

11. **Voi** pagate (*You're paying*)

12. **Tu** cerchi (*You look for*)

13. **Noi** giochiamo (*We play, We're playing*)

14. **Noi** dimentichiamo (*We forget*)

15. **Io** stacco (*I unplug*)

16. **Dimentichi** sempre i libri! (*You always forget your books!*)

17. Emilia **stanca** il cane! (*Emilia is tiring the dog!*)

18. **Nevica** domani? (*Is it going to snow tomorrow?*)

19. Noi **giochiamo** a calcio domenica. (*We're playing soccer on Sunday.*)

20. Mio marito ed io **litighiamo** poco. (*My husband and I don't argue much.*)

21. Dove **mangi** tu? (*Where are you eating?*)

22. A che ora **comincia** la partita? (*At what time does the game begin?*)

23. Noi **viaggiamo** in Italia in autunno. (*We're traveling to Italy in the fall.*)

24. **Studiate** meglio di notte o di giorno? (*Do you (pl.) study better at night or in the day?*)

25. Io **ringrazio** mia madre per la sua gentilezza. (*I'm thanking my mom for her kindness.*)

26. Maria **cerca** la mamma. (*Maria's looking for her mom.*)

27. Marinella e Gianni **comprano** una casa. (*Marinella and Gianni are buying a house.*)

28. Mio padre **canta** bene. (*My dad sings well.*)

29. Giancarlo ed io **abitiamo** a Ravenna. (*Giancarlo and I live in Ravenna.*)

30. Tu **parli** italiano? (*Are you speaking Italian; Do you speak Italian?*)

31 Tu e Emilia **mangiate** a casa questa sera? (*Are you and Emilia eating at home tonight?*)

32 Loro **desiderano** visitare l'Italia quest'estate. (*They wish to visit Italy this summer.*)

33 Io non **guardo** mai la televisione. (*I never watch television.*)

34 Mamma, **paghi** con la carta di credito? (*Mom, are you paying with a credit card?*)

35 Noi **dimentichiamo** sempre i libri! (*We always forget our books!*)

36 **scrivo**	**38** **riceve**	**40** **ripetiamo**	**42** **viviamo**	**44** **corriamo**
37 **prendo**	**39** **scrive**	**41** **leggono**	**43** **perde**	**45** **rispondi**

46 Io **offro** la cena! (*Dinner is my treat!*)

47 A che ora **parti** tu? (*What time are you leaving?*)

48 Emilia **dorme** bene! (*Emilia sleeps well!*)

49 Io **sento** uno strano rumore. (*I hear a strange noise.*)

50 Loro **servono** la cena alle otto. (*They're serving dinner at eight.*)

51 Noi **finiamo** sempre il compito. (*We always finish our homework.*)

52 Gli studenti **capiscono** bene l'italiano! (*The students understand Italian well!*)

53 Il babbo **pulisce** la casa? (*Is daddy cleaning the house?*)

54 Voi **restituite** tutto? (*Are you (pl.) giving everything back?*)

55 Tu **preferisci** questi stivali? (*Do you prefer these boots?*)

56 Sandro: Abi, **studi** per l'esame d'italiano questa sera? (*Abi, are you studying for the Italian exam tonight?*)

Abi: No, **preferisco** dormire! (*No, I prefer to sleep!*)

57 Nina: Mamma, cosa **mangiamo** stasera? (*Mom, what are we eating tonight?*)

Mamma: **Preparo** un po' di pollo. (*I'm making some chicken.*)

58 Anna Maria: Daniel, Giancarlo, e Maria, perchè non **pulite** le vostre camere oggi? (*Daniel, Giancarlo, and Maria, why don't you clean your rooms today?*)

Daniel, Giancarlo, Maria: Perchè **giochiamo** a calcio tutto il giorno. (*Because we're playing soccer all day.*)

59 Nicole: L'anno prossimo **frequento** il primo anno dell'università. (*Next year I'll be attending my first year of college.*)

Maria Paola: **Pensi** di guidare all'università? (*Do you think that you're going to drive to school?*)

Nicole: No, Mamma, **prendo** il treno o l'autobus, o **mi porti** tu! (*No, Mom, I'll take the bus, or you can bring me!*)

60 Laurie: **Compro** queste scarpe nere. (*I'm going to buy these black shoes.*)

John: Come **paghi,** in contanti o con la carta di credito? (*How are you going to pay, with cash or a credit card?*)

Chapter 3

Talking in the Present Tense with Irregular Verbs

In This Chapter

▶ Addressing the most common irregular verbs

▶ Speaking of movement with **venire** and **andare**

▶ Announcing your needs, wants, and abilities

▶ Mastering the essentials: Telling and going

▶ Rewarding yourself with a lesson in drinks

▶ Mingling with uncommon irregular verbs

Italian features some frequently used verbs that are irregular in the present tense (in other words, the verbs aren't conjugated in the regular way). (For a discussion of the uses of regular present tense verbs, see Chapter 2.) You need these verbs for basic daily communication and function in Italian. The language also features some not-so-common verbs that are irregular in the present tense; these verbs come in handy when reading and writing and when talking about more complex issues.

In this chapter, you work on conjugating various irregular verbs. Some are grouped according to similarities in their conjugation and frequency of use (like the verbs **dare, fare,** and **stare**); others (like **andare** and **venire**) are grouped together because you can talk about coming and going with those two very common irregular verbs (even though their conjugations are completely different). The verbs **dovere, volere,** and **potere** are grouped together because they often function as helping verbs and are always presented together in a classroom. In another section, I've placed **dire** and **uscire** together because there are some similarities in pronunciation. Finally, I include a section of three different types of irregular verbs — verbs that all follow the same conjugation pattern.

Conjugating the "Little Verbs": Dare, Stare, and Fare

The irregular verbs **dare** (*to give*), **stare** (*to be* or *to stay*), and **fare** (*to do* or *to make*) are bound to enter many sentences that appear in everyday conversation, and, thankfully, they share some similarities in conjugation for the present tense — especially in the loro form (third-person plural). In the tables that follow, I present their conjugations.

dare (*to give*)	
io d**o**	noi d**iamo**
tu d**ai**	voi d**ate**
lui, lei, Lei d**à**	loro d**anno**
Loro **mi danno** un bacio. (*They give me a kiss.*)	

The most common translation and use of the verb **dare** is *to give*. But it can also mean *to take* — **dare** un esame (*an exam*) — and *to have* — **dare** una festa (*a party*). Giving (money), taking (exams), and partying . . . necessary words for any scholar!

stare (*to be* or *to stay*)	
io st**o**	noi st**iamo**
tu st**ai**	voi st**ate**
lui, lei, Lei st**a**	loro st**anno**
Come **stai?** Io **sto** bene, grazie, e tu? (*How are you? I'm well, thanks, and you?*)	

The verb **stare's** primary translation is *to be,* but it also means *to pay attention/to be careful* — **stare attento/a/i/e** — and *to be quiet* — **stare zitto/a/i/e.** Words necessary for any loving/nagging parent or significant other. The adjectives "attento" and "zitto" must agree in gender and number with the subject. (For more on adjectives agreeing with subjects, please see Chapter 4.)

fare (*to do* or *to make*)	
io **faccio**	noi **facciamo**
tu **fai**	voi **fate**
lui, lei, Lei **fa**	loro **fanno**
Fate i compiti ogni giorno? (*Do you* (pl.) *do your homework every day?*)	

The verb **fare** means *to do* or *to make,* as in *to do* your homework or *to make* a cake. **Fare** also serves an idiomatic purpose with a great many common expressions. Table 3-1 provides you with a list of some of **fare's** different meanings when coupled with nouns.

Table 3-1	Common Idiomatic Uses of the Verb Fare		
Infinitive	*Translation*	*Infinitive*	*Translation*
fare una passeggiata	*to take a walk*	**fare** un pisolino	*to take a nap*
fare due passi	*to take a short walk*	**fare** la spesa	*to go shopping* (grocery)
fare due chiacchiere	*to chat*	**fare** le spese	*to shop* (like for clothing)
fare una telefonata	*to make a phone call*	**fare** bella figura	*to impress; to make a good impression*

Infinitive	Translation	Infinitive	Translation
fare una foto	*to take a picture*	**fare** benzina	*to get gas*
fare le fusa	*to purr*	**fare** autostop	*to hitchhike*
fare la valigia	*to pack a suitcase*	**fa** bello	*it's nice out* (weather)
fare un viaggio	*to take a trip*	**fa** brutto	*it's not nice out* (weather)
fare la fila	*to wait in line*	**fa** caldo	*it's hot* (temperature)
fare una domanda	*to ask a question*	**fa** freddo	*it's cold* (temperature)
fare colazione	*to have breakfast*	**fa** fresco	*it's cool* (temperature)
fare merenda	*to have a snack*	**fare** schifo	*to disgust*

As you can see from Table 3-1, you'll often opt to use the third-person singular form of **fare** (**fa**) to describe the weather. You can use the expression "Che tempo **fa?**" to ask about the weather.

Time to practice what you've discovered about irregular verbs in the present tense. For this exercise, provide subject pronouns for the already conjugated verbs. Remember, you may have more than one subject pronoun for the third-person singular! Follow my example:

Q. _____ do

A. **io** do (*I give*)

1. _____ fai

2. _____ dà

3. _____ stanno

4. _____ fate

5. _____ facciamo

6. _____ sto

7. _____ danno

Now you can put your brain in reverse and answer the following personal questions by conjugating the verbs. Use sì for "yes" and no, non for "no." Here's an example to show you how the sì and no format works (your answers will be purely subjective, as mine are in the answer key):

Q. Stai attenta quando guidi? (*Are you* (fam.) *careful when you drive?*)

A. Sì, **sto** attenta quando **guido.** (*Yes, I am careful when I drive.*)

A. No, non **sto** attenta quando **guido.** (*No, I'm not careful when I drive.*)

8. Fai sempre colazione?

_____

9. Fai un viaggio in Italia quest'estate?

_____

10. Dai una festa domani?

_____

11. Stai zitto o preferisci parlare quando conosci qualcuno per la prima volta?

_____

12. Dai regali spesso (often)?

_____

13. Stai male?

_____

For this final **dare, stare, fare** exercise, put your knowledge together to conjugate the verbs in parentheses and translate the sentences. Here's an example to get you going:

Q. Emilia _____ merenda ogni pomeriggio dopo scuola. (fare)

A. Emilia **fa** merenda ogni pomeriggio dopo scuola. _Emilia has a snack every afternoon after school._

14. Noi _____ molte domande. (fare)

_____

15. _____ la valigia tuo marito? (fare)

_____

16. Emilia _____ zitta. (stare)

_____

17. Io _____ un esame domani. (dare)

_____

18. Loro _____ sempre una mano a tutti. (dare)

_____

19. _____ bello oggi! (fare)

_____

20. Voi _____ attenti quando parlo? (stare)

_____

Coming and Going with Venire and Andare

You need the verbs **venire** (*to come*) and **andare** (*to go*) in your verbal toolbox if you want to make busy plans in Italy, ask your teacher if you can go to the restroom, or impress a date at an Italian restaurant. Although their use in Italian is very similar to their use in English, these verbs often pair up with different prepositions: "**Vengo** dal ristorante" (*I'm coming from the restaurant*) and "**Vado** al cinema" (*I'm going to the movies*), for example. I present the conjugations of the verbs **venire** and **andare** in the following tables.

venire (*to come*)	
io **vengo**	noi ven**iamo**
tu **vieni**	voi ven**ite**
lui, lei, Lei **viene**	loro **vengono**
Venite alla mia festa? (*Are you* (pl.) *coming to my party?*)	

andare (*to go*)	
io **vado**	noi and**iamo**
tu **vai**	voi and**ate**
lui, lei, Lei **va**	loro **vanno**
Vai in Italia? (*Are you going to Italy?*)	

Conjugate the verbs **venire** and **andare** in the following problems, according to the subjects at hand. Here's an example:

Q. Tu e Maria _____. (andare)

A. Tu e Maria **andate.** (*You and Maria go.*)

21. Io _____. (venire)

22. I miei amici _____. (andare)

23. Noi _____. (venire)

24. Tu _____. (venire)

25. Matteo _____. (andare)

26. Tu e Sofia _____. (andare)

27. Francesca e Fabrizio _____. (venire)

28. Noi _____. (andare)

29. Tu _____. (andare)

In Italian, the phrases for the different means of transportation take different prepositions. Just like in English, you can go *by* car, *by* train, *on* foot, and so on from one place to another. Similarly, you use different prepositions when talking about the different places you go and how you plan to get there. Table 3-2 can help you find out which prepositions and expressions you should use with the verbs **andare** and **venire.**

Table 3-2	Prepositions Often Paired with Andare and Venire
Andare/Venire Prepositional Phrase	*Translation*
andare/venire a piedi	*to walk* or *to go/to come on foot*
andare a cavallo	*to go horseback riding*
andare/venire in macchina	*to go/to come by car*
andare/venire in autobus	*to go/to come by bus*
andare in bici	*to go by bike*
andare/venire in treno	*to go/to come by train*
andare/venire in aereo	*to go/to come by plane*
andare/venire in traghetto	*to go/to come by ferry*
andare in barca a vela	*to go sailing*
andare a + città, isola piccola, . . .	*to go to a city, small island, . . .*
andare in + paese, stati, regioni, isole grandi, . . .	*to go to a country, a state, a region, a large island, . . .*
venire da	*to come from*

The following sentences describe a trip you're taking with a couple of friends to Italy to visit your friend Pino who lives in Taormina. Pino is very curious to know how you plan to get there, not to mention get from one place to another when you *are* there. Address all his worrisome questions by conjugating the verbs in the answers I provide. Follow my example.

Keep these guidelines in mind for answering questions as you proceed with this exercise:

✔ If a question appears in the tu (second-person singular), answer in the io (first-person singular) form of the verb.

✔ If a question appears in the voi (second-person plural), answer in the noi (first-person plural).

✔ If a question appears in the lui/lei (third-person singular) or loro (third-person plural), answer in those persons as well.

Q. Come vieni in Italia? (*How are you coming to Italy?*) _____ in aereo. (Venire)

A. **Vengo** in aereo. (*I'm coming by plane.*)

30. Come andate da Roma a Napoli? _____ in treno. (andare)

31. Come vieni dalla Calabria in Sicilia? _____ in traghetto. (venire)

32. I tuoi amici come vanno da Roma a Frosinone? _____ in macchina. (venire)

33. Il tuo amico Giorgio viene anche a Taormina? Sì, Giorgio _____ a Taormina. (venire)

34. Dove vai dopo che visiti Agrigento? _____ a Siracusa. (venire)

35. Perchè non venite tutti a trovarmi? _____ a trovarti solo io e Giorgio perchè gli altri amici vanno a trovare i parenti a Palermo. (venire)

Declaring Your Needs, Wants, and Abilities: Dovere, Volere, and Potere

Mastering the irregular verbs **volere** (*to want*), **dovere** (*to need to, to have to, must, should, ought*), and **potere** (*to be able to, can*) puts you on the road to building more sophisticated sentences and allows you to declare your needs, wants, and abilities. I group these remarkable verbs because they share some similarities in conjugation — for example, the io (first-person singular) and the loro (third-person plural) share the same stem, and the voi (second-person plural) has a regular **-ere** ending. Furthermore, you often conjugate these three verbs and then follow them with an infinitive: "**Devo studiare**" (*I need to/I have to/I must/I should study*), for example. The only downside? You really need to memorize these verbs in order to learn them. I'm sure that you can.

Volere almost always means *to want*, but it can also mean *I love you* — "Ti **voglio** bene!" — in the idiomatic expression often addressed to a friend or relative, and sometimes to your partner.

The following three tables present the conjugations of **volere, dovere,** and **potere.**

volere (*to want*)	
io **voglio**	noi **vogliamo**
tu **vuoi**	voi vol**ete**
lui, lei, Lei **vuole**	loro **vogliono**
Volete andare al cinema stasera? (*Do you* (pl.) *want to go to the movies tonight?*)	

Dovere's stem becomes **dev-** in the first three singular persons (io, tu, and lui) and in the third-person plural (loro). After you've adjusted the stem to **dev-** or **dobb-** (for the noi person), just add the regular **-ere** endings (see Chapter 2).

dovere (*to need to, to have to, must, should, ought*)	
io **devo**	noi **dobbiamo**
tu **devi**	voi dov**ete**
lui, lei, Lei **deve**	loro **devono**
Dobbiamo fare la valigia. (*We need to pack.*)	

potere (*to be able to, can, may*)	
io **posso**	noi **possiamo**
tu **puoi**	voi pot**ete**
lui, lei, Lei **può**	loro **possono**
Scusi, **può dirmi** dov'è il Palazzo Pitti, per favore? (*Excuse me, can you* (form., sing.) *please tell me where the Pitti Palace is?*)	

The noun "potere" means *power*. If you use some creative liberties, you can pull the word "potent" from potere. This may help you remember the meaning of the verb **potere**. When you're potent and empowered, you can do it!

Put the need, want, and ability verbs to use by conjugating the verbs in parentheses in the following exercise. Here's an example:

Q. Non _____ andare a scuola oggi! (volere)

A. Non **voglio** andare a scuola oggi! (*I don't want to go to school today!*)

36. Noi _____ telefonare a casa. (dovere)

37. La mamma _____ fare la spesa. (volere)

38. Tu _____ giocare a tennis oggi? (potere)

39. Maria e Domenico _____ andare in Florida. (dovere)

40. Che cosa _____ mangiare questa sera? (volere [voi])

41. Io _____ venire alla festa ma non _____: _____ studiare! (volere, potere, dovere)

For this exercise, imagine you're taking a trip to Cortona, a wonderful Tuscan hillside town, and you need to make plans. Conjugate the verbs in parentheses, and then translate the sentences into English. Here's an example:

Q. Io _____ andare al mercato sabato mattina. (dovere)

A. Io **devo** andare al mercato sabato mattina. *I have to go to the market on Saturday morning.*

42. Loro _____ visitare Cortona, un bel paese in Toscana. (volere)

_____

43. A Cortona _____ mangiare al ristorante il Cacciatore! (dovere [voi])

_____

44. _____ provare la "torta della nonna." (dovere [tu])

_____

45. _____ anche fare una passeggiata fino alla fortezza. (potere)

_____

46. _____ vedere un pò di arte spettacolare? (volere, [voi])

_____

47. Io _____ fare delle (some) belle foto. (potere)

_____

48. _____ anche visitare la chiesa di Santa Margherita. (potere [voi])

_____

49. _____ vedere il bel panorama dalle mura del paese. (dovere [tu])

_____

50. _____ venire con me a trovare i funghi porcini nel bosco? (volere)

_____

Volere can also mean a couple of other things you may want to keep in mind:

✔ **Vuole dire** means *to mean:* "Cosa **vuole dire** 'flattery'?" (*What does "flattery" mean?*) Or, when speaking, you can say "**Voglio dire**" (*I mean*) or "Cosa **vuoi dire?**" (*What do you mean?*)

✔ **Volerci** means *to need/it takes* and is used in the third-person singular and third-person plural, depending on whether the noun is singular or plural. For example: "Quanto tempo **ci vuole** per **arrivare** a Bologna?" (*How long does it take to get to Bologna?*) "Quante persone **ci vogliono** per **preparare** la cena?" (*How many people does it take to prepare dinner?*)

I'm Telling You, Don't Leave Home without Dire and Uscire!

The verbs **dire** (*to say, to tell*) and **uscire** (*to go out*) are irregular verbs that constantly come up in dialogue. Gossip isn't complete without a little he said, she said (lui **ha detto,** lei **ha detto**), not to mention talking about who's going out with whom. These verbs also share some similarities in conjugation:

✔ **Dire** takes the stem **dic-** in the first three singular persons (io, tu, and lui), in the first-person plural (noi), and in the third-person plural (loro).

✔ **Uscire** takes the stem **esc-** in the first three singular persons and in the third-person plural.

✔ Both verbs have regular **-ire** second-person plural (voi) endings.

You can compare the verbs **dire** and **uscire** in the following tables.

dire (*to say*)	
io **dico**	noi **diciamo**
tu **dici**	voi **dite**
lui, lei, Lei **dice**	loro **dicono**
Lui **dice** sempre la verità. (*He always tells the truth.*)	

Uscire means *to go out,* but when you put it with "di casa," it means *to leave the house.*

uscire (*to go out*)	
io **esco**	noi usc**iamo**
tu **esci**	voi usc**ite**
lui, lei, Lei **esce**	loro **escono**
Antonio **esce** con Samanta stasera. (*Antonio is going out with Samantha tonight.*)	

Practice conjugating the verbs **dire** and **uscire** in the following exercise by altering the forms of the verbs in parentheses. You can follow my example:

O. La mamma _____ di andare a letto. (dire)

A. La mamma **dice** di andare a letto. (*Mom says to go to bed.*)

51. _____ questa sera? (uscire [noi])

52. Che cosa _____ quando conosci qualcuno per la prima volta? (dire [tu])

53. Io non _____ domani sera: Devo studiare! (uscire)

54. Pinocchio _____ sempre le bugie. (dire)

55. Mamma e papà _____ con la zia. (uscire)

56. Voi _____ tutto quello che pensate? (dire)

Drink It All In with Bere

The verb **bere** (*to drink*) is almost a regular verb. After you form the stem **bev-,** all you have to do to conjugate the verb is add the endings for regular **-ere** verbs (see Chapter 2), as you can see in the following table. You generally use the verb **prendere** (*to take, to buy*) when you want to get or order something to drink. If you want to talk about drinking, you use the verb **bere.**

bere (*to drink*)	
io **bevo**	noi **beviamo**
tu **bevi**	voi **bevete**
lui, lei, Lei **beve**	loro **bevono**
Che cosa **bevi** con i pasti? (*What do you drink with your meals?*)	

Provide the correct conjugation of the verb **bere** in the following sentences. Here's an example to get you started:

Q. Giancarlo _____ il vino o la birra durante la cena?

A. Giancarlo **beve** il vino o la birra durante la cena? (*Does Giancarlo drink wine or beer with supper?*)

57. La bambina _____ poca acqua.

58. Io _____ molta acqua.

59. Che cosa _____ (voi) di più, la Coca-Cola o lo Sprite?

60. Noi _____ spesso il Campari quando siamo in Italia.

Utilizing Some Not-So-Common (But Not-So-Uncommon) Irregular Verbs

You use the irregular verbs that appear in the previous sections of this chapter in almost every conversation. Other irregular verbs gather a bit more dust in your verbal toolbox, but you use them often enough that you should be able to recognize them when you encounter them. You can see four general groupings in Table 3-3: verbs that end in **-porre**, verbs that end in **-gliere**, verbs that end in **-tenere,** and verbs that end in **-durre.** All four groupings share similarities in conjugation after you have the stems. Table 3-3 shows you the irregular verbs, translations, and their conjugations.

Table 3-3	Conjugations of Lesser-Used Irregular Verbs	
Irregular Infinitive	**Translation**	**Conjugation**
porre	*to place*	**pongo, poni, pone, poniamo, ponete, pongono**
proporre	*to propose*	**propongo, proponi, propone, proponiamo, proponete, propongono**
disporre	*to dispose, to make available*	**dispongo, disponi, dispone, disponiamo, disponete, dispongono**
imporre	*to impose*	**impongo, imponi, impone, imponiamo, imponete, impongono**
cogliere	*to pick* (flowers)	**colgo, cogli, coglie, cogliamo, cogliete, colgono**
accogliere	*to welcome*	**accolgo, accogli, accoglie, accogliamo, accogliete, accolgono**
scegliere	*to choose*	**scelgo, scegli, sceglie, scegliamo, scegliete, scelgono**
raccogliere	*to gather*	**raccolgo, raccogli, raccoglie, raccogliamo, raccogliete, raccolgono**
togliere	*to take off, take away*	**tolgo, togli, toglie, togliamo, togliete, tolgono**

(continued)

Table 3-3 *(continued)*

Irregular Infinitive	Translation	Conjugation
sostenere	to support	sostengo, sostieni, sostiene, sosteniamo, sostenete, sostengono
tenere	to keep, to hold	tengo, tieni, tiene, teniamo, tenete, tengono
ottenere	to obtain	ottengo, ottieni, ottiene, otteniamo, ottenete, ottengono
tradurre	to translate	traduco, traduci, traduce, traduciamo, traducete, traducono
indurre	to induce, to persuade	induco, induci, induce, induciamo, inducete, inducono
dedurre	to deduce	deduco, deduci, deduce, deduciamo, deducete, deducono
condurre	to lead, to take for a drive	conduco, conduci, conduce, conduciamo, conducete, conducono

Use Table 3-3 to translate the following sentences into English. I've selected the most frequently used uncommon irregular verbs, with their most common meanings implied (quite a mouthful!). Here's an example to get you started:

Q. Quanto tempo rimane fino alla fine del volo?

A. How much time is left before the end of the flight?

61. Tolgo le scarpe prima di entrare in casa.

_____

62. Loro salgono sul treno.

_____

63. Alan propone di andare a sciare.

_____

64. Induco il mio amico a restare.

_____

65. Traduciamo dall'italiano in inglese.

_____

66. Colgo il momento per scriverti.

_____

67. Che cosa ottieni con questo atteggiamento (attitude)?

_____

68. Ci opponiamo a tutte le guerre.

_____

69. Tieni il coltello con la destra o la sinistra?

_____

70. Rimango a casa stasera.

_____

Answer Key

1. **tu** fai (*you do, you make, you're doing, you're making*)

2. **lui, lei, Lei** dà (*he, she, you* (form.) *gives, are giving, do give*)

3. **loro** stanno (*they are*)

4. **voi** fate (*you* (pl.) *do, are doing*)

5. **noi** facciamo (*we do, are doing*)

6. **io** sto (*I am*)

7. **loro** danno (*they give, are giving, they do give*)

8. No, non **faccio** sempre colazione. (*I don't always have breakfast.*)

9. Sì, **faccio** un viaggio in Italia. (*Yes, I'm taking a trip to Italy.*)

10. No, non **do** una festa domani. (*No, I'm not throwing a party tomorrow.*)

11. Sì, **sto** zitta quando **conosco** qualcuno per la prima volta. (*Yes, I'm quiet when I meet someone for the first time.*)

12. Sì, **do** spesso regali. (*Yes, I often give gifts.*)

13. No, non **sto** male: **Sto** bene, grazie! (*No, I'm not feeling poorly: I'm well, thanks!*)

14. Noi **facciamo** molte domande. (*We ask a lot of questions.*)

15. **Fa** la valigia tuo marito? (*Is your husband packing?*)

16. Emilia **sta** zitta. (*Emilia is being quiet.*)

17. Io **do** un esame domani. (*I'm taking a test tomorrow.*)

18. Loro **danno** sempre una mano a tutti. (*They're helping out.*)

19. **Fa** bello oggi! (*It's nice out today!*)

20. Voi **state** attenti quando parlo? (*Are you all paying attention when I'm speaking?*)

21. Io **vengo.** (*I'm coming.*)

22. I miei amici **vanno.** (*My friends are going.*)

23. Noi **veniamo.** (*We're coming.*)

24. Tu **vieni.** (*You're coming.*)

25. Matteo **va.** (*Matteo is going.*)

26. Tu e Sofia **andate.** (*You and Sofia are going.*)

27   Francesca e Fabrizio **vengono.** (*Francesca and Fabrizio are coming.*)

28   Noi **andiamo.** (*We're coming.*)

29   Tu **vai.** (*You're going.*)

30   **Andiamo** in treno. (*We're coming by train.*)

31   **Vengo** in traghetto. (*I'm coming by ferry.*)

32   **Vanno** in macchina. (*They're going by car.*)

33   Sì, Giorgio **viene** a Taormina. (*Yes, Giorgio is coming to Taormina.*)

34   **Vado** a Siracusa. (*I'm going to Syracuse.*)

35   **Veniamo** a trovarti solo io e Giorgio perchè gli altri amici vanno a trovare i parenti a Palermo. (*Only Giorgio and I are coming to visit you because the other friends are going to visit relatives in Palermo.*)

36   Noi **dobbiamo** telefonare a casa. (*We have to phone home.*)

37   La mamma **vuole** fare la spesa. (*Mom wants to go shopping.*)

38   Tu **puoi** giocare a tennis oggi? (*Can you play tennis today?*)

39   Maria e Domenico **devono** andare in Florida. (*Maria and Domenico have to go to Florida.*)

40   Che cosa **volete** mangiare questa sera? (*What do you* (pl.) *want to eat tonight?*)

41   Io **voglio** venire alla festa ma non **posso: Devo** studiare! (*I want to come to the party but I can't: I need to study!*)

42   Loro **vogliono** visitare Cortona, un bel paese in Toscana. *They want to visit Cortona, a beautiful town in Tuscany.*

43   A Cortona **dovete** mangiare al ristorante il Cacciatore! *In Cortona you have to eat at the restaurant called Il Cacciatore!*

44   **Devi** provare la torta della nonna. *You must try la torta della nonna* [a type of cake].

45   **Possiamo** anche fare una passeggiata fino alla fortezza. *We can take a walk to the fortress.*

46   Voi **volete** vedere un po' di arte spettacolare? *Do you all want to see some spectacular art?*

47   Io **posso** fare delle belle foto. *I can take some nice pictures.*

48   **Potete** anche visitare la chiesa di Santa Margherita. *You all can visit the church of Saint Marguerite as well.*

49   **Devi** vedere il bel panorama dalle mura del paese. *You have to see the beautiful view from the town's walls.*

50   **Vuoi** venire con me a trovare i funghi porcini nel bosco? *Do you want to come with me to look for porcini mushrooms in the woods?*

51 **Usciamo** questa sera? (*Are we going out tonight?*)

52 Che cosa **dici** quando conosci qualcuno per la prima volta? (*What do you say when you meet someone for the first time?*)

53 Io non **esco** domani sera: Devo studiare! (*I'm not going out tomorrow night: I have to study!*)

54 Pinocchio **dice** sempre le bugie. (*Pinocchio always tells lies.*)

55 Mamma e papà **escono** con la zia. (*Mom and Dad are going out with aunty.*)

56 Voi **dite** tutto quello che pensate? (*Do you* (pl.) *say everything you're thinking?*)

57 La bambina **beve** poca acqua. (*The little girl drinks little water.*)

58 Io **bevo** molta acqua. (*I drink a lot of water.*)

59 Che cosa **bevete** di più, la Coca-Cola o lo Sprite? (*What do you drink more of, Coca-Cola or Sprite?*)

60 Noi **beviamo** spesso il Campari quando siamo in Italia. (*We often drink Campari when we're in Italy.*)

61 *I take off my shoes before going in the house.*

62 *They're getting on the train.*

63 *Alan is proposing to go skiing.*

64 *I'm persuading my friend to stay.*

65 *We translate from Italian to English.*

66 *I'm grabbing the opportunity to write you.* (Literally: *I welcome the moment to write you.*)

67 *What are you going to obtain with this attitude?*

68 *We are against all wars.*

69 *Do you hold the knife with your right or left hand?*

70 *I'm staying home tonight.*

Chapter 4

Shakespeare, Italian Style: To Be or Not to Be; To Have and Have Not

In This Chapter

▶ Molding **essere** into its many forms

▶ Grasping the forms of the possessive **avere**

▶ Creating idiomatic expressions with **avere**

▶ Recognizing when to use **essere** or **avere**

▶ Handling questions that involve **essere** or **avere**

The two most common verbs used in the Italian language are **essere** (*to be*) and **avere** (*to have*). And as luck would have it, the two most common verbs are irregular, meaning that they don't follow the regular **-ere** conjugation pattern from Chapter 2; rather, they enjoy their own unique conjugations like the irregular verbs in Chapter 3. Because of their importance, you get a chapter's worth of practice dedicated to these two verbs. In this chapter, you practice conjugating **essere** and **avere**, create idiomatic expressions with **avere**, and handle questions involving these two verbs.

To Be: Conjugating Essere

You use the verb **essere** (*to be*) to describe people, items, and situations, just as you do in English. You *are* a reader of this book. This book *is* awesome. You *are* excited for Italian class. See what I mean? (You also use the verb **essere** when forming compound tenses in Part III.) The following table shows the present-tense conjugation of **essere**.

essere (*to be*)	
io **sono**	noi **siamo**
tu **sei**	voi s**iete**
lui, lei, Lei **è**	loro **sono**
Io **sono** stanca. (*I am tired.*)	

You often use the verb **essere** (and **avere**) with adjectives. For example,

> Lui **è** italiano. (*He is Italian*)
>
> Lei **è** italiana. (*She is Italian*)
>
> Loro **hanno** amici italiani. (*They have Italian friends.*)

Therefore, it helps to brush up on your adjectives.

I provide only a cursory explanation of using **essere** and **avere** with adjectives here. For a more in-depth look at adjectives, you can check out *Italian For Dummies,* by Francesca Romana Onofri, or just type the words Italian Adjectives into a good Internet search engine.

Some adjectives only agree in number with the nouns that they modify. These adjectives end in -e. Common adjectives in this category include inglese (*English*), intelligente (*intelligent*), francese (*French*), and verde (*green*). These adjectives end in -e in the singular and -i in the plural:

> ✔ la benzina verde (*green gasoline*) — sing.
>
> ✔ il politico verde (*the green politician*) — sing.
>
> ✔ le scarpe verdi (*the green shoes*) — pl.
>
> ✔ i colori verdi (*the green colors*) — pl.

Other adjectives end in -o and agree in both number and gender with the nouns that they modify. A few examples of these adjectives include americano (*American*), rosso (*red*), and buono (*good*). These adjectives end in -a or -o in the singular and -i or -e in the plural, depending upon the gender of the noun. Take americano, for example:

> ✔ la studentessa americana (*American student*) — fem./sing.
>
> ✔ L'aereo **è** americano. (*The plane is American.*) — masc./sing.
>
> ✔ le banche americane (*American banks*) — fem./pl.
>
> ✔ i film americani (*American films*) — masc./pl.

Practice conjugating the verb **essere** in the following sentences by placing the right form of the verb in the blanks. Take note of how the adjectives italiano and bella agree. Here's an example:

Q. Io _____ italiana.

A. Io **sono** italiana. (*I am Italian.*)

1. Tu _____ italiano?

2. Mia madre _____ italiana.

3. Isabella e Claudio _____ italiani.

4. Donna ed io _____ italiane.

5. Michele _____ italiano.

6. Tu e Ines _____ italiani.

7. Taormina _____ bella! (*Note:* All cities are feminine singular.)

8. Le donne italiane _____ belle.

9. I vestiti italiani _____ belli.

10. Marco, come _____ bello!

For these practice exercises, I give you the verbs and you make the adjectives agree with either the subjects or the nouns. Here's an example to get you started:

Q. La macchina è _____. (rosso)

A. La macchina è **rossa.** (*The car is red.*)

11. I capelli sono _____. (rosso)

12. La penna è _____. (rosso)

13. Anna Maria ed io (fem.) siamo _____. (americano)

14. Tu e Giulia siete _____. (americano)

15. I miei studenti sono _____. (intelligente)

To Have: Conjugating Avere

The verb **avere** means *to have.* You *have* this book in your hands. The other people in the coffee house *have* noise issues. You *have* an out-of-sight IQ. (*Note:* You also use the present tense of **avere** when forming the compound tenses in Part III of this book.)

In Italian, the "h" is always silent. Keep this in mind as you repeat the verb in the following table to yourself a few times while memorizing it. The table shows how you conjugate **avere** in the present tense.

avere *(to have)*	
io **ho**	noi **abbiamo**
tu **hai**	voi **avete**
lui, lei, Lei **ha**	loro **hanno**
Hanno un altro numero di telefono adesso. (*They have a different phone number now.*)	

Allow me to use the following practice exercises to tell you about my family. Conjugate the verb **avere** and then translate each sentence. I start you off with the following example:

Q. Mio cugino Paul _____ due bambini, Cole ed Ava.

A. Mio cugino Paul **ha** due bambini, Cole ed Ava. *My cousin Paul has two children, Cole and Ava.*

16. Loro _____ una casa in North Carolina.

_____

17. Mia sorella Anna _____ un buon lavoro in Connecticut.

_____

18. Mio marito ed io _____ una barca che non usiamo!

_____

19. Tu e Susan _____ molti film.

_____

20. Io _____ una figlia che si chiama Emilia Rosa.

_____

21. Tu, Sandro, _____ una moglie gentile.

_____

22. Mio fratello John _____ due bambine, Jenny e Lucy.

_____

23. Noi _____ una grande famiglia.

_____

24. Quanti cugini _____ voi?

_____

25. Tu _____ un padre veneziano?

_____

Forming Idiomatic Expressions with Avere

The main meaning of the verb **avere** is *to have,* but it can also mean *to be,* along with other less common meanings, such as *to need.* If this sounds confusing, don't worry! **Avere** means different things only when you use certain idiomatic expressions (espressioni idiomatiche). For example, when you say "I am hungry" in English, you use the verb "to be" (I am, you are, he is, and so on). In Italian, you say "**Ho** fame," or *I am hungry* (Literally: *I have hunger*). Table 4-1 gives you most of the common idiomatic expressions used with **avere.**

Table 4-1	Idiomatic Expressions of *to Have*		
Expression	*Translation*	*Example*	*Translation*
avere . . . anni	*to be . . . years old*	Emilia **ha** cinque anni.	*Emilia is 5 years old.*
avere bisogno di	*to need*	**Hai** bisogno di una mano?	*Do you need a hand?*
avere caldo	*to be hot*	Il cane **ha** caldo.	*The dog is hot.*
avere fame	*to be hungry*	**Avete** fame?	*Are you* (pl.) *hungry?*
avere freddo	*to be cold*	I bambini **hanno** freddo.	*The children are cold.*
avere fretta	*to be in a hurry*	**Abbiamo** fretta!	*We're in a hurry!*
avere paura di	*to be afraid of*	**Ho** paura di Dracula.	*I'm afraid of Dracula.*
avere sete	*to be thirsty*	Non **hai** sete?	*Aren't you thirsty?*
avere sonno	*to be sleepy*	Vado a dormire: **Ho** sonno.	*I'm going to sleep: I'm sleepy.*
avere voglia di	*to feel like*	Chi **ha** voglia di uscire?	*Who feels like going out?*

The following list provides you with some additional information you need when using the idiomatic expressions found in Table 4-1.

- ✔ After the preposition "di" in the expressions "**avere** bisogno di," "**avere** paura di," and "**avere** voglia di," you should use an infinitive rather than a conjugated verb. Here are some examples:

  - **Hai** voglia di **mangiare?** (*Do you feel like eating?*)

  - Lui **ha** paura di **innamorarsi.** (*He's afraid of falling in love.*)

  - **Ho** bisogno di **dormire.** (*I need to sleep.*)

- ✔ Use "**avere** caldo" and "**avere** freddo" when you're talking about a living being in a hot or cold state. If you're talking about an inanimate object, you use the verb **essere** (see the section "To Be: Conjugating Essere" earlier in this chapter). Here are some examples:

  - Io **ho** caldo perchè questa stanza **è** calda. (*I'm hot because this room is hot.*)

  - La mamma **ha** freddo perchè **è** fredda dentra la macchina. (*Mom is cold because it's cold inside the car.*)

In the following exercises, try to figure out which idiomatic expressions you need by analyzing the context of the sentences, and place the expressions together with the right forms of the verb **avere** in the spaces provided. (See Table 4-1 for a list of idiomatic expressions.) Here's an example:

Q. Quanti _____ tuo padre se è nato nel '38?

A. Quanti **anni ha** tuo padre se è nato nel '38? (*How old is your father if he was born in '38?*)

26. Brrr! Chiudi la finestra per favore. Io _____.

27. Luisa accende l'aria condizionata perchè _____.

28. Vai a dormire? _____?

29. Noi _____: Ordiniamo due pizze.

30. La bambina _____ di Cruella De Vil.

31. Non volete un po' d'acqua? Non _____?

32. Chi _____ un gelato? Offro io!

33. Lisa _____ aiuto.

34. Dan, _____ studiare questa sera?

35. Chi _____ di andare al cinema?

Here you can practice translating a few sentences into Italian by using the idiomatic expressions I present in Table 4-1. Here's an example to get you going:

Q. We are thirsty.

A. **Abbiamo** sete.

36. Colin and Katherine are in a hurry. _____

37. Belinda is 14 years old. _____

38. Abi is always cold. _____

39. I feel like sleeping. _____

40. Are you (sing.) afraid of dying? _____

41. Matteo is sleepy today. _____

42. Mike, how old are you? _____

43. Giuseppe and I are thirsty. _____

44. Pina is afraid of dogs. _____

45. Daniel and Maria are hot! _____

Inserting Essere or Avere into Sentences

In the previous sections of this chapter, you tackle the common verbs **essere** (*to be*) and **avere** (*to have*). This section, devoted solely to practice, gives you the opportunity to put your knowledge of the verbs together.

In the following exercises, decide which of the two verbs you need to insert in the sentence, conjugate it, and place it in the blank space. Here's an example:

Q. _____ caldo? (voi)

A. **Avete** caldo? (*Are you* (pl.) *hot?*)

46. Tu _____ italiana o americana?

47. Quanti anni _____ tuo padre?

48. Quando _____ stanca vado a letto; adesso io non _____ sonno.

49. Beviamo una limonata perchè _____ sete.

50. (Io) _____ una macchina italiana, una FIAT; la mia macchina _____ rossa.

Asking and Answering Questions

Asking and answering questions affirmatively and negatively is pretty straightforward in Italian. To ask a question, you can simply alter the intonation of your voice: **Mangi** (*You're eating*) becomes **Mangi?** (*Are you eating?*), simply by adding a questioning tone to your voice. When answering a question in the affirmative, you can add "sì" (*yes*) or "certo che" (*of course*), or you can simply use the verb — Sì, **mangio!** Certo che **mangio! Mangio!**

Another tactic you can use is reversing your word order, placing the subject at the end of the sentence (although this order isn't always necessary):

Maria è italiana (*Maria is Italian*) becomes **È** italiana Maria? (*Is Maria Italian?*)

When asking a question in the negative, you begin the sentence with "non":

Non vuoi una bella fetta di cocomero? (*Don't you want a nice piece of watermelon?*)

When answering a question in the negative, you simply add the word "non" in front of the verb:

Maria non **è** italiana. (*Maria isn't Italian.*)

The "non" you add, however, can also mean "*aren't you?*" (*he, she, we*)? For example, "Non **mangi?**" translates to "*Aren't you eating?*"

Answer the following questions affirmatively or negatively, using the conjugations of the verbs **essere** or **avere**. Here's an example:

Q. Sei un avvocato? (*Are you a lawyer?*)

A. Sì, **sono** un avvocato. (*Yes, I am a lawyer.*)

51. Hai fame in questo momento? No, _____.

52. Hai parenti in Italia? Sì, _____.

53. Sei triste? No, _____.

54. Hai molti amici? Sì, _____.

55. Sei medico? No, _____.

The Italian language provides you with some more tools for your job of asking and answering questions. Namely, you can use the phrases **c'è** (*there is*) and **ci sono** (*there are*) in interrogative and declarative sentences. The sound in both is the soft "ch," as in the English word "cheetah."

By itself, the question "Cosa **c'è?**" means "*What's up?/What's wrong?*" "Cosa **c'è** che non **va?**" is another way of asking what's wrong.

Here are a couple examples of using **c'è** and **ci sono** in declarative and interrogative sentences:

- ✔ **C'è** una mosca nella mia minestra! (*There's a fly in my soup!*)

- ✔ **Ci sono** 9 studenti nella classe. (*There are 9 students in the class.*)

- ✔ Chi non **c'è** a lezione oggi? (*Who's not in class today?*)

Practice using the phrases **c'è** and **ci sono** by answering the following questions; some of your answers will be subjective. I provide my subjective answers in the Answer Key. Here's an example:

Q. C'è la posta? (*Is there any mail?*)

A. Sì, **c'è.** (*Yes, there is.*)

56. Quante persone ci sono nella tua famiglia? _____

57. Cosa c'è a Roma da vedere? _____

58. Cosa c'è nel frigo? _____

59. Quante regioni ci sono in Italia? _____

60. Cosa c'è di nuovo? _____

In addition to the phrases **c'è** and **ci sono,** you have many other ways to ask questions that sometimes combine with the verb **essere** (*to be*). Table 4-2 presents a short list of common interrogatives.

Table 4-2		Common Interrogative Words	
Interrogative	*Definition*	*Example*	*Translation*
chi	*who*	Chi **c'è?**	*Who's there?/Who is it?*
come	*how*	Come si **dice** "help!"?	*How do you say "help!"?*
com'è	*how is*	**Com'è** la tua famiglia?	*What's your family like?*
come **sono**	*how are*	Come **sono** i calamari qui?	*How are the calamari here?*
dove	*where*	Dove **vai?**	*Where are you going?*
di dove	*from where*	Di dove **siete?**	*Where are you from?*
dov'è	*where is*	**Dov'è** Anna?	*Where's Anna?*

Interrogative	Definition	Example	Translation
dove **sono**	where are	Dove **sono** le chiavi?	Where are the keys?
quale/i	which, what	Quale film **preferisci?**	Which film do you prefer?
qual **è**	what is	Qual è il problema?	What's the problem?
quali **sono**	which are	Quali **sono** le tue valige?	Which are your suitcases?
quando	when	Quando **venite** a **trovarmi?**	When are you coming to visit me?
quanto/a/i/e	how much, how many	Quanto pane **mangiate?**	How much bread are you eating?
		Quanta birra **bevi?**	How much beer do you drink?
		Quanti soldi **ha** lui?	How much money does he have?
		Quante amiche **vengono?**	How many (girl)friends are coming?
perchè	why (and because)	Perchè **piangono?** Perchè **hanno** sonno.	Why are they crying? Because they're sleepy.

You've just met a new Italian friend online, and he/she wants to know all about you. Answer the following personal questions in Italian in a subjective manner, and I'll provide my subjective answers in the Answer Key. *Note:* You never need the interrogative pronoun or adjective in your response.

Q. Quando vai in Italia?

A. **Vado** in Italia ad agosto. (*I'm going to Italy in August.*)

61. Di dove sei? _____

62. Come sei? (*Note:* This doesn't mean "*How are you?*", which is "Come **stai?**" This means "*What are you like?*") _____

63. Dov'è casa tua? _____

64. Com'è la tua città? _____

65. Come sono i tuoi amici? _____

66. Perchè studi l'italiano? _____

67. Quanti anni hai? _____

68. Quante persone ci sono nella tua famiglia? _____

69. Hai figli? _____

70. Quando vai in Italia? _____

Answer Key

1 Tu **sei** italiano? (*Are you Italian?*)

2 Mia madre **è** italiana. (*My mother is Italian.*)

3 Isabella e Claudio **sono** italiani. (*Isabella and Claudio are Italian.*)

4 Donna ed io **siamo** italiane. (*Donna and I are Italian.*)

5 Michele **è** italiano. (*Michael is Italian.*)

6 Tu e Ines **siete** italiani. (*You and Ines are Italian.*)

7 Taormina **è** bella! (*Taormina is beautiful!*)

8 Le donne italiane **sono** belle. (*Italian women are beautiful.*)

9 I vestiti italiani **sono** belli. (*Italian clothes are beautiful.*)

10 Marco, come **sei** bello! (*Marco, how nice you look; Marco, how beautiful you are!*)

11 I capelli sono **rossi.** (*The hair is red.*)

12 La penna è **rossa.** (*The pen is red.*)

13 Anna Maria ed io siamo **americane.** (*Anna Maria and I are American.*)

14 Tu e Giulia siete **americani/e.** (*You and Giulia are American.*) **Note:** The gender of the tu isn't specified here, so you have to go with the masculine gender.

15 I miei studenti sono **intelligenti.** (*My students are intelligent.*)

16 Loro **hanno** una casa in North Carolina. *They have a house in North Carolina.*

17 Mia sorella Anna **ha** un buon lavoro in Connecticut. *My sister Anna has a good job in Connecticut.*

18 Mio marito ed io **abbiamo** una barca che non usiamo! *My husband and I have a boat that we don't use.*

19 Tu e Susan **avete** molti film. *You and Susan have many films.*

20 Io **ho** una figlia che sì chiama Emilia Rosa. *I have a daughter whose name is Emilia Rosa.*

21 Tu, Sandro, **hai** una moglie gentile. *You, Sandro, have a nice wife.*

22 Mio fratello John **ha** due bambine, Jenny e Lucy. *My brother John has two girls, Jenny and Lucy.*

23 Noi **abbiamo** una grande famiglia. *We have a big family.*

24 Quanti cugini **avete** voi? *How many cousins do you have?*

25 Tu **hai** un padre veneziano? *Do you have a Venetian father?*

26 Brrr! Chiudi la finestra per favore. Io **ho freddo.** (*Brrr! Close the window please. I'm cold.*)

27 Luisa accende l'aria condizionata perchè **ha caldo.** (*Luisa is turning on the air conditioner because she's hot.*)

28 Vai a dormire? **Hai sonno?** (*Are you going to sleep? Are you tired?*)

29 Noi **abbiamo fame:** Ordiniamo due pizze. (*We're hungry: Let's order two pizzas.*)

30 La bambina **ha paura** di Cruella De Vil. (*The baby [girl] is afraid of Cruella De Vil.*)

31 Non volete un po' d'acqua? Non **avete sete?** (*Don't you* (pl.) *want some water? Aren't you thirsty?*)

32 Chi **ha voglia di** un gelato? Offro io! (*Who feels like having an ice cream? My treat!*)

33 Lisa **ha bisogno di** aiuto. (*Lisa needs help.*)

34 Dan, **hai bisogno di/hai voglia di** studiare questa sera? (*Dan, do you need to/feel like studying tonight?*)

35 Chi **ha voglia** di andare al cinema? (*Who feels like going to the movies?*)

36 Colin e Caterina **hanno** fretta.

37 Belinda **ha** quattordici anni.

38 Abi **ha** sempre freddo.

39 **Ho** voglia di **dormire.**

40 **Hai** paura di **morire?**

41 Matteo **ha sonno** oggi.

42 Mike, quanti anni **hai?**

43 Giuseppe ed io **abbiamo** sete.

44 Pina **ha** paura dei cani.

45 Daniel e Maria **hanno** caldo.

46 Tu **sei** italiana o americana? (*Are you Italian or American?*)

47 Quanti anni **ha** tuo padre? (*How old is your father?*)

48 Quando **sono** stanca vado a letto; adesso, io non **ho** sonno. (*When I'm tired I go to bed; right now, I'm not sleepy.*)

49 Beviamo una limonata perchè **abbiamo** sete. (*We're drinking a lemonade because we're thirsty.*)

50 **Ho** una macchina italiana, una FIAT; la mia macchina **è** rossa. (*I have an Italian car, a FIAT; my car is red.*)

51 No, non **ho** fame. (*No, I'm not hungry.*)

52 Sì, **ho** parenti in Italia. (*Yes, I have relatives in Italy.*)

53   No, non **sono** triste. (*No, I'm not sad.*)

54   Sì, **ho** molti amici. (*Yes, I have many friends.*)

55   No, non **sono** medico. (*No, I'm not a doctor.*)

56   **Ci sono** tre persone nella mia famiglia. (*There are three people in my family.*)

57   **C'è** il Colosseo. (*There's the Colosseum.*)

58   **Ci sono** il latte, il succo di frutta, e le uova./Non **c'è** niente nel frigo. (*There are milk, fruit juice, and eggs./There's nothing in the fridge.*)

59   **Ci sono** 20 regioni in Italia. (*There are 20 regions in Italy.*)

60   **Abbiamo** un nuovo cane; **si** chiama Toby./Non **c'è** niente di nuovo. (*We have a new dog; his name is Toby./There's nothing new.*)

61   **Sono** del Connecticut. (*I'm from Connecticut.*)

62   **Sono** bassa, bruna, onesta, e gentile. (*I'm short, dark-haired, honest, and kind.*)

63   Casa mia **è** a Fairfield. (*My house is in Fairfield.*)

64   La mia città **è** piccola ma carina. **È** vicino al mare ed **ha** un bel centro. (*My city is small but cute. It's near the sea and has a nice center.*)

65   I miei amici **sono** intelligenti. (*My friends are smart.*)

66   **Studio** l'italiano perchè **amo** l'Italia, il cibo italiano, i film italiani, e i miei amici italiani. (*I study Italian because I love Italy, Italian food, Italian films, and my Italian friends.*)

67   **Ho** quarantaquattro anni. (*I'm 44 years old.*)

68   **Ci sono** cinque persone nella mia famiglia. (*There are five people in my family.*)

69   Sì, **ho** 3 figli. (*Yes, I have 3 children.*)

70   **Vado** in Italia a luglio. (*I'm going to Italy in July.*)

Chapter 5

Waking Up to Reflexive Verbs

∙∙∙

In This Chapter

▶ Replacing personal pronouns with reflexive pronouns

▶ Determining the proper forms of reflexive verbs

▶ Changing the position of reflexive pronouns with **dovere, volere,** and **potere**

▶ Addressing the reciprocal form of reflexive verbs

∙∙∙

*Y*ou need *reflexive verbs* (i verbi riflessivi) — verbs whose actions are directed back to their subjects — to express a wide variety of actions in Italian, from waking up in the morning to falling asleep at night. Reflexive verbs end in **-arsi, -ersi,** and **-irsi,** a fact that leads me to some good news: After you deal with the **-si** endings, the reflexive verbs actually follow the same three conjugation patterns of **-are, -ere,** and **-ire** verbs, respectively (which I cover in Chapter 2).

Very often, you can translate a reflexive verb as including the term *oneself.* The reflexive verb **lavarsi,** for example, means *to wash oneself* (*get washed*), and the verb **divertirsi** means *to enjoy oneself* (*to have a good time*). Other reflexive verbs, however, don't translate to *oneself* in English. For example, the reflexive verbs **sposarsi** (*to get married*) and **rendersi conto** (*to realize*) focus their action on the subjects of the sentences, but you can't marry "oneself" — technically, I suppose. What can I say? That's why you need to practice these verbs and make use of the exercises in this chapter.

In this chapter, you replace personal pronouns with reflexive pronouns, practice conjugating reflexive verbs in the present tense, and work with *reciprocal verbs* (verbs where the general meanding is *each other*).

Reflexive verbs are very common, helpful tools that you use in all the tenses I cover in this book, but in this chapter, I focus on reflexive verbs in the present tense. Chapter 15 presents the reflexive verbs in the past tense, and most of the other chapters contain reflexive verbs as well.

Pairing Reflexive Pronouns with Reflexive Verbs

The first rule of the reflexive-verb club? A reflexive verb always requires a reflexive pronoun — it wouldn't be a reflexive verb without it! The second rule? Refer to rule one (and feel free to talk about reflexive verbs all you want). These pronouns usually take the place of the personal pronouns in sentences and generally precede the conjugated verbs: "**Mi alzo** alle 6" (*I get up at 6*), for example, where "Mi" is the reflexive pronoun. (On occasion, however — such as with the imperatives I cover in Chapter 6 — you attach the pronouns to the verb forms; you may also attach them to infinitives.) Table 5-1 provides a list of the reflexive pronouns that accompany your favorite reflexive verbs.

Avoid using personal pronouns with reflexive verbs — unless you want to emphasize a part of your statement. For example, you could say, "Mio marito **si addormenta** subito; io, invece, non **mi addormento** facilmente." (*My husband falls asleep right away; I, on the other hand, don't fall asleep easily.*) In this sentence, I compare myself to my husband, so I can use the personal pronoun "I" for emphasis.

Table 5-1	Reflexive Pronouns Taking the Place of Personal Pronouns		
Personal Pronoun	*Reflexive Pronoun*	*Personal Pronoun*	*Reflexive Pronoun*
io	**mi**	noi	**ci**
tu	**ti**	voi	**vi**
lui/lei/Lei	**si**	loro	**si**

Before you move on to conjugating reflexive verbs, run through the following exercises to see if you know which pronouns to pair with reflexive verbs. I provide you with the subject in each sentence, and you write the appropriate reflexive pronoun. I stick with the verb **alzarsi** (*to get up*), conjugated just like an **-are** verb. Follow my cue from the example. (***Here's a hint:*** The commas after the subjects in Questions 3 through 5 are your hints that the sentences feature direct speech and that you need to use the tu, Lei [formal], or voi forms.)

I use the reflexive pronoun "si" in the example because when I talk about my daughter (or anyone), I speak in the third-person singular. In this example, the pronoun "si" doesn't translate into English; nonetheless, the pronoun is always necessary!

O. Mia figlia _____ alza alle 7:00.

A. Mia figlia **si** alza alle 7:00. (*My daughter gets up at 7:00.*)

1. Io e te _____ alziamo alle 7:00.

2. Gli studenti _____ alzano alle 7:00.

3. Lei, Professor Mariani, _____ alza alle 7:00?

4. Josh, _____ alzi alle 7:00?

5. Samantha e Antonio, _____ alzate alle 7:00?

6. (io) _____ alzo alle 7:00.

7. (noi) _____ alziamo alle 7:00.

8. Marie _____ alza alle 7:00.

9. (tu) _____ alzi alle 7:00.

10. (voi) _____ alzate alle 7:00.

Conjugating Reflexive Verbs

The infinitive forms of reflexive verbs end in **-arsi, -ersi,** or **-irsi.** When you conjugate these verbs (in any tense), the first step is to cut the **-si** endings off the infinitives and drag them in front of the verbs. In this position, the "si" becomes a placeholder for all the reflexive pronouns (see the previous section). You place the proper reflexive pronoun in this position and make it agree with your subject and verb form. At that point, you conjugate the verb as if it's an **-are, -ere,** or **-ire** verb (which you can find in Chapters 2 and 3). In other words, cut the verb at its root (dropping the **-are, -ere,** or **-ire**) and add the appropriate ending.

Many students get confused about where to cut off the reflexive pronouns and how to form the stems, even though they've mastered the present tense. For example, look at the infinitives **lavarsi** (*to wash*), **mettersi** (*to put something on,* like glasses or clothing), **divertirsi** (*to have fun, to have a good time, to enjoy oneself*), and **trasferirsi** (*to move,* like to another city; this verb takes the **-isc** ending, like **finire** [*to finish*]). For these verbs, and all other reflexive verbs, you cut off the **-si** ending, bring it in front of the verb, and then cut off the new ending, creating your stem. Here are the steps:

- **lavarsi** → lavar~~si~~ → si lav~~are~~ → **si lav-**

- **mettersi** → metter~~si~~ → si mett~~ere~~ → **si mett-**

- **divertirsi** → divertir~~si~~ → si divert~~ire~~ → **si divert-**

- **trasferirsi** → trasferir~~si~~ → si trasfer~~ire~~ → **si trasferisc-** (except for noi and voi, which take the stem **trasfer-**)

When you have the **-si** ending in its place, you can insert the proper reflexive pronoun that agrees with the subject/verb form in the sentence at hand.

The following tables show the conjugations of the four examples I present in this section.

lavarsi (*to wash oneself*)	
(io) mi lav**o**	(noi) ci lav**iamo**
(tu) ti lav**i**	(voi) vi lav**ate**
(lui, lei, Lei) si lav**a**	(loro) si lav**ano**
Paola, **ti lavi** i capelli oggi? (*Paola, are you washing your hair today?*)	

mettersi (*to put something on, to wear*)	
(io) mi mett**o**	(noi) ci mett**iamo**
(tu) ti mett**i**	(voi) vi mett**ete**
(lui, lei, Lei) si mett**e**	(loro) si mett**ono**
Io **mi metto** una gonna lunga nera, e Giancarlo **si mette** i jeans. (*I'm wearing a long black skirt, and Giancarlo is wearing jeans.*)	

divertirsi (*to have fun, to have a good time, to enjoy oneself*)	
(io) mi divert**o**	(noi) ci divert**iamo**
(tu) ti divert**i**	(voi) vi divert**ite**
(lui, lei, Lei) si divert**e**	(loro) si divert**ono**
Ci divertiamo sempre in Italia! (*We always have fun in Italy!*)	

trasferirsi (*to move* [to another town, or at a specified time])	
(io) mi trasfer**isco**	(noi) ci trasfer**iamo**
(tu) ti trasfer**isci**	(voi) vi trasfer**ite**
(lui, lei, Lei) si trasfer**isce**	(loro) si trasfer**iscono**
I Marotti **si trasferiscono** a Torino a maggio. (*The Marotti's are moving to Torino in May.*)	

Time to flex your reflexive muscle. Conjugate the following verbs in parentheses, using the correct reflexive pronoun in each case, and then translate.

Try to use *cognates* (words that are similar in English) to help you understand the gist of the sentences.

Here's an example to get you started:

Q. Mamma, perchè non _____ gli occhiali da sole? (mettersi)

A. Mamma, perchè non **ti metti** gli occhiali da sole? *Mom, why don't you put on your sunglasses?*

11. _____ le mani prima di cenare. (lavarsi [io])

_____

12. Pina, _____ i denti? (lavarsi)

_____

13. Il gatto _____ le zampe. (lavarsi)

_____

14. Emma e Giuseppe _____ la giacca. (mettersi)

_____

15. Carla ed io _____ i pantaloni. (mettersi)

_____

16. Carla, tu e Daniele _____ le lenti a contatto la mattina? (mettersi)

_____

17. _____ a imparare l'italiano? (divertirsi [noi])

_____

18. Dove _____ di più, al mare o in montagna? (divertirsi [tu])

_____

19. Alessandro e Guglielmo _____ a sciare. (divertirsi)

_____

20. _____ facilmente. (innamorarsi [io])

After you discover how to use reflexive pronouns and how to conjugate reflexive verbs, you can start building on your reflexive vocabulary. Table 5-2 presents a list of some common and not-so-common reflexive verbs that you can add to your verb repertoire. *Note:* Table 5-2 is only a preliminary list; the more you study Italian, the more verbs you can add to this list!

Table 5-2	Some Common (and Some Rare) Reflexive Verbs		
Reflexive Verb	*Translation*	*Reflexive Verb*	*Translation*
abituarsi	to get used to	**pettinarsi**	to comb your hair
accorgersi	to realize	**prepararsi**	to get ready
annoiarsi	to be bored, to be annoyed	**rendersi conto**	to realize
arrabbiarsi	to get angry	**rilassarsi**	to relax
bruciarsi	to get burned	**sbagliarsi**	to make a mistake
cambiarsi	to get changed	**scusarsi**	to say you're sorry, to say "excuse me"
chiamarsi	to be called	**sedersi***	to sit down
dimenticarsi	to forget something	**sentirsi (bene, male, triste)**	to feel (well, poorly, sad)
diplomarsi	to graduate from high school	**sistemarsi**	to settle down
farsi la barba	to shave (your beard, for instance)	**slogarsi**	to dislocate (an ankle, perhaps)
farsi male	to get hurt, to hurt	**spazzolarsi**	to brush your hair
fermarsi	to stop	**sporcarsi**	to get dirty
godersi	to enjoy	**sposarsi**	to get married
guardarsi	to look at yourself	**spostarsi**	to move
impegnarsi	to make an effort, to work hard	**stabilirsi**	to settle into a place
innamorarsi	to fall in love	**svegliarsi**	to wake up
lamentarsi di	to complain about	**trovarsi**	to get settled in, to like being in a place
laurearsi	to graduate from a university	**truccarsi**	to put makeup on, to wear makeup
mangiarsi le unghie	to bite your nails	**vestirsi**	to dress
muoversi	to move (yourself)	**voltarsi**	to turn (around)

*(Note: **Sedersi** is a stem-changing verb: **mi siedo, ti siedi, si siede, ci sediamo, vi sedete**, and **si siedono**)*

For the following exercise, conjugate the reflexive verbs I provide for you in parentheses and attach the appropriate reflexive pronouns. I start you off with an example:

0. Maria Francesca _____ alle 7:30. (svegliarsi)

A. Maria Francesca **si sveglia** alle 7:30. (*Maria Francesca wakes up at 7:30.*)

21. Dopo 5 minuti, Maria Francesca _____ dal letto. (alzarsi)

22. Riccardo e Giuditta _____ dell'insegnante. (lamentarsi)

23. Dopo un caffè, _____ per uscire. (prepararsi [io])

24. _____ subito, in 5 minuti, ma con cura. (vestirsi [tu])

25. _____ troppo! (truccarsi [voi])

26. Non _____ mai. (pettinarsi [io])

27. Andiamo a lavorare, dove _____ molto, ma _____ anche!
(impegnarsi, divertirsi [noi])

28. Dopo lavoro _____ a casa con la famiglia. (rilassarsi [voi])

29. I miei figli _____ sempre verso le 11:00 di sera. (addormentarsi)

30. Non _____ mai! (annoiarsi [noi])

You can really give yourself a reflexive workout by focusing on multiple reflexive verbs and pronouns in a sentence. In the following mini-dialogues, conjugate the verbs in parentheses to agree with the subjects at hand. Here's an example:

0. A: Ciao, _____ Teresa. Come _____ tu? (chiamarsi)

   B: _____ Marisa.

A. A: Ciao, **mi chiamo** Teresa. Come **ti chiami** tu? (*Hi, my name is Teresa. What's yours?*)

   B: **Mi chiamo** Marisa. (*My name is Marisa.*)

31. A: Dove _____ dopo che _____? (stabilirsi, sposarsi [voi])

   B: _____ a Ferrara dopo che _____. (stabilirsi, sposarsi [noi])

32. A: Daniele, quando _____? (sistemarsi)

   B: _____ quando _____. (sistemarsi, innamorarsi [io])

33. A: Tuo padre _____ ad essere in pensione (to be retired)? (rilassarsi)

   B: Sì, molto: _____ la vita, e non _____ mai! (godersi, annoiarsi)

34. A: Amalia _____ a scuola? (impegnarsi)

   B: Certo che _____! _____ che è necessario impegnarsi per fare sempre bene! (impegnarsi, rendersi conto)

35. A: Come _____? (sentirsi [tu])

   B: _____ benissimo! (sentirsi [io])

Of course, constantly talking about washing oneself (one's hair, one's teeth, and so on), for example, is boring and, frankly, not very useful. In many cases, you need to talk about the act of washing another object (or person, I suppose). In such cases, you don't need the reflexive verb **lavarsi** (_to wash oneself_); you need the verb **lavare** (_to wash_). You can also compare the verbs **svegliarsi** (_to wake up_) and **svegliare** (_to wake up someone else_), and **chiamarsi** (_to be called_) and **chiamare** (_to call_), in the same way. (This information is especially useful when you conjugate transitive and intransitive verbs in the passato prossimo and other compound tenses; see Chapters 14 and 15.)

Compare the following sentences:

Emilia **si lava** il viso (_Emilia's washing her face_) versus Emilia **lava** i piatti (_Emilia's washing the dishes_)

Ci svegliamo tardi la domenica (_We wake up late on Sundays_) versus **Svegliamo** il babbo (_We're waking up daddy_)

Mi chiamo Teresa (_My name is Teresa_) versus **Chiamo** il medico (_I'm calling the doctor_)

Altering the Position of Reflexive Pronouns

At times, you have to deal with reflexive verbs in their infinitive forms. The infinitive form becomes necessary when the reflexive verbs accompany the conjugated verbs **dovere** (_to have to_), **volere** (_to want_), and **potere** (_to be able to_) (see Chapter 3). With these verbs already conjugated, the reflexive verbs remain in the infinitive, with one caveat: You need to change the **-si** endings of the reflexive infinitives (which become the reflexive pronouns) to agree with the subjects of the verbs. Before attaching the reflexive pronoun, drop the final **-e** of the infinitive. In these cases, the reflexive pronouns will either precede the conjugated verbs or attach themselves to the reflexive verbs. Even though the path you take is perfectly optional, the latter is more common.

Note the following examples, which show both possible positions for the reflexive verb cases where the reflexive pronouns precede the conjugated verbs:

- **Dovere** (with **alzarsi**): **Dobbiamo alzarci./Ci dobbiamo alzare.** (_We need to get up._) After you remove the reflexive pronoun "si" from the infinitive **alzarsi,** you're left with **alzare.** Take the final **-e** off and you're left with **alzar-.** Now, you can attach the appropriate reflexive pronoun to the infinitive.

- **Volere** (with **sposarsi**): **Vogliamo sposarci** a Roma./**Ci vogliamo sposare** a Roma. (_We want to get married in Rome._)

- **Potere** (with **sedersi**): **Posso sedermi** qui?/**Mi posso sedere** qui? (_May I sit here?_)

In this exercise, provide me with the second way of saying the same thing. Here's an example to get you going:

_**Q.**_ Voglio svegliarmi presto. (_I want to get up early tomorrow._)

_**A.**_ **Mi voglio svegliare** presto.

36. Dobbiamo fermarci in farmacia.

37. Finalmente i nonni possono rilassarsi

_____

38. Volete sedervi vicino alla finestra?

_____

39. Posso laurearmi con lode, se lavoro duro.

_____

40. Non devi arrabbiarti così tanto!

_____

Other verb constructions require that you attach the reflexive pronoun to the reflexive infinitive only. Constructions like this occur with the verbs **piacere** (_to like_) (see Chapter 7) and **preferire** (_to prefer_):

✔ **Mi piace alzarmi** presto! (_I like to get up early!_)

✔ No grazie, **preferisco sedermi** qui. (_No thanks, I prefer to sit here._)

Try your hand at a couple of exercises that require you to attach the appropriate reflexive pronouns to the reflexive infinitives. Follow my example lead:

_Q._ Ti piace _____ di nero. (vestirsi)

_A._ Ti piace **vestirti** di nero. (_You like to dress in black._)

41. Sì, ma a volte mi piace _____ di rosso. (vestirsi)

42. Noi preferiamo _____ presto. (alzarsi)

43. Ad Amanda piace _____! (divertirsi)

44. Preferite _____ a Roma o a Milano? (trasferirsi)

45. Alle bambine piace _____ allo specchio. (guardarsi)

Focusing on "Each Other" with the Reciprocal Form

The reciprocal form is a form of a reflexive verb. The _reciprocal form_ (forma reciproca), in most areas of expertise, implies two or more parties that cancel each other out. When it comes to Italian verbs, the focus on "each other" doesn't change: You translate reciprocal forms as _each other_. The focus on multiple parties is the same, also; therefore, the persons that you use are always plural: first-, second-, and third-person plural. You can turn many verbs that are normally transitive (meaning verbs that can take a direct object and are conjugated with **avere** in compound tenses; see Chapter 14) into the reciprocal form by adding **-si** to their infinitive endings. For example, the verb **vedere** means _to see,_ but **vedersi** means _to see each other;_ **scrivere** means _to write,_ but **scriversi** means _to write to each other._

The reciprocal form in the present tense needs the following before it can come out and play:

- ✔ The plural reflexive pronouns: ci, vi, and si
- ✔ The plural verb endings corresponding to noi (first person), voi (second person), and loro (third person)

The following table presents three examples of verbs conjugated in the reciprocal form.

amarsi (to love each other)	scriversi (to write each other)	sentirsi (to hear from each other)
noi **ci** am**iamo**	noi **ci** scriv**iamo**	noi **ci** sent**iamo**
voi **vi** am**ate**	voi **vi** scriv**ete**	voi **vi** sent**ite**
loro **si** am**ano**	loro **si** scriv**ono**	loro **si** sent**ono**
Gix e Teresa **si amano.** (*Gix and Teresa love each other.*)	Laura ed io **ci scriviamo** spesso. (*Laura and I write to each other often.*)	**Vi sentite** spesso, tu e tuo figlio? (*Do you and your son speak to each other often?*)

The following is a short list of some more very common verbs (for good or for bad, but I try to keep it positive) in the reciprocal form:

- ✔ **abbracciarsi** (*to hug each other*)
- ✔ **amarsi** (*to love each other;* only for partners, not for family, friends, and casual romantic relationships)
- ✔ **baciarsi** (*to kiss each other*)
- ✔ **darsi appuntamento** (*to make a date with each other*)
- ✔ **incontrarsi** (*to meet each other*)
- ✔ **odiarsi** (*to hate each other*)
- ✔ **salutarsi** (*to greet each other*)
- ✔ **volersi bene** (*to love each other;* for family/friends/a relationship that's beginning or has weathered time)

For this exercise, write in your journal, describing the Italians you're watching from your table (tavolino) at the Piazza della Signoria in Florence. Switching focus, talk about your budding romance with Gualtiero (or Matilde). Finally, talk about your friends Silvia and Lorenzo who have just split up. For all your musings, conjugate the verbs in the parentheses, focusing on the reciprocal form. Here's an example:

O. Quando gli amici _____, sono contenti. (vedersi)

A. Quando gli amici **si vedono,** sono contenti. (*When friends see each other, they are happy.*)

46. Quando gli italiani _____, _____ e _____ due volte. (incontrarsi, abbracciarsi, baciarsi)

47. Quando _____, fanno la stessa cosa. (salutarsi)

48. Gualtiero ed io _____ tante e-mail durante il giorno. (scriversi)

49. Matilde ed io _____ appuntamento in piazza. (darsi [noi])

50. Silvia e Lorenzo non _____ più; anzi, _____! (amarsi, odiarsi)

Answer Key

1 Io e te **ci** alziamo alle 7:00. (*You and I are getting up/get up at 7:00.*)

2 Gli studenti **si** alzano alle 7:00. (*The students get up at 7:00.*)

3 Lei, Professor Mariani, **si** alza alle 7:00? (*Professor Mariani, do you get up at 7:00?*)

4 Josh, **ti** alzi alle 7:00? (*Josh, do you get up at 7:00?*)

5 Samantha e Antonio, **vi** alzate alle 7:00? (*Samantha and Antonio, do you get up at 7:00?*)

6 **Mi** alzo alle 7:00. (*I get up at 7:00.*)

7 **Ci** alziamo alle 7:00. (*We get up at 7:00.*)

8 Marie **si** alza alle 7:00. (*Marie gets up at 7:00.*)

9 **Ti** alzi alle 7:00. (*You get up at 7:00.*)

10 **Vi** alzate alle 7:00. (*You (pl.) get up at 7:00.*)

11 **Mi lavo** le mani prima di cenare. *I'm going to wash my hands before dinner.*

12 Pina, **ti lavi** i denti? *Pina, are you going to brush your teeth?*

13 Il gatto **si lava** le zampe. *The cat is washing his paws.*

14 Emma e Giuseppe **si mettono** la giacca. *Emma and Giuseppe are putting on their jackets.*

15 Carla ed io **ci mettiamo** i pantaloni. *Carla and I are wearing pants.*

16 Carla, tu e Daniele **vi mettete** le lenti a contatto la mattina? *Carla, do you and Daniele put in your contact lenses in the morning?*

17 **Ci divertiamo** a imparare l'italiano? *Are we having fun learning Italian?*

18 Dove **ti diverti** di più, al mare o in montagna? *Where do you have more fun, at the beach or in the mountains?*

19 Alessandro e Giuglielmo **si divertono** a sciare. *Alex and Giuglielmo have fun skiing.*

20 **Mi innamoro** facilmente. *I fall in love easily.*

21 Dopo 5 minuti, Maria Francesca **si alza** dal letto. (*After 5 minutes, Maria Francesca gets out of bed.*)

22 Riccardo e Giuditta **si lamentano** dell'insegnante. (*Riccardo and Giuditta complain about their teacher.*)

23 Dopo un caffè, **mi preparo** per uscire. (*After a coffee, I get ready to go out.*)

24 **Ti vesti** subito, in 5 minuti, ma con cura. (*You dress quickly, but with care, in 5 minutes.*)

25 **Vi truccate** troppo! (*You're putting too much makeup on!/You wear too much makeup!*)

26   Non **mi pettino** mai. (*I never comb my hair.*)

27   Andiamo a lavorare, dove **ci impegniamo** molto, ma **ci divertiamo** anche! (*We're going to work, where we work hard, but also have fun!*)

28   Dopo lavoro **vi rilassate** a casa con la famiglia. (*After work you relax at home with your family.*)

29   I miei figli **si addormentano** sempre verso le 11:00 di sera. (*My children always fall asleep around 11:00 p.m.*)

30   Non **ci annoiamo** mai! (*We never get bored!*)

31   **A:** Dove **vi stabilite** dopo che **vi sposate?** (*Where are you going to live after you get married?*)

     B: Ci stabiliamo a Ferrara dopo che **ci sposiamo.** (*We're going to live in Ferrara after we get married.*)

32   **A:** Daniele, quando **ti sistemi?** (*Daniel, when are you going to settle down?*)

     B: Mi sistemo quando **mi innamoro.** (*I'm going to settle down when I fall in love.*)

33   **A:** Tuo padre **si rilassa** ad essere in pensione? (*Is your dad relaxing now that he's retired?*)

     B: Sì, molto: **Sì gode** la vita, e non **si annoia** mai! (*Yes, very much: He's enjoying life, and he's bored!*)

34   **A:** Amalia **si impegna** a scuola? (*Does Amalia work hard in school?*)

     B: Certo che **si impegna! Si rende conto** che è necessario impegnarsi per fare sempre bene! (*She certainly does work hard! She realizes that it's necessary to work hard in order to do well always.*)

35   **A:** Come **ti senti?** (*How do you feel?*)

     B: Mi sento benissimo! (*I feel very well!*)

36   **Ci dobbiamo fermare** in farmacia. (*We have to stop at the pharmacy.*)

37   Finalmente, i nonni **si possono rilassare.** (*Finally, my grandparents can relax.*)

38   **Vi volete sedere** vicino alla finestra? (*Do you want to sit near the window?*)

39   **Mi posso laureare** con lode, se lavoro duro. (*I can graduate with honors if I work hard.*)

40   Non **ti devi arrabbiare** così tanto! (*You don't have to get so angry!*)

41   Sì, ma a volte mi piace **vestirmi** di rosso. (*Yes, but sometimes I like to dress in red.*)

42   Noi preferiamo **alzarci** presto. (*We prefer to get up early.*)

43   Ad Amanda piace **divertirsi!** (*Amanda likes to have fun!*)

44   Preferite **trasferirvi** a Roma o a Milano? (*Do you prefer to move to Rome or Milan?*)

45   Alle bambine piace **guardarsi** allo specchio. (*Children like to look at themselves in the mirror.*)

46   Quando gli italiani **si incontrano, si abbracciano** e **si baciano** due volte. (*When Italians meet each other, they hug each other and kiss each other twice.*)

47   Quando **si salutano,** fanno la stessa cosa. (*When they greet each other/say goodbye to each other, they do the same thing.*)

48   Gualtiero ed io **ci scriviamo** tante e-mail durante il giorno. (*Gualtiero and I write each other many e-mails during the day.*)

49   **Ci diamo** appuntamento in piazza. (*We're making a date with each other in the piazza.*)

50   Silvia e Lorenzo non **si amano** più: anzi, **si odiano!** (*Silvia and Lorenzo don't love each other anymore: on the contrary, they hate each other!*)

Chapter 6

Giving a Command(ing) Performance with the Imperative

*L*ike a five-star chef barking out orders to his cooks at 7:00 p.m. on a Friday night, you can use the imperative (imperativo) to issue commands like "**Vieni** qua!" (*Come here!*) But you can also use the imperative to give advice, such as "**Lascialo stare!**" (*Just forget about it!*)

You hear the command form primarily in oral interactions, but you also see it in letters and e-mails — for example, "**Scrivimi** presto!" (*Write me soon!*) Whether you know it or not, you use the command form frequently in English, which is why you need the tool for Italian as well.

Nat King Cole immortalized the song "**Non dimenticar**" while inadvertently teaching everyone who heard it the structure of the negative tu command! And Rosemary Clooney made an indelible imprint (at least in my mind) of the positive tu command form with her "Ba ba **baciami baby** sulla bo bo bocca piccolina." The commands in Italian are used more often than you might think, and remembering the titles of these two songs — "**Non dimenticar**" and "**Baciami, baby!**" — will help you to construct your positive and negative tu commands from now on.

In this chapter, I explain how to give orders and make polite requests by using the imperative. I start out by showing you the ropes with the tu (second-person singular), noi (first-person plural), and voi (second-person plural) forms that you use with people (and pets) whom you know or whom you're angry with. I also explain how to make requests with the Lei (third-person singular, formal) and loro (third-person plural) forms, which come in handy for polite conversation and interacting with everyone from the judge who's ready to hand down a verdict to the shopkeeper from whom you want the best sausages. Along the way, I help you get a handle on using direct and indirect objects, too. Now get going!

Constructing Commands (Of the Tu, Noi, and Voi Variety)

The imperative is really about your tone of voice, which you can tell when you work with the tu (second-person singular), noi (first-person plural), and voi (second-person plural) forms. You form commands with these persons just like you conjugate the verbs in the present tense (see Chapters 2 and 3). However, as you often find throughout the Italian language, you must account for one exception: The tu affirmative imperative of **-are** verbs ends in **-a** — **Mangia!** (*Eat!*), for example — unlike the present-tense conjugation that ends in an **-i — mangi** (*you eat*). And as you find out a bit further, the tu form of various commands always seems to be a bit different than the others.

The following tables contain examples of **-are**, **-ere**, and **-ire** verb endings. You also see an **-ire** ending for which you have to add an **"isc"** before the tu **-ire** ending.

parlare (*to speak*)	
	noi parl**iamo**
tu parl**a**	voi parl**ate**
Parlate solo italiano! (*Speak* [you, pl.] *only Italian!*)	

leggere (*to read*)	
	noi legg**iamo**
tu legg**i**	voi legg**ete**
Josh, **leggi** ad alta voce, per favore. (*Josh, read aloud, please.*)	

partire (*to leave*)	
	noi part**iamo**
tu part**i**	voi part**ite**
Ragazzi, **partiamo** subito! (*Hey guys, let's leave right away!*)	

finire (*to finish*)	
	noi fin**iamo**
tu fin**isci**	voi fin**ite**
Emilia, **finisci** il tuo succo d'arancia! (*Emilia, finish your orange juice!*)	

A tavola! (*Everyone come to the table; the food's ready!* Literally: *Come to the table!*) For this exercise, practice the affirmative imperative in the tu, noi, and voi forms by commanding the different people in your house during suppertime. I provide you with the infinitive of the verb and the person (tu, noi, voi) in parentheses, and you conjugate the verb into the imperative. If the verb is irregular, I place an asterisk by it so that you can look it up in Chapter 3 (if you don't remember it, that is). Here's an example to get you started:

0. _____ la televisione! (spegnere [tu])

A. **Spegni** la televisione! (*Turn off the television!*)

1. _____ a tavola! (venire [voi])

2. _____! (mangiare [noi])

3. _____ una bottiglia di vino! (aprire [tu])

4. _____ il vino rosso! (bere* [noi])

5. _____ un brindisi! (fare* [noi])

6. _____ tu, Alan, con la pasta! (cominciare [tu])

7. _____ che bella cena! (guardare [voi])

8. _____ il pane, per favore! (passare [voi])

9. _____ la mamma! (ringraziare [noi])

10. _____ l'insalata, per favore, Emilia! (finire [tu])

Taking a negative approach

Forming the negative tu command is simple; you just take the word "non" (*not, don't*) and add the infinitive:

> non + infinitive — **Non Dimenticare!** (*Don't forget!*)

The noi (first-person plural) and voi (second-person plural) forms are the same as the affirmative forms (see the intro to this section). You just add the negation "non" in front of them.

Compare the following negative examples to the affirmative commands in the intro to this section:

✔ Non **parlare!** (*Don't speak!* [tu])

✔ Non **parliamo!** (*Let's not speak!* [noi])

✔ Non **parlate!** (*Don't speak!* [voi])

Your tone of voice is an essential part of the command, especially when the affirmative and the negative are essentially the same. For the negative, you want to emphasize what you're saying and imagine an exclamation point ending it.

You can't make up your mind today! First, you tell someone to do something, and then you tell him not to. For the purposes of this exercise, assume that you've already used the affirmative imperative; now you need to restate the phrase, but in the negative imperative, changing the conjugation of the verb in question. An asterisk means that the verb is irregular in the present indicative and also in the imperative. Here's an example for you:

Q. Mamma, vieni* a cena stasera!

A. Mamma, non **venire** a cena stasera! (*Mom, don't come for supper this evening!*)

11. Puliamo il frigo oggi!

_____

12. Uscite* stasera!

_____

13. Prendiamo gli spaghetti alla carbonara!

_____

14. Finisci tutto quel gelato!

15. Andate a Volterra in macchina!

16. Studia stasera!

17. Mangiamo a casa stasera!

18. Parla!

19. Fai il compito!

20. Dite tutto alla mamma!

Dealing with irregular imperatives

Some very common verbs have irregular affirmative "you" imperative forms. (The negative is always non + the infinitive of the verb.) The verbs in Table 6-1 have two forms: one that corresponds to the irregular present-tense verb conjugation, and one that's shortened with an apostrophe. These two forms are interchangeable, except when you have to attach a pronoun to the verb form. In that case, you must use the shorter one: for example, "**Fammi** un favore!" (*Do me a favor!*) = **fa'** + mi, rather than **fai** + mi, which would be awkward enough to say. (I talk about pronouns in the section "Adding Pronouns to the Imperative" later in this chapter.)

Table 6-1		Irregular tu Forms
Infinitive	*Tu Affirmative Imperative*	*Example*
andare (*to go*)	**va' (vai)**	**Va'** in camera! (*Go to your room!*)
dare (*to give*)	**da' (dai)**	**Da'** una mano alla mamma! (*Give mom a hand!*)
fare (*to make, to do*)	**fa' (fai)**	**Fai** le lasagne! (*Make lasagne!*)
stare (*to be, to stay*)	**sta' (stai)**	**Stai** zitto! (*Be quiet!*)
dire (*to say, to tell*)	**di'***	**Di'** a tuo padre che la nonna ha telefonato. (*Tell your dad that grandma called.*)

Unlike the other verbs in Table 6-1, **dire has only one form.*

The noi (first-person plural) and voi (second-person plural) imperative forms of the verbs in Table 6-1, affirmative and negative, are the same as their present-tense conjugations.

Not so fast: Before you jump into an exercise dealing with irregular tu imperatives, I need to add two more irregular verbs: **essere** (*to be*) and **avere** (*to have*). These two verbs don't follow the pattern of the verbs in Table 6-1. (Note that the voi person is also irregular, unlike the the other voi imperative forms, which are the same as the present indicative.) The voi, lei, and loro persons of these two verbs share their conjugations with the present subjunctive (see Chapter 12), as you can see in Tables 6-2 and 6-3.

The differences between the affirmative and negative commands of **essere** and **avere** are the same as the differences between the affirmative and negative commands for all verbs in the command form: Only the tu negative becomes an infinitive. For the other negatives, just place a "non" in front of the imperative.

Table 6-2   Comparing Affirmative and Negative Essere Commands

Affirmative	*Negative*
(tu) **Sii** buono! (*Be good!*)	Non **essere** cattivo! (*Don't be naughty!*)
(noi) **Siamo** ragionevoli! (*Let's be reasonable!*)	Non **siamo** in ritardo! (*Let's not be late!*)
(voi) **Siate** tranquilli! (*Be calm!*)	Non **siate** maleducati! (*Don't be rude!*)

Table 6-3   Comparing Affirmative and Negative Avere Commands

Affirmative	*Negative*
(tu) **Abbi** pazienza! (*Have patience!*)	Non **avere** paura! (*Don't be afraid!*)
(noi) **Abbiamo** paziena! (*Let's be patient!*)	Non **abbiamo** paura! (*Let's not be afraid!*)
(voi) **Abbiate** pazienza! (*Be patient!*)	Non **abbiate** paura! (*Don't be afraid!*)

Now you have the chance to put together the irregular affirmative and negative imperative forms from Tables 6-1 through 6-3. (I also throw in a regular verb or two.) Maria Cortina is talking to her eight children. Help her out by conjugating the verbs in parentheses into the affirmative or negative imperative.

If you see one name with a comma following it, you use the tu command form. If you see more than one name, you use the voi command form. If I specify to use the noi form, it should be obvious that you need to use the noi!

Here's an example:

Q. Francesca e Maria, _____ i letti! (fare)

A. Francesca e Maria, **fate** i letti! (*Francesca and Maria, make the beds!*)

21. Rocco, _____ al mercato e _____ del salame! (andare, comprare)

22. Viola, _____ a casa con le bambine oggi: Non _____ a lavorare. (stare, andare)

23. Giulio, non _____ parolacce (cuss words)! (dire)

24. Annunziata e Lino, non _____ fretta! (avere)

25. Maria e Francesca, _____ contente; _____ dei buoni mariti, e
_____ delle buone madri! (essere, trovare, fare)

26. Bambini, non _____ troppo rumore! (fare [noi])

27. Tutti quanti _____ zitti! (stare)

28. _____ una mano a Filippo! (dare [noi])

29. Maria, _____ un po' di pazienza: arrivo! (avere)

30. Rocco, per favore, _____ sempre onesto, e _____ sempre il
meglio per le tue sorelle. (essere, fare)

Adding Pronouns to the Imperative

You really can't talk about commands, much less use them, without knowing what to
do with the pronouns that often accompany them — including reflexive pronouns,
which I cover in Chapter 5, and direct- and indirect-object pronouns, which I cover
here. I mean, can you imagine saying "Give," "Take," or "Wash" without following up
with the appropriate pronoun?

- A **direct-object pronoun** substitutes for a direct object and agrees in gender and
  number with that object. For example, in the sentence "**Leggi** il libro!" (*Read the
  book!*), *the book* is the direct object. A direct object answers the question "Who?"
  or "What?" If you want to say "Read it" (**Leggilo!**), you have to replace *the book*
  with the masculine singular direct-object pronoun *lo*.

- An **indirect-object pronoun** replaces an indirect object, generally indicated in
  Italian by the preposition "a" (*to*): "**Parla** al professore!" (*Speak to the professor!*)
  Here, *to the professor* is the indirect object. An indirect object answers the question "To whom?" If you want to say "*Speak to him!*" (**Parlagli!**), you have to
  replace *to the professor* with the masculine singular indirect-object pronoun *gli*.

Check out Table 6-4, where I conveniently place all the personal, reflexive, direct-
object, and indirect-object pronouns. But don't use the personal pronouns with the
imperative.

Table 6-4		Pronouns		
Person	*Personal*	*Reflexive*	*Direct Object*	*Indirect Object*
First-person singular	io	mi	mi	mi
Second-person singular	tu	ti	ti	ti
Third-person singular	lui/lei/Lei	si	lo/la/La	gli/le/Le
First-person plural	noi	ci	ci	ci
Second-person plural	voi	vi	vi	vi
Third-person plural	loro/Loro	si	li/le	gli/loro/Loro

Here are some pronoun rules to keep in mind, along with plenty of examples:

✔ All reflexive, direct-, and indirect-object pronouns are attached to the tu, noi, and voi affirmative forms of the imperative:

- **Baciami!** (*Kiss me!*)

- **Alzati!** (from the reflexive verb **alzarsi**) (*Get up!*)

- **Vestitevi!** (from the reflexive verb **vestirsi**) (*Get dressed!*)

- **Prendi** i soldi: **Prendili!** ("I soldi" is the direct object) (*Take the money: Take it!*)

- **Telefoniamo** al babbo subito; **telefoniamogli** subito! ("al babbo" is the masculine singular indirect object) (*Let's call dad right away; let's call him right away!*)

- **Tagliamo** la torta; **tagliamola!** (*Let's cut the cake; let's cut it!*)

✔ The monosyllabic imperative forms in Table 6-1 double up on the **m** and sometimes **l** when combined with direct- and indirect-object pronouns:

- **Di'** la verità a me! ("a me" is the indirect object) → **Dimmi** la verità! (*Tell me the truth!*)

- **Da'** una mano a me! ("a me" is the indirect object) → **Dammi** una mano! (*Give me a hand!*)

- **Fa'** un piacere a me! ("a me" is the indirect object) → **Fammi** un piacere! (*Do me a favor!*)

- **Fa'** un favore a me! ("un favore" is the masculine singular direct object) → **Fallo** per me! (*Do it for me!*)

✔ In the negative forms of the imperative, the pronouns may come before or be attached to the command forms of the verbs:

- Non **baciarmi!** or Non **mi baciare!** (*Don't kiss me!*)

- Non **vestitevi** così! or Non **vi vestite** così! (*Don't dress that way!*)

- Non **dirmi** bugie! or Non **mi dire** bugie! (*Don't tell me lies!*)

✔ When you attach a pronoun to the negative tu, you just drop the final **e** from the infinitive and add the pronoun:

- Non **parlarmi!** (Non **parlare** + mi) (*Don't talk to me!*)

- Non **guardarlo!** (Non **guardare** + lo) (*Don't look at him!*)

Finally, here's a reflexive verb in the imperative that everyone needs to know, whether you're in the classroom or in Italy.

scusarsi (*to excuse onself, to be sorry*)	
	(noi) scus**iamoci!**
(tu) scus**ami!**	(voi) scus**atevi!**
Scusatemi! (*Excuse me!*) In a crowded train, this could mean, *Sorry, please let me through!*	

For this exercise, test your tu, noi, and voi prowess in the affirmative and negative imperative forms with either the direct- or indirect-object pronouns. Consult Table 6-4 to rewrite the sentences, substituting the underlined words with the direct- or indirect-object pronouns that apply. I give you the imperative and tell you in parenthesis if you need the direct-object pronoun (d.o.p.) or the indirect-object pronoun (i.o.p.). Here's an example:

Q. Saluta <u>la mamma</u>! (d.o.p.) (*Say hi to your mom [for me]*. Literally: *Greet your mom for me;* hence, "mom" is the direct object here.)

A. **Salutala!** (*Say hi to her!*)

31. Leggi <u>la poesia</u>! (d.o.p.) _____

32. Mangia <u>i ravioli</u>! (d.o.p.) _____

33. Non parlare <u>con lui</u>! (i.o.p.) _____

34. Non dite bugie <u>a noi</u>! (i.o.p) _____

35. Bevi <u>il latte</u>! (d.o.p.) _____

Now you can try an exercise with a couple of reflexive verbs in the imperative. Your mom is giving you advice. She tells you to do one thing with the affirmative imperative and not to do its opposite with the negative imperative. Create the tu forms of the affirmative and negative imperatives and then translate the whole thing! You can refer to Table 6-4 and the structure of the reflexive verb **scusarsi.** Here's an example to get you started:

Q. alzarsi presto/non alzarsi tardi

A. **Alzati** presto! Non **alzarti** tardi! (or, alternatively, Non **ti alzare** tardi!) *Get up early! Don't get up late!*

36. mettersi questi vestiti (these clothes)/non mettersi quei vestiti _____

_____

37. muoversi/non muoversi _____

_____

38. lavarsi i capelli domani/non lavarsi i capelli domani _____

_____

39. divertirsi/non divertirsi troppo _____

_____

40. sposarsi giovane/non innamorarsi mai _____

_____

In this exercise, you put together the different parts of the imperative you've seen in the chapter up to this point. Gigio has gone to see his friend Gianni, who's also his doctor. Gianni examines Gigio and gives him advice. Transform Gianni's sentences by conjugating the infinitives you see in parentheses into the tu (affirmative or negative) imperative and then adding the rest of whatever is in the parentheses. Here's an example:

Q. _____! (accomodarsi)

A. **Accomodati!** (*Come on in!*)

41. _____! (spogliarsi)

42. _____! (aprire la bocca)

43. _____! (dire trentatrè — this is like saying "Ahhhh" when you stick your tongue out)

44. _____! (toccare il naso)

45. _____! (respirare forte)

46. Non _____! (fumare più)

47. Non _____! (bere più la birra)

48. _____ alle 10 ogni sera! (andare a letto)

49. _____ un po' di ginnastica ogni giorno! (fare)

50. _____ ogni mattina! (svegliarsi presto)

Commanding Politely: Forming the Lei and Loro Forms of the Imperative

The Lei (third-person singular, formal) and Loro (third-person plural, formal) forms of the imperative are important forms to use with people you aren't familiar with or who deserve the proper respect: shopkeepers, hotel staff, policemen, strangers on trains, and so on. The Lei and Loro command forms are especially useful when you want to buy something at a store — for example, you can say, "**Mi dia** 12 paste, per favore; **metta** due di ogni tipo." (*Please give me 12 pastries; put in two of each kind.*)

In the following two ways, the Lei and Loro forms are much simpler than the tu, noi, and voi forms (see the previous sections of this chapter):

- ✔ The verb forms are the same for the affirmative and negative imperative.

- ✔ The applicable pronouns always proceed, in both the affirmative and negative, Lei and Loro in the imperative.

The following list presents the Lei and Loro imperative forms. Notice that the **-are, -ere,** and **-ire** verbs switch their characteristic letters. In other words, **-are** verb endings begin with **-i** and **-ere** and **-ire** verb endings begin with **-a:**

- ✔ **parlare: parl-** is the stem; **-i** and **-ino** are the Lei and Loro endings.

- ✔ **mettere: mett-** is the stem; **-a** and **-ano** are the Lei and Loro endings.

- ✔ **partire: part-** is the stem; **-a** and **-ano** are the Lei and Loro endings.

- ✔ **finire: finisc-** is the stem; **-a** and **-ano** are the Lei and Loro endings.

Information for later: The imperative Lei form resembles the regular and irregular forms of the io, tu, lui/lei/Lei persons of the present subjunctive; and the imperative Loro form is the same as the loro/Loro person of the present subjunctive. (This will be one less thing to memorize when you get to the present subjunctive in Chapter 12!)

Table 6-5 shows examples of regular, very common irregular, and reflexive forms of the Lei and Loro imperative. (I put an asterisk by the irregular verb forms — for more irregular forms, see Chapter 12.) With this table, you can do all the exercises that follow, and you can communicate in a hotel, at the doctor's office, and at a fruit market in Italy!

You often accompany these commands with "per favore," "per cortesia," or "per piacere" (*please*), but your polite tone of voice is the most important factor (it implies the "please"). You often see the word "pure" (*by all means*) with commands, too.

The pronoun "ne" means *some,* acts like a direct-object pronoun, and often replaces a quantity within a sentence.

Table 6-5	Lei and Loro Imperative Forms		
Infinitive	*Lei*	*Loro*	*Translation*
parlare (*to speak*)	**Parli!, Mi parli!**	**Mi parlino!**	*Please Speak! Speak to me!*
prendere (*to have, to take*)	Ne, **prenda!**	Ne, **prendano!**	*Please, take some!*
aprire (*to open*)	**Apra** la valigia per favore!	**Aprano...!**	*Open your suitcases please!*
finire (*to finish*)	**Finisca** con calma!	**Finiscano** con calma!	*Please finish at your leisure!*
dire* (*to say or tell*)	**Mi dica!**	**Mi dicano!**	*How can I help you?* (Literally: *Tell me what you'd like!*)
andare* (*to go*)	**Vada** pure!	**Vadano** pure!	*By all means, go!* or *After you!*
dare* (*to give*)	**Mi dia** mezzo chilo, per favore!	**Mi diano...!**	*Please give me half a chilo!*
avere* (*to have*)	**Abbia** pazienza!	**Abbiano** pazienza!	*Have patience* (please)!
essere* (*to be*)	**Sia** presente alla riunione!	**Siano** presenti...!	(Please) *Be at the meeting!*
stare* (*to be, to stay*)	**Stia** tranquilla!	**Stiano** tranquilli!	*Don't worry!*

Infinitive	Lei	Loro	Translation
sedersi (*to sit*)	**Si sieda,** prego!	**Si siedano,** prego!	*Please have a seat!* (*Sit down!*)
scusarsi (*to excuse oneself*)	**Mi scusi!**	**Mi scusino!**	*Oh, I'm sorry! Excuse me!*

You and your friend are at the market in Pienza, and you want to buy some cheese to bring back to the United States. The venditore (*vendor;* V) will use the Loro imperative, and you and your friend (A for amici) will use the Lei imperative. Conjugate the verbs in parentheses like I do in the following example:

Q. V: Buon giorno, mi _____! (dire)

A: Buon giorno, ci _____ del formaggio, per favore. (dare)

A. V: Buon giorno, mi **dicano!** (*Good morning, what can I get for you* [pl.]?)

A: Buon giorno, ci **dia** del formaggio, per favore. (*Good morning, please give us some cheese.*)

51. V: Prego, _____ pure quello che vogliono! (scegliere*)

52. A: Ci _____ un formaggio locale, per favore! (consigliare)

53. V: _____ questo pecorino fresco di Pienza; è molto buono! (assaggiare)

54. A: Che buono! Ce ne _____ un pezzo grande, per cortesia. Ci _____ un pacco ben chiuso (da portare in aereo)! (tagliare, fare*)

55. V: Lo _____ al fresco! (tenere*)

56. V: Serve altro? _____ anche questi bei funghi porcini! (vedere)

57. V: _____ tranquilli che sono freschissimi! (essere)

58. A: Allora, ci _____ un pacchetto do 500 grammi, per cortesia! (preparare)

59. A: Grazie _____! (tenere*)

60. V: Arrivederci, e _____ buon viaggio! (fare*)

Answer Key

1. **Venite** a tavola! (*Come to the table!*)

2. **Mangiamo!** (*Let's eat!*)

3. **Apri** una bottiglia di vino! (*Open a bottle of wine!*)

4. **Beviamo** il vino rosso! (*Let's drink red wine!*)

5. **Facciamo** un brindisi! (*Let's make a toast!*)

6. **Comincia** tu, Alan, con la pasta! (*You start, Alan, with the pasta!*)

7. **Guardate** che bella cena! (*Look at the beautiful supper!*)

8. **Passate** il pane, per favore! (*Pass the bread, please!*)

9. **Ringraziamo** la mamma! (*Let's thank mom!*)

10. **Finisci** l'insalata, per favore, Emilia! (*Finish your salad, please, Emilia!*)

11. Non **puliamo** il frigo oggi! (*Let's not clean the fridge today!*)

12. Non **uscite** stasera! (*Don't (pl.) go out tonight!*)

13. Non **prendiamo** gli spaghetti alla carbonara! (*Let's not get spaghetti alla carbonara!*)

14. Non **finire** tutto quel gelato! (*Don't finish all that ice cream!*)

15. Non **andate** a Volterra in macchina! (*Don't go to Volterra by car!*)

16. Non **studiare** stasera! (*Don't study tonight!*)

17. Non **mangiamo** a casa stasera! (*Let's not eat at home tonight!*)

18. Non **parlare!** (*Don't speak!*)

19. Non **fare** il compito! (*Don't do your homework!*)

20. Non **dite** tutto alla mamma! (*Don't tell Mom everything!*)

21. Rocco, **va'** al mercato e **compra** del salame! (*Rocco, go to the market and buy some salami!*)

22. Viola, **sta'** a casa con le bambine oggi: Non **andare** a lavorare. (*Viola, stay at home with the little girls today: Don't go to work.*)

23. Giulio, non **dire** parolacce! (*Giulio, don't say cuss words!*)

24. Annunziata e Lino, non **abbiate** fretta! (*Annunziata and Lino, don't rush!*)

25. Maria e Francesca, **siate** contente; **trovate** dei buoni mariti, e **fate** delle buone madri! (*Maria and Francesca, be happy; find good husbands, and be good mothers!*)

26. Bambini, non **facciamo** troppo rumore! (*Children, let's not make too much noise!*)

27 Tutti quanti **state** zitti! (*Everyone be quiet!*)

28 **Diamo** una mano a Filippo! (*Let's give Filippo a hand.*)

29 Maria, **abbi** un po' di pazienza: arrivo! (*Maria, have patience: I'm coming!*)

30 Rocco, per favore, **sii** sempre onesto, e **fa'** sempre il meglio per le tue sorelle. (*Rocco, please, be honest always, and always do what's best for your sisters.*)

31 **Leggila!** (*Read it!*)

32 **Mangiali!** (*Eat them!*)

33 Non **parlargli!**/Non gli **parlare!** (*Don't speak to him!*)

34 Non **ci dite** bugie!/Non **diteci** bugie! (*Don't tell us lies!*)

35 **Bevilo!** (*Drink it!*)

36 **Mettiti** questi vestiti. Non **metterti** (or non **ti mettere**) quei vestiti. *Put on these clothes. Don't put on those clothes.*

37 **Muoviti.** Non **muoverti** (or non **ti muovere**). *Move! Don't move!*

38 **Lavati** i capelli domani. Non **lavarti** (or non **ti lavare**) i capelli domani. *Wash your hair tomorrow. Don't wash your hair tomorrow.*

39 **Divertiti!** Non **divertirti** (or non **ti divertire**) troppo! *Have fun! Don't have too much fun!*

40 **Sposati** giovane. Non **innamorarti** (or non **ti innamorare**) mai! *Get married young. Don't ever fall in love!*

41 **Spogliati!** (*Undress!*)

42 **Apri** la bocca! (*Open your mouth!*)

43 **Di'** trentatrè! (*Say 33!*)

44 **Tocca** il naso! (*Touch your nose!*)

45 **Respira** forte! (*Breathe deeply!*)

46 Non **fumare** più! (*Don't smoke anymore!*)

47 Non **bere** più la birra! (*Don't drink anymore beer!*)

48 **Va'** a letto alle 10 ogni sera! (*Go to bed at 10 every evening!*)

49 **Fa'** un po' di ginnastica ogni giorno! (*Do some exercise every day!*)

50 **Svegliati** presto ogni mattina! (*Wake up early every morning!*)

51 V: Prego, **scelgano** pure quello che vogliono! (*Please, by all means choose whatever you like!*)

52 A: Ci **consigli** un formaggio locale, per favore! (*Please recommend a local cheese for us!*)

53 V: **Assaggino** questo pecorino fresco di Pienza; è molto buono! (*Taste this fresh pecorino from Pienza; it's very good!*)

54 A: Che buono! Ce ne **tagli** un pezzo grande, per cortesia. Ci **faccia** un pacco ben chiuso (da portare in aereo)! (*How good it is! Please cut us a big piece. And* [please] *make us a tightly sealed package* [*to bring on the plane*]*.*)

55 V: Lo **tengano** al fresco! (*Keep it in a cool spot!*)

56 V: Serve altro? **Vedano** anche questi bei funghi porcini! (*Do you need anything else? Take a look at these beautiful porcini mushrooms!*)

57 V: **Siano** tranquilli che sono freschissimi! (*Be assured that they are very fresh!*)

58 A: Allora, ci **prepari** un pacchetto di 500 grammi, per cortesia! (*Well then, please prepare us a package of 500 grams!*)

59 A: Grazie, **tenga**! (*Thanks, here you go!/Take this!*) **Note:** If you're handing money or anything else over, you should use this verb.

60 V: Arrivederci e **facciano** buon viaggio! (*Goodbye and have a good trip!*)

Chapter 7

Declaring Your Likes (and Dislikes) with Piacere

In This Chapter

▶ Pairing **piacere** with indirect-object pronouns

▶ Forming the third-person singular and plural of **piacere**

▶ Passing through the tenses of **piacere**

▶ Tackling forms of **piacere** other than third-person singular and plural

▶ Noting the similarities of **mancare** and **piacere**

*I*f you plan on traveling to Italy, or if you've already been (and now want to learn the beautiful language you heard time and again), you should become familiar with the verb **piacere,** which most people take to mean, "*It's a pleasure to meet you!*" However, **piacere** is also the closest Italian equivalent to the English infinitive "to like." **Piacere** literally means *to be pleasing to* someone or something (and non **piacere,** quite simply, means *to not like*). In this chapter, you see **piacere** in all its glory. You practice with indirect-object pronouns, conjugate the two most common persons of **piacere** in the present, and take a trip with **piacere** through the different possible tenses. After you finish the exercises, you'll be able to express your likes and dislikes in a variety of ways. I hope this chapter is pleasing to you!

The Indirect Object of Piacere's Affection

As a verb, **piacere** (*to like, to be pleasing to*) is unique in that it takes indirect-object pronouns rather than personal pronouns. For example, "I like milk" becomes "Milk is pleasing to me," or "**Mi piace** il vino." Similarly, you need the preposition "a" (*to*) when using proper nouns. For example, you translate "A Domenico **piace** la pasta" as (literally) *Pasta is pleasing to Domenick* (or *Domenick likes pasta*).

I cover both indirect- and direct-object pronouns in Chapter 6, but here's a refresher on the indirect-object pronouns:

✔ **mi:** *to me*

✔ **ti:** *to you* (fam. sing.)

✔ **gli:** *to him*

✔ **le:** *to her*

✔ **Le:** *to you* (form. sing.)

✔ **ci:** *to us*

✔ **vi:** *to you* (form. pl.)

✔ **loro:** *to them* (this indirect object follows the verb)

The indirect-object pronoun loro always follows the verb **piacere;** all the other indirect-object pronouns precede the verb. Loro, however, is interchangeable with gli when you want to say "They like" or "To them": "Gli **piace** fumare?" "**Piace** loro fumare?" (*Do they like to smoke?*) Loro is more correct grammatically, but gli is more common and colloquial.

Of course, working with a sentence that contains the verb **piacere** isn't the only time you use an indirect-object pronoun in Italian; you use one every time you'd normally do so in English — for example, "Gli **dai** il libro?" (*Are you giving him the book?*) But for the purpose of this chapter, concentrate on using the pronouns when conjugating the verbs **piacere** and **mancare** (*to miss;* see the section "Missing You! Conjugating **Mancare**").

Don't forget that the indirect-object pronoun "gli" also means *to him* (or *he*). You can use gli to replace both *to him* and *to them*. This can save you time when speaking and writing and eliminate the question of where to put the pronoun (because gli always comes before).

Now you can try some exercises that focus on including indirect-object pronouns. In the following problems, I include a sentence with a specific subject, and then I provide the object of the sentence preceded by a blank; you give me the corresponding indirect-object pronoun. Here's an example for you:

0. A Teresa piace il teatro. _____ piace il teatro.

A. **Le** piace il teatro. (*She likes theater; theater is pleasing to her.*)

1. Al babbo piace nuotare. _____ piace nuotare.

2. A noi piace il gelato italiano. _____ piace il gelato italiano.

3. A voi piace l'Italia? _____ piace l'Italia?

4. A Maria Paola piace il Campari. _____ piace il Campari.

5. Ai miei studenti piace quel film. Piace _____ quel film (or _____ piace quel film).

6. A me piacciono gli spaghetti alla carbonara. _____ piacciono gli spaghetti alla carbonara.

7. A te piace l'Italia? _____ piace l'Italia?

8. Signora Costa, a Lei piacciono gli Stati Uniti? Signora Costa, _____ piacciono gli Stati Uniti?

9. A John e Laurie piacciono le Hawaii. _____ piacciono le Hawaii (or Piacciono _____ le Hawaii).

10. Julia, _____ piace ballare?

Choosing between Piace and Piacciono

The verb **piacere** enjoys a couple of very unique conjugations (if you were paying close attention, you may have caught on in the practice exercises in the previous section), in that the most common conjugation forms are the third-person singular (**piace**) and the third-person plural (**piacciono**). For most verbs, you use all six persons when conjugating so that the verbs agree with the subjects of the sentences — for example,

"Io **mangio** la carne" (*I eat meat*). With the verb **piacere,** what's typically the object in an English construction becomes the subject in an Italian construction. For example, *I like spaghetti* becomes (literally) *To me, spaghetti is pleasing,* or "**Mi piacciono** gli spaghetti."

Here are some guidelines on when to choose **piace** or **piacciono:**

> ✔ You use **piace** when what you like is singular or to keep a verb in its infinitive form. For example, "Gli **piace** la pizza di Pepe" (*He likes Pepe's pizza*) or "Gli **piace mangiare**" (*He likes to eat*).

> ✔ You use **piacciono** when what you like is plural. For example, "Gli **piacciono** i frutti di mare" (*He likes shellfish* [the word for shellfish is plural in Italian]; *Shellfish are pleasing to him*) or "**Mi piacciono** i film italiani" (*I like Italian films; Italian films are pleasing to me*).

After you decide which form to use, all you need to change is the indirect object or indirect-object pronoun (see the previous section for a list of these).

You use the same cases for all the tenses when dealing with **piacere:** the third-person singular and third-person plural.

For the following practice exercise, place the correct form of the verb **piacere** (**piace** or **piacciono**) in the space provided. Follow my example:

0. A Maria _____ le patate.

A. A Maria **piacciono** le patate. (*Maria likes potatoes.*)

11. Ci _____ la Florida.

12. A Domenico _____ gli spaghetti.

13. Vi _____ i panini al prosciutto?

14. Ai miei studenti non _____ gli esami.

15. A Gina _____ essere magra.

16. Ti _____ la pizza ai funghi?

17. Gli _____ i cani?

18. Mi _____ andare in Italia.

19. Le _____ i ragazzi italiani!

20. Non mi _____ fumare.

You may want to expand on the conjugations of **piace** and **piacciono** by talking about your likes and dislikes. One vehicle for such discussions is the process of asking and answering questions. When you ask a question in Italian, the word "do" is understood.

Ti piace Ravenna? (*Do you like Ravenna?*)

When a statement or question calls for you to say "it" or "them," these words, too, are understood. In other words, you don't need a direct-object pronoun to substitute whatever object or person you want to declare you like or to query about liking:

> **Ti piace** Ravenna? Sì, **mi piace!** (*Yes, I like it!*) The *it* is understood.

> **Ti piacciono** i cappelletti? Sì, mi **piacciono.** (*Do you like cappelletti* [a wonderful pasta dish from the Emilia Romagna region]? *Yes, I like them.*) The term *them* is understood.

When you want to declare that you don't like an object, event, or person, you use the word "non" (*not*). You place non in front of **piacere** if you have a proper noun or regular noun, and you place non in front of the indirect-object pronoun when it has been substituted for a noun.

> A Teresa non **piace** quel ragazzo. (*Teresa doesn't like that boy.*) The non is right before **piace.**

> Ai ragazzi non **piace** l'insegnante. (*The kids don't like the teacher.*) The non is right before **piace.**

> Non **mi piace** quel ragazzo. (*I don't like that boy.*) The non is in front of the indirect-object pronoun.

For this exercise, ask your friend Jacopo some questions about his likes and dislikes by using the correct form of the verb **piacere** and any necessary pronouns, and then answer the questions (in the affirmative or negative when necessary). Don't worry about answering for Jacopo . . . he's used to such abuse. Follow my lead with this example:

Q. Jacopo, _____ la poesia italiana? Sì, _____.

A. Jacopo, **ti piace** la poesia italiana? Sì, **mi piace** (or Sì, **mi piace** la poesia italiana). (*Jacopo, do you like Italian poetry? Yes, I like it* [or *I like Italian poetry*].)

21. Jacopo, quali scrittori italiani _____? _____ Leopardi e Foscolo.

22. Jacopo, _____ la lotta (wrestling)? No, _____, ma _____ molto il calcio.

23. Jacopo, _____ studiare l'italiano? Sì, _____.

24. Jacopo, _____ le ragazze italiane? No, _____.

25. Jacopo, _____ questa scuola? Sì, _____.

Time to head to il mercato (*the market*)! For this exercise, practice translating from English into Italian, using the correct forms of the verb **piacere** along with the proper indirect objects or indirect-object pronouns. Here's an example:

Q. I like to shop at the market.

A. **Mi piace fare** la spesa al mercato.

26. I like the fresh fruit (la frutta fresca).

_____

27. I like to buy pecorino from Pienza, too.

_____

28. I don't like the supermarket (il supermercato).

_____

29. My mother likes the eggs (le uova) at the market.

_____

30. She likes to go to the market every morning (ogni mattina).

_____

Expressing Likes (And Dislikes) in Any Tense

Just like the verb **piacere** in the present tense, **piacere** in other tenses features the third-person singular and plural as its most common forms. Table 7-1 gives you a quick overview of **piacere** through some common tenses. You can come back to this table whenever you need to after you go through the different uses of the verb tenses in other chapters — it will prove invaluable!

Table 7-1	Piacere 1st and 3rd Person Through the Tenses	
Tense	*1st- and 3rd-Person Verb Conjugation*	*Example*
Future	**piacerà**	John, **ti piacerà** Cortona. (*John, you're going to like Cortona.*)
	piaceranno	John, **ti piaceranno** questi vini. (*John, you're going to like these wines.*)
Present perfect	**è piaciuto/a**	Le **è piaciuta** l'opera ieri. (*She liked the opera last night.*)
	sono piaciuti/e	Non le **sono piaciute**, però, le penne alla vodka. (*She didn't like, however, the penne with vodka sauce.*)
Conditional	**piacerebbe**	**Mi piacerebbe andare** ad Assisi. (*I'd like to go to Assisi.*)
	piacerebbero	**Mi piacerebbero** questi jeans se **costassero** di meno. (*I'd like these jeans if they cost less.*)
Past absolute	**piacque**	Al nonno **piacque** l'America. (*Grandfather liked America.*)
	piacquero	Al nonno **piacquero** gli americani. (*Grandfather liked Americans.*)

(continued)

Table 7-1 (continued)

Tense	1st- and 3rd-Person Verb Conjugation	Example
Imperfect	**piaceva**	Quando **eri** piccola, **ti piaceva cantare?** (*When you were little, did you like to sing?*)
	piacevano	Quando **eri** piccola, **ti piacevano** i ragazzi? (*When you were little, did you like boys?*)
Pres. subjunctive	**piaccia**	Non **credo** che gli **piaccia.** (*I don't think [that] he likes it.*)
	piacciano	Non **credo** che gli **piacciano.** (*I don't think [that] he likes them.*)
Past subjunctive	**sia piaciuto/a**	**Spero** che vi **sia piaciuto** questo capitolo. (*I hope that you all liked this chapter.*)
	siano piaciuti/e	**Spero** che vi **siano piaciute** le lasagne. (*I hope that you liked the lasagne.*)
Imperf. subjunctive	**piacesse**	Non **sapevo** che **ti piacesse** il gorgonzola! (*I didn't know that you like gorgonzola!*)
	piacessero	Non **sapevo** che **ti piacessero** le sfogliatelle! (*I didn't know that you like sfogliatelle!*)

The following exercises allow you to work with the tenses I present in Table 7-1. Translate the sentences into English; I tell you what tenses you should put the verb **piacere** in. Here's an example:

Q. Ci sarebbe piaciuto fermarci di più. (past conditional)

A. *We would've liked to stay longer.*

31. Non so se gli sia piaciuta la cena. (past subjunctive)

_____

32. Ci piaceva giocare fuori quando eravamo piccole. (imperfect)

_____

33. Sono contenta che ti piaccia questa poesia. (present subjunctive)

_____

34. A Maria sono piaciuti i regali. (present perfect)

_____

35. Mi piacerebbe un caffè. (conditional)

_____

The following exercise problems allow you to practice using the third-person singular or the third-person plural of the verb **piacere.** However, you have to concentrate on the present perfect tense. You use the present perfect tense (or passato prossimo) quite a bit if you travel to Italy, and it may be necessary for corresponding with, for example, an Italian e-pal. For the following exercise, fill in the blanks with the correct forms of the verb **piacere** in the present perfect tense.

Here are a few points to keep in mind as you complete these practice problems (for more information on the present perfect, see Chapters 14 and 15):

> ✔ **Piacere** takes **essere** (*to be*) in the present perfect.
>
> ✔ **Piacere's** past participle is **piaciuto.**
>
> ✔ **Piaciuto** has to agree with what was liked, not with who liked it.

Here's an example to get you started:

Q. Non mi _____ quella birra italiana.

A. Non mi **è piaciuta** quella birra italiana. (*I didn't like that Italian beer.*)

36. Ti _____ i ristoranti a Roma?

37. Sì, ma mi _____ la pizzeria *Da Ivo* di più.

38. Che altro hai mangiato? Mi _____ molto i carciofi alla giudia.

39. A mio marito _____ le tagliatelle con i funghi.

40. Ci _____ soprattutto visitare Frascati una sera.

Piacere: The Rest of the Story

If you've worked through the practice exercises in the previous sections of this chapter, you're becoming an expert in conjugating the verb **piacere** in the third-person singular and plural persons. However, just because these forms are **piacere's** most common forms doesn't mean that the other persons don't exist!

Let me break it down in more likeable terms. What I mean is that when some people go to Italy or spark a friendship with an Italian person, they inevitably find that they need to be able to say, "I like you" or "Do you like me?" Showing your feelings gets a little tricky with the common forms of the verb **piacere,** which literally means *to be pleasing to.* So, allow me to present the full conjugation in the following table.

piacere (*to like, to be pleasing to*)	
io pia**cc**io	noi pia**cc**iamo
tu piac**i**	voi piac**ete**
lu, lei, Lei piac**e**	loro pia**cc**iono
(lei) **Ti piaccio?** (lui) Sì, **mi piaci** molto. ([she] *Do you like me?* [he] *Yes, I like you a lot.*)	

Notice in the following examples that I use "gli" rather than "lui" for "he":

Io **piaccio** a Marco./Gli **piaccio.** (*Marco likes me/He likes me;* Literally: *I am pleasing to Marco.*)

Tu **piaci** a Marco./Gli **piaci.** (*Marco likes you./He likes you.*)

Lei **piace** a Marco./Lei gli **piace.** (*Marco likes her./He likes her.*)

Noi **piacciamo** a Marco./Gli **piacciamo.** (*Marco likes us./He likes us.*)

Voi **piacete** a Marco./Gli **piacete.** (*Marco likes you./He likes you.*)

Loro **piacciono** a Marco./Loro gli **piacciono.** (*Marco likes them./He likes them.*)

In the following exercise, substitute the indirect object with an indirect-object pronoun, noting the uses of the less-common forms of **piacere,** and then translate. Here's an example:

O. Io piaccio a Marco.

A. Io **gli** piaccio. *He likes me.* (Literally: *I am pleasing to him.*)

41. Piaci a Marianna. (*MaryAnn likes you.*) _____

_____

42. Piacete ai vostri insegnanti? (*Do your teachers like you?*) _____

_____

43. Piacciamo al professore. (*The professor likes us.*) _____

_____

44. Fabrizio piace a Francesca? (*Does Francesca like Fabrizio?*) _____

_____

45. Piaccio a voi? (*Do you all like me?*) _____

_____

Missing You! Conjugating Mancare

The verb **mancare,** which means *to miss* or *to lack*, functions in precisely the same manner as the verb **piacere** (*to like*). In other words, you generally use it with indirect objects and indirect-object pronouns, and it translates literally as *Something is missing to me.* Therefore, I think this chapter is the perfect spot for it! The following table shows the initial conjugation of **mancare.**

mancare (*to miss*)	
io man**co**	noi man**chiamo**
tu man**chi**	voi man**cate**
lui, lei, Lei man**ca**	loro man**cano**
Cara mamma e papà, **mi mancate!** (*Dear mom and dad, I miss you!*)	

Here are some more examples of **mancare** conjugations:

Io **ti manco?** (*Do you miss me?* Literally: *Am I missing to you?*)

Sì, tu **mi manchi.** (*Yes, I miss you.*)

Mi manca mia madre. (*I miss my mother.*)

For this practice exercise, simply choose between the third-person singular and the third-person plural of **mancare.** If what you're missing is singular, use **manca;** if what you're missing is plural, use **mancano.** Here's an example:

Q. Ti _____ l'Italia?

A. Ti **manca** l'Italia? (*Do you miss Italy?*)

46. Che cosa ti _____ dell'Italia?

47. Mi _____ i miei amici.

48. Ad Emilia _____ la piadina romagnola.

49. Ti _____ lavorare là?

50. A Giancarlo _____ il ritmo di vita, gli amici, e la sua città.

For the final exercise of the chapter, translate the sentences dealing with **mancare** into English, keeping an eye on the forms of the verbs and the pronouns around them. Follow the example:

Q. A Giancarlo manca Ravenna. Gli manca Ravenna.

A. *Giancarlo misses Ravenna. He misses Ravenna.*

51. Cosa manca per la cena? Mancano gli spaghetti e il pesce.

_____

52. Manchi a tua madre; le manchi molto.

_____

53. So che manco ai miei genitori. So che gli manco.

_____

54. Samanta manca ad Antonio. Samanta gli manca.

_____

55. Mi mancano i miei vecchi studenti.

_____

Answer Key

1 **Gli** piace nuotare. (*He likes to swim.*)

2 **Ci** piace il gelato italiano. (*We like Italian ice cream.*)

3 **Vi** piace l'Italia? (*Do you like Italy?*)

4 **Le** piace il Campari. (*She likes Campari.*)

5 Piace **loro** quel film (or **gli** piace quel film). (*They like that film.*)

6 **Mi** piacciono gli spaghetti alla carbonara. (*I like spaghetti alla carbonara.*)

7 **Ti** piace l'Italia? (*Do you like Italy?*)

8 Signora Costa, **Le** piacciono gli Stati Uniti? (*Mrs. Costa, do you like the United States?*)

9 **Gli** piacciono le Hawaii (or Piacciono **loro** le Hawaii). (*They like Hawaii.*)

10 Julia, **ti** piace ballare? (*Julia, do you like to dance?*)

11 Ci **piace** la Florida. (*We like Florida.*)

12 A Domenico **piacciono** gli spaghetti. (*Domenick likes spaghetti.*)

13 Vi **piacciono** i panini al prosciutto? (*Do you (pl.) like prosciutto sandwiches?*)

14 Ai miei studenti non **piacciono** gli esami. (*My students don't like exams.*)

15 A Gina **piace** essere magra. (*Gina likes to be thin.*)

16 Ti **piace** la pizza ai funghi? (*Do you like pizza with mushrooms?*)

17 Gli **piacciono** i cani? (*Does he like dogs?/Do they like dogs?*)

18 Mi **piace** andare in Italia. (*I like to go to Italy.*)

19 Le **piacciono** i ragazzi italiani! (*She likes Italian boys!*)

20 Non mi **piace** fumare. (*I don't like to smoke.*)

21 Jacopo, quali scrittori italiani **ti piacciono? Mi piacciono** Leopardi e Foscolo. (*Jake, which Italian writers do you like? I like Leopardi and Foscolo.*)

22 Jacopo, **ti piace** la lotta? No, non **mi piace**, ma **mi piace** molto il calcio. (*Jake, do you like wrestling? No, I don't like it, but I like soccer very much.*)

23 Jacopo, **ti piace** studiare l'italiano? Sì, **mi piace** (or **mi piace** studiare l'italiano). (*Jake, do you like studying Italian? Yes, I like it [or I like studying Italian].*)

24 Jacopo, **ti piacciono** le ragazze italiane? No, non **mi piacciono** (or non **mi piacciono** le ragazze italiane). (*Jake, do you like Italian girls? No, I don't like them [or No, I don't like Italian girls].*)

25 Jacopo, **ti piace** questa scuola? Sì, **mi piace.** (*Jake, do you like this school? Yes, I like it.*)

26 **Mi piace** la frutta fresca.

27 **Mi piace** anche **comprare** il pecorino di Pienza.

28 Non **mi piace** il supermercato.

29 A mia madre **piacciono** le uova al mercato.

30 Le **piace andare** al mercato ogni mattina.

31 *I don't know if he liked the dinner.*

32 *We used to like to play outside when we were little.*

33 *I'm pleased that you like this poem.*

34 *Maria liked the presents.*

35 *I'd like a coffee.*

36 Ti **sono piaciuti** i ristoranti a Roma? (*Did you like the restaurants in Rome?*)

37 Sì, ma mi **è piaciuta** la pizzeria *Da Ivo* di più. (*Yes, but I liked the pizzeria Da Ivo the most.*)

38 Che altro hai mangiato? Mi **sono piaciuti** molto i carciofi alla giudia. (*What else did you eat? I liked the Jewish-style artichokes very much.*)

39 A mio marito **sono piaciute** le tagliatelle con i funghi. (*My husband liked the tagliatelle with mushrooms.*)

40 Ci **è piaciuto** soprattutto visitare Frascati una sera. (*Above all, we liked visiting Frascati one evening.*)

41 **Le piaci.** *She likes you.*

42 **Piacete loro?** *Do they like you?*

43 **Gli piacciamo.** *He likes us.*

44 **Le piace** Fabrizio? *Does she like Fabrizio?*

45 **Vi piaccio?** *Do you all like me?*

46 Che cosa ti **manca** dell'Italia? (*What do you miss about Italy?*)

47 Mi **mancano** i miei amici. (*I miss my friends.*)

48 Ad Emilia **manca** la piadina romagnola (piadina is a flat bread made in the Romagna region). (*Emilia misses the piadina.*)

49 Ti **manca** lavorare là? (*Do you miss working there?*)

50 A Giancarlo **mancano** il ritmo di vita, gli amici, e la sua città. (*Giancarlo misses the pace of life, his friends, and his city.*)

51 *What do we still need for the dinner?* (Literally: *What's missing for dinner?*) *We still need the spaghetti and the fish.*

52 *Your mother misses you; she misses you a lot.*

53 *I know my parents miss me. I know that they miss me.*

54 *Antonio misses Samantha. He misses Samantha.*

55 *I miss my old students.*

Part II
Looking to the Past and the Future

The 5th Wave   By Rich Tennant

"You want me to use the passato remoto? What does the channel changer that came with our Japanese television set have to do with learning Italian verbs?"

and the Future

In this part . . .

You cover a lot of territory here: the future, the past, and even a different mood — the subjective subjunctive! This part should be the most challenging, but think of how proud you'll be when you master it! Here, I cover two of the main past tenses: the imperfect and the past absolute. You also start talking about the future with the future tense and conditionally with the conditional tense. I introduce the subjunctive mood as well, through the scope of the present and imperfect subjunctive tenses.

Chapter 8

Once Upon a Time: The Imperfect Tense

In This Chapter
▶ Becoming familiar with the uses of the imperfect tense
▶ Putting perfect imperfect sentences together
▶ Conjugating and practicing the imperfect tense

As they say, you don't know where you're going unless you know where you've been. In Italian, the imperfect tense is one of several past tenses that you need to utilize in order to dwell on the past (a good thing, in this chapter anway). The *imperfect* (or *imperfetto*) tense is the tense of a verb that indicates a past action or a state as uncompleted, continuous, or ongoing. The imperfect is very common and indispensable for everyday speech, narrating, and reading.

Often called the *past descriptive tense,* the imperfect tense has its own specific uses that set it apart from the other tenses that you use to speak about past actions in Italian — the passato prossimo (the present perfect; see Chapters 14 and 15) and the passato remoto (the past absolute; see Chapter 9). You often find it in fairy tales and literature — hence this chapter's title, "Once Upon a Time." In this chapter, you discover how to conjugate verbs in the imperfect tense and when to use the imperfect, with plenty of practice exercises to master your craft.

Perfecting the Uses of the Imperfect

In addition to fairy tales, the imperfect tense has a number of uses. Bulk up your knowledge by checking out the following list.

To describe a repeated or habitual action in the past

This use translates as *used to* or *would.* Expressions denoting the frequency of the action you're describing, such as the following, often signal this use of the imperfect:

 ✔ **sempre:** *always, all the time*

 ✔ **spesso:** *often*

 ✔ **ogni estate:** *every summer*

 ✔ **quando:** *when*

 ✔ **a volte:** *sometimes*

 ✔ **di solito:** *usually*

 ✔ **di notte/di giorno:** *in the evening/during the day*

 ✔ **la domenica, il lunedì, il martedì . . . :** *on Sundays, on Mondays, on Tuesdays . . .*

Here are some specific examples outlined in complete sentences:

✔ **Andavamo** <u>sempre</u> a Urbino con la scuola. (*We used to go to Urbino all the time with our school.*)

✔ <u>Spesso</u> **prendevo** il gelato dopo cena. (*I would often get ice cream after dinner.*)

✔ <u>Ogni estate</u> i miei amici **lavoravano.** (*My friends would work every summer.*)

✔ <u>Quando</u> **eri** piccolo, dove **andavi** in vacanza? (*When you were little, where did you go on vacation?*)

To express an ongoing action in the past

This use also may include two simultaneous actions, both of which appear in the imperfect. You often see the word "mentre" (*while, during*) in this circumstance. Here are a couple examples:

✔ **Frequentavo** un programma estivo. (*I was attending a summer program.*)

✔ I bambini **giocavano** <u>mentre</u> Enzo **preparava** da **mangiare.** (*The children were playing while Enzo was preparing something to eat.*)

To describe an ongoing action in the past that eventually gets interrupted

In this case, the ongoing action is in the imperfect tense, and the action that interrupts is in the present perfect, or passato prossimo (see Chapter 14). In this usage, you often see the word "quando" (*when*) or the less common "all'improvviso" (*all of a sudden*). Here a couple examples:

✔ Cosa **facevi** <u>quando</u> **hai saputo?** (*What were you doing when you found out?*)

✔ **Cenavamo,** e <u>all'improvviso</u> la luce **è saltata.** (*We were having dinner, and all of a sudden the electricity went out.*)

At times, you can interchange this particular use with the present progressive tense (see Chapter 23).

To describe weather, time, and age in the past

Here are a couple dark and dreary examples of this usage:

✔ Ieri **faceva** freddo e **tirava** vento. (*It was cold and windy yesterday.*)

✔ **Era** mezzanotte quando **sono rientrata.** (*It was midnight when I got home.*)

To describe a physical, mental, or emotional state in the past

Here's where you can get sentimental:

✔ Giancarlo **era** magro 15 anni fa. (*Giancarlo was thin 15 years ago.*)

✔ Noi **eravamo** bambini felici. (*We were happy children.*)

✔ **Ci volevamo** bene. (*We loved each other.*)

You can also use the imperfect with verbs denoting knowing, wanting, believing, and doubting (**sapere, volere, credere,** and **dubitare,** respectively):

✔ **Sapevo** tutto di te. (*I knew everything about you.*)

✔ **Volevi** un'altra risposta? (*Did you want a different answer?*)

✔ **Mi credevano** morto! (*They thought I was dead!*)

You can find some other uses of the imperfect tense in Chapter 13 (together with the imperfect subjunctive) and in Chapter 21 (with some hypothetical phrases).

Forming Perfect Sentences with the Imperfect

To form the imperfetto tense, you start with the infinitive form of **-are**, **-ere**, and **-ire** verbs (that is, the whole verb — **parlare, mettere, partire**). You take the stem of the infinitives and add the imperfect endings for these verbs (for examples, see the following tables). Italian features only a few irregular verbs in the imperfetto, and I cover those in this section as well.

Here's a a breakdown of the imperfect endings for **-are**, **-ere**, and **-ire** verbs. Say these endings to yourself aloud a few times before moving on to conjugating the verbs and reviewing the upcoming tables. This practice will help you commit the endings to memory.

> With an **-are** verb like **parlare**, the stem is **parl-**; the possible endings include **-avo, -avi, -ava, -avamo, -avate,** and **-avano**.

> With an **-ere** verb like **vendere**, the stem is **vend-**; the possible endings include **-evo, -evi, -eva, -evamo, -evate,** and **-evano**.

> With an **-ire** verb like **capire**, the stem is **cap-**; the possible endings include **-ivo, -ivi, -iva, -ivamo, -ivate,** and **-ivano**.

parlare (*to speak, to talk*)	
io parl**avo**	noi parl**avamo**
tu parl**avi**	voi parl**avate**
lui, lei, Lei parl**ava**	loro parl**avano**
La mamma **parlava** al telefonino mentre io **guidavo**. (*Mom was talking on her cell phone while I was driving.*)	

vendere (*to sell*)	
io vend**evo**	noi vend**evamo**
tu vend**evi**	voi vend**evate**
lui, lei, Lei vend**eva**	loro vend**evano**
I nonni **vendevano** l'uva che **coltivavano**. (*My grandparents would sell the grapes that they would grow.*)	

capire (*to understand*)	
io cap**ivo**	noi cap**ivamo**
tu cap**ivi**	voi cap**ivate**
lui, lei, Lei cap**iva**	loro cap**ivano**
Una volta **capivo** il russo, ma ora non più. (*I used to understand Russian, but not anymore.*)	

PRACTICE

Quando ero piccolo/piccola . . . (*When I was little . . .*) Here's your chance to talk about what life was like when you were little. Conjugate the following verbs in parentheses into the imperfetto tense. I provide the full translation in the Answer Key. Here's an example:

Q. _____ in Connecticut. (abitare)

A. **Abitavo** in Connecticut. (*I lived in Connecticut.*)

1. Mio padre _parlava_ l'italiano. (parlare)

2. Noi _andavamo_ in vacanza in Italia. (andare)

3. Io _mangiava_ il gelato tutti i giorni. (mangiare)

4. Al ritorno, _ci fermavamo_ ad Amsterdam. (fermarsi [noi])

5. Io _avevo_ 3 conigli. (avere)

6. Mia sorella _seguiva_ lezioni di danza. (seguire)

7. I miei genitori _uscirivano_ spesso con i loro amici. (uscire)

8. Mia madre _preparava_ il sugo e gli gnocchi la domenica. (preparare)

9. Mia sorella, mio fratello ed io _giocavamo_ fuori tutto il giorno. (giocare)

10. Il passatempo che _preferivano_ tutti era cantare. (preferire)

11. E tu, _ti divertivi_ quando eri piccolo/a? (divertirsi)

12. Ci _piacevamo_ mangiare la pizza a New Haven. (piacere)

13. Mio fratello _si vestiva_ sempre in pantaloncini rossi. (vestirsi)

14. Noi _facevamo_ le gite scholastiche. (fare)

15. E tu, cosa _facevi_ quando _eri_ piaccolo/a? (fare, essere)

Some verbs that you frequently use in Italian have an irregular form in the imperfect tense. With these common verbs, such as **bere, dire, fare, porre,** and **tradurre,** all you have to do is add the regular **-ere** imperfect endings (see the example tables earlier in this section) to the irregular stems that I list in Table 8-1.

Table 8-1	Changing Common Irregular Stems to Form the Imperfect
Infinitive	*Imperfect Stem*
bere (*to drink*)	**bev-**
dire (*to say, to tell*)	**dic-**
fare (*to do, to make*)	**fac-**
introdurre (*to introduce*)	**introduc-**
porre (*to place, to pose*)	**pon-**
tradurre (*to translate*)	**traduc-**

The verbs **comporre, imporre, proporre,** and **opporsi** form stems in the same manner as **porre,** and **indurre, condurre,** and **dedurre** form stems in the same manner as **tradurre.**

As opposed to simply having an irregular stem, the verb **essere's** entire conjugation is irregular and in a category all by itself.

essere (*to be*)	
io er**o**	noi er**avamo**
tu er**i**	voi er**avate**
lui, lei, Lei er**a**	loro er**ano**
C'eravate tutti alla festa? (*Were you all at the party?*)	

Practice the irregular forms of the imperfect tense by conjugating the following verbs in parentheses. And why not pile on the practice? Follow up the conjugation by translating the full sentence. Follow my example:

Q. Com'_eri_____ da piccola? (essere [tu])

A. Com'**eri** da piccola? *What were you like when you were little?*

16. Che cosa _dicevi_____? (dire [tu])

_____

17. Che tempo _faceva_____ al mare ieri? (fare)

_____

18. Noi _traducevamo_____ per mia nonna che non parlava inglese. (tradurre)

_____

19. Dove _eravate_____ durante l'estate del 1990? (essere [voi])

_____

20. La mamma _bevano_____ il Campari quando _era_____ in Italia. (bere, essere)

_____

21. Pinocchio _diceva_____ tante bugie. (dire)

_____

22. _Ponevi_____ molte domande al liceo? (porre [tu])

_____

23. Maria e Amalia _facevano_____ una passeggiata in centro ogni sera. (fare)

_____

24. Mio marito _si opponava_ a tutte le guerre. (opporsi)

_____

25. _Conducavo_ una vita tranquilla. (condurre [io])

_____

Putting It All Together

Try the following exercises to test your accumulated knowledge of the imperfect tense from the previous sections in this chapter.

This first exercise allows you to put the imperfect microscope on parents and other relatives. Translate the following expressions into English, paying attention to the imperfect implications. Take the following example into consideration:

0. Mio padre lavorava tanto.

A. *My father used to work a lot.*

26. La nonna si arrabbiava.
    The grandmother always used to get angry

27. Facevamo passaggiate.
    We to used to go on walks

28. Lo zio beveva.
    Uncle used to drink

29. I miei cugini venivano a trovarci.
    My cousins would come + stay w us

30. Io volevo essere veterinaria.
    I used to want to be a vet

31. Voi eravate a Ravenna?
    Did you used to go to Ravenna

32. Ci scrivevamo.
    We would write eachother

33. I miei genitori ci dicevano di non parlare con gli estranei.
    My parents told us to not talk to strangers

34. Mio fratello giocava a football Americano.
    My brother used to play american potbl

35. Mia sorella ed io litigavamo spesso.

My sister & I used to argue alot

PRACTICE

You use the imperfect tense to describe events, physical or emotional states of mind, or situations in the past, such as what life was like when you were younger or when you lived and worked in a different place. The following problems give you my little story about a very specific chapter of my life. After you conjugate the verbs in my story, you can try writing your own! Here's an example conjugation:

Q. Quando avevo 30 anni, _abitavo_ e _lavoravo_ nel New Hampshire. (abitare, lavorare)

A. Quando avevo 30 anni, **abitavo** e **lavoravo** nel New Hampshire. (_When I was 30 years old, I worked and lived in New Hampshire._)

36. Io _insegnavo_ l'italiano in un piccolo college. (insegnare)

37. _Avevo_ degli studenti bravissimi. (avere)

38. I miei amici migliori _erano_ Liora e Alan, ma _avevo_ tante buone amiche. (essere, avere)

39. Liora _era_ generosa e tranquilla. (essere)

40. Faith ed io _andavamo_ a pattinare. (andare)

41. Graziella ed io _facevamo_ aerobica. (fare)

42. Kate ed io _ci parlavamo_ di tutto, e _ci aiutavamo_. (parlarsi, aiutarsi)

43. Nel New Hampshire d'inverno _era_ molto freddo, ma d'estate noi _nuotavamo_ nel fiume Connecticut. (fare, nuotare)

44. Io _ero_ molto felice. (essere)

45. I miei studenti _venivano_ a casa mia a volte per le lezioni. (venire)

PRACTICE

For the following problems, use the terms I outline in the sections "Perfecting the Uses of the Imperfect" and "Forming Perfect Sentences with the Imperfect" to translate the following sentences into Italian. Follow my example:

Q. During the day we would go to the beach, and in the evening we would go out.

A. Di giorno **andavamo** alla spiaggia, e di sera **uscivamo.**

46. Every summer we would go to Italy.

Ogni estate andavamo in Italia

47. I used to love Clark Gable.

Amavo Clark Gable

48. Marcella would usually have her cappuccino at the bar.

Marcella di solito prendeva il cappuccino al bar

49. Toby was sleeping while we were watching a film.

Toby dormiva mentre guardavam eau film

50. What were you (pl.) doing when Uncle John arrived?

Che cose facevate quando è arrivato zoo John

51. I would always play with Anna Maria.

Giocavo sempre con Anna Maria

52. They wanted to eat at home.

Volevano mangiare a casa

53. On Sundays we went to church.

La domenica, andavamo a chiesa

54. Sometimes Emilia slept well.

Qualche volte dormiva bene Emilia

55. We used to get up at 6:00.

Ci alzavamo alle sei

Answer Key

1. Mio padre **parlava** l'italiano. (*My father would speak Italian.*)

2. Noi **andavamo** in vacanza in Italia. (*We used to go to Italy on vacation.*)

3. Io **mangiavo** il gelato tutti i giorni. (*I would eat ice cream everyday.*)

4. Al ritorno, **ci fermavamo** ad Amsterdam. (*On the way back, we would stop in Amsterdam.*)

5. Io **avevo** 3 conigli. (*I had three rabbits.*)

6. Mia sorella **seguiva** lezioni di danza. (*My sister took dance lessons.*)

7. I miei genitori **uscivano** spesso con i loro amici. (*My parents would often go out with their friends.*)

8. Mia madre **preparava** il sugo e gli gnocchi la domenica. (*My mom used to prepare sauce and gnocchi on Sundays.*)

9. Mia sorella, mio fratello, ed io **giocavamo** fuori tutto il giorno. (*My sister, brother, and I would play outside all the time.*)

10. Il passatempo che **preferivano** era cantare. (*Singing was our favorite pastime.*)

11. E tu, **ti divertivi** quando eri piccolo/a? (*And you, did you have fun when you were little?*)

12. Ci **piaceva** mangiare la pizza a New Haven. (*We used to like to eat pizza in New Haven.*)

13. Mio fratello **si vestiva** sempre in pantaloncini rossi. (*My brother would always wear red shorts.*)

14. Noi **facevamo** le gite scolastiche. (*We used to go on class trips.*)

15. E tu, cosa **facevi** quando **eri** piccolo/a? (*And you, what did you do when you were little?*)

16. Che cosa **dicevi**? *What were you saying?*

17. Che tempo **faceva** al mare ieri? *What was the weather like at the beach yesterday?*

18. Noi **traducevamo** per mia nonna che non parlava inglese. *We used to translate for my grandmother who didn't speak English.*

19. Dove **eravate** durante l'estate del 1990? *Where were you during the summer of 1990?*

20. La mamma **beveva** il Campari quando **era** in Italia. *Mom would drink Campari when she was in Italy.*

21. Pinocchio **diceva** tante bugie. *Pinocchio told many lies.*

22. **Ponevi** molte domande al liceo? *Did you pose a lot of questions in high school?*

23. Maria e Amalia **facevano** una passeggiata in centro ogni sera. *Maria and Amalia used to take a walk every evening.*

24. Mio marito **si opponeva** a tutte le guerre. *My husband protested all wars.*

25. Io **conducevo** una vita tranquilla. *I led a peaceful life.*

26. *Grandma would get angry.*

27. *We used to take walks.*

28 *My uncle drank (as in, "My uncle drank homemade wine when we were little").*

29 *My cousins would/used to come visit us.*

30 *I wanted to be a veterinarian.*

31 *Were you (pl.) in Ravenna?*

32 *We used to write to each other.*

33 *My parents used to tell us not to speak with strangers.*

34 *My brother used to play football.*

35 *My sister and I would often argue.*

36 Io **insegnavo** l'italiano in un piccolo college. (*I used to teach Italian in a small college.*)

37 **Avevo** studenti bravissimi. (*I had excellent students.*)

38 I miei amici migliori **erano** Liora e Alan, ma **avevo** tante buone amiche. (*My best friends were Liora and Alan, but I had many good women friends.*)

39 Liora **era** generosa e tranquilla. (*Liora was generous and calm.*)

40 Faith ed io **andavamo** a pattinare. (*Faith and I would go skating.*)

41 Graziella ed io **facevamo** aerobica. (*Graziella and I would do aerobics.*)

42 Kate ed io **ci parlavamo** di tutto, e **ci aiutavamo.** (*Kate and I would talk to each other about everything, and we helped each other.*)

43 Nel New Hampshire d'inverno **faceva** molto freddo, ma d'estate noi **nuotavamo** nel fiume Connecticut. (*In New Hampshire it was very cold in the winter, but in the summer we would go swimming in the Connecticut River.*)

44 Io **ero** molto felice. (*I was very happy.*)

45 I miei studenti **venivano** a casa mia a volte per le lezioni. (*My students used to come to my house sometimes for class.*)

46 Ogni estate **andavamo** in Italia.

47 **Amavo** Clark Gable.

48 Di solito Marcella **prendeva** il cappuccino al bar.

49 Toby **dormiva** mentre noi **guardavamo** un film.

50 Che cosa **facevate** quando **è arrivato** lo zio John?

51 **Giocavo** sempre con Anna Maria.

52 **Volevano mangiare** a casa.

53 La domenica **andavamo** in chiesa.

54 A volte Emilia **dormiva** bene.

55 **Ci alzavamo** alle sei.

Chapter 9

Reckoning Back to the Old Days: The Past Absolute Tense

In This Chapter
▶ Covering the uses of the past absolute tense
▶ Conjugating regular verbs in the past absolute
▶ Working with irregular verbs in the past absolute
▶ Combining the past absolute with the imperfect

Many textbooks tell you that you use the past absolute tense, or the passato remoto, for events that occurred only in the distant past, and that the tense seldom makes appearances in everyday speech. They lie! Well, maybe *lie* is a bit too harsh, but this assertion isn't entirely true. Although the passato prossimo (the present perfect), which I discuss in Chapter 14, is the more common of the two past tenses for describing events completed in the past, you often use the passato remoto in everyday speech to refer to events that happened some time ago. For example, you may say, "Mio padre **comprò** questa casa nel 1983" (*My dad bought this house in 1983*) or "**Andammo** in Turchia l'estate scorsa" (*We went to Turkey last summer*). Many Italians in Southern Italy (from Rome on down) often use the past absolute rather than the present perfect to talk about events that occurred as recently as an hour ago! (This is a natural outgrowth of many Southern dialects.) And, if you look for it, you'll realize that the past absolute appears quite often in literature.

In this chapter, you discover the uses of the past absolute tense, its conjugations, and its relationship with irregular verbs. The past absolute also has a few unique issues, which I share with you in this chapter, along with plenty of exercises for conjugating regular and irregular verbs in the passato remoto.

Patrolling for Uses of the Past Absolute

The following list outlines some uses of the passato remoto:

✔ To describe an event begun and completed in the distant past. You may use the expression "molti anni fa" (*many years ago*) or "anni fa" (*years ago*), or you may use a date — "Nel 1916 . . ." (*In 1916 . . .*).

✔ To refer to a completed action in literature, which covers a broad range: from children's stories and fairy tales, to popular literature, to the classics of Italian literature. Here's a famous example: "Ricciolidoro **guardò** i tre orsi e **disse** . . ." (*Goldilocks looked at the three bears and said . . .*).

✔ In historical texts and historical narratives: "Giuseppe Garibaldi **nacque** a Nizza." (*Giuseppe Garibaldi was born in Nice.*)

The past absolute differs from the imperfect tense (see Chapter 8) in the same way that the present perfect does (see Chapter 14). You often find the imperfect and the past absolute in the same sentence, and each tense corresponds to a different function. (See the section "Alternating the Past Absolute with the Imperfect" for more.)

Conjugating Regular Verbs

The regular forms of the past absolute are fairly straightforward: You take the stem of the verbs and simply add the past absolute endings (first-, second-, and third-person singular and plural) for **-are, -ere,** and **-ire** verbs. The stems of verbs in the past absolute take the following pattern:

- ✔ **parlare** (*to speak*): The stem is **parl-,** and the endings are **-ai, -asti, -ò, -ammo, -aste,** and **-arono.**
- ✔ **vendere** (*to sell*): The stem is **vend-,** and the endings are **-ei, -esti, -è, -emmo, -este,** and **-erono.**
- ✔ **scolpire** (*to sculpt*): The stem is **scolp-,** and the endings are **-ii, -isti, -ì, -immo, -iste,** and **-irono.**

Repeat these endings — just the endings — at a lively pace to yourself a few times to commit them to memory before you conjugate the verbs in the following tables.

parlare (*to speak*)	
io parl**ai**	noi parl**ammo**
tu parl**asti**	voi parl**aste**
lui, lei, Lei parl**ò**	loro parl**arono**
I due mercanti **parlarono** a lungo e poi **si salutarono.** (*The two merchants spoke for a long time and then parted.*)	

The verb **vendere,** like many **-ere** verbs, carries regular past absolute **-ere** endings and some irregular endings (in the first- and third-person singular and in the third-person plural; see the following section). Both endings are perfectly acceptable and interchangeable. Two other common **-ere** verbs that follow the same pattern as **vendere** (in other words, having both regular and irregular forms) are **dovere** (*to have to*) and **credere** (*to believe*).

vendere (*to sell*)	
io vend**ei** (or vend**etti**)	noi vend**emmo**
tu vend**esti**	voi vend**este**
lui, lei, Lei vend**è** (or vend**ette**)	loro vend**erono** (or vend**ettero**)
Il nonno **vendè** la sua terra ed **immigrò** negli Stati Uniti. (*Grandfather sold his land and emigrated to the United States.*)	

scolpire (to sculpt)	
io scolp**ii**	noi scolp**immo**
tu scolp**isti**	voi scolp**iste**
lui, lei, Lei scolp**ì**	loro scolp**irono**
Lo **sai** quando Bernini **scolpì** l'Estasi di Santa Teresa? (*Do you know when Bernini sculpted The Ecstasy of Saint Teresa?*)	

You follow the same format to use reflexive verbs, whose endings are **-arsi, -ersi,** and **-irsi,** in the past absolute (the verb's subject and an object in the sentence refer to the same person or thing). The only difference is that you have to add the reflexive pronouns. Reflexive verbs always require reflexive pronouns; they aren't reflexive verbs without them! The pronouns usually take the place of the personal pronouns. (See Chapter 5 for more on reflexive verbs.)

Conjugate the following verbs into the past absolute tense. Here's an example to get you started:

Q. Cappuccetto Rosso _____ alla porta. (bussare)

A. Cappuccetto Rosso **bussò** alla porta. (*Little Red Riding Hood knocked on the door.*)

1. Romeo e Giulietta *si amarono* così tanto che *morirono* per il loro amore. (amarsi, morire)

2. Quando *finì* la Seconda Guerra Mondiale in Italia? Nel 1945. (finire)

3. Dove *morì* Dante? A Ravenna. (morire)

4. Perchè *andaste* in Argentina? (andare [voi])

5. Nonna, è vero che tu *studiasti* all'Università di Roma? (studiare)

6. Noi *credemmo* a quello che diceva lui. (credere)

7. I greci *si stabilirono* in Magna Grecia 2,500 anni fa. (stabilirsi)

8. *Dovei* tornare in Italia per vendere la casa dei nonni. (dovere [io])

9. Ricciolidoro *mangiò* tutta la pappa degli orsi. (mangiare)

10. Quando *partirono* i primi immigranti? (partire)

Addressing Irregular Verbs

The past absolute tense becomes more complicated when you (or, more likely, your schedule-oriented instructor) introduce all the irregular verbs into the picture. Many verbs in the past absolute follow a 1-3-3 pattern, which simply means that the verbs are irregular in the

- ✔ First-person singular
- ✔ Third-person singular
- ✔ Third-person plural

All the other persons take the regular past-absolute stems and endings (see the previous section). In the following table, you see the verb **mettere** (which follows the 1-3-3 pattern) conjugated in the past absolute.

mettere (*to put or place*)	
io **misi**	noi mett**emmo**
tu mett**esti**	voi mett**este**
lui, lei, Lei **mise**	loro **misero**
Dante **mise** gli eretici nel decimo canto. (*Dante put the Heretics in the tenth canto.*)	

Table 9-1 contains many commonly used verbs that follow the same 1-3-3 pattern in the past absolute tense.

Table 9-1	Verbs Following a 1-3-3 Pattern in the Past Absolute		
Infinitive	*1-3-3 Conjugation*	*Infinitive*	*1-3-3 Conjugation*
accendere (*to light*)	accesi, accese, accesero	rompere (*to break*)	ruppi, ruppe, (like **ruppero** e**rompere**)
cadere (*to fall*)	caddi, cadde, caddero	sapere (*to know*)	seppi, seppe, seppero
chiudere (*to close*)	chiusi, chiuse, chiusero	scegliere (*to choose*)	scelsi, scelse, scelsero (like **raccogliere, cogliere**)
confondere (*to confuse*)	confusi, confuse, confusero	scrivere (*to write*)	scrissi, scrisse, scrissero (like **iscrivere**)
conoscere (*to know, meet*)	conobbi, conobbe, conobbero	sorridere (*to smile*)	sorrisi, sorrise, sorrisero (like **ridere**)
decidere (*to decide*)	decisi, decise, decisero	spegnere (*to put out, extinguish*)	spensi, spense, spensero
dipingere (*to paint*)	dipinsi, dipinse, dipinsero (like **spingere, fingere**)	succedere (*to happen*)	successe, successero (3rd-person sing., pl.; *something happens*)
leggere (*to read*)	lessi, lesse, lessero	tenere (*to keep, hold*)	tenni, tenne, tennero
mettere (*to put, place*)	misi, mise, misero (like **smettere, mettersi, promettere**)	vedere (*to see*)	vidi, vide, videro
nascere (*to be born*)	nacqui, nacque, nacquero	venire (*to come*)	venni, venne, vennero
perdere (*to lose*)	persi, perse, persero	vincere (*to win*)	vinsi, vinse, vinsero
rimanere (*to remain*)	rimasi, rimase, rimasero	vivere (*to live*)	vissi, visse, vissero
rispondere (*to answer, respond*)	risposi, rispose, risposero	volere (*to want*)	volli, volle, vollero

For this exercise, try conjugating the verbs **scrivere, accendere,** and **conoscere** in the past absolute tense (verbs that follow the 1-3-3 pattern). Here's an example to get you off on the right foot with **scrivere:**

Q. Io _____ lettere d'amore. (scrivere)

A. Io **scrissi** lettere d'amore. (*I wrote love letters.*)

11. Tu, Amanda _____ lettere d'amore. (scrivere)

12. Io e Caterina _____ lettere d'amore. (scrivere)

13. Samanta e Antonio _____ lettere d'amore. (scrivere)

14. Io _____ il suo cuore. (accendere)

15. Tu, Jacopo _____ il suo cuore. (accendere)

16. Emma e Carla _____ il suo cuore. (accendere)

17. Tu, Dani _____ Claudio 26 anni fa? (conoscere)

18. Alessandro _____ Claudio 26 anni fa. (conoscere)

19. Tu e tuo marito _____ Claudio 26 anni fa. (conoscere)

20. Maristella e Rosaria _____ Claudio 26 anni fa. (conoscere)

For this exercise, conjugate the verbs in parentheses according to the persons indicated. Here's an example:

Q. _____ di partire con l'alba. (decidere [loro])

A. **Decisero** di partire con l'alba. (*They decided to leave at dawn.*)

21. _____ la gara di poesia. (vincere [io])

22. Dove _____ la barca l'anno scorso? (mettere [voi])

23. _____ bene quando _____ Robert. (scegliere, sposare [tu])

24. _____ le relazioni diplomatiche. (rompere [loro])

25. _____ a bocca aperta. (rimanere [lui])

26. _____ il Colosseo per la prima volta nel 1976. (vedere [noi])

27. Io _____ Claudio molti anni fa. (conoscere)

28. Leopardi _____: "_____ i fiori." (scrivere, vivere)

29. Geppetto _____ che Pinocchio era davvero vivo. (sapere)

30. Pinocchio _____ di essere un bravo ragazzo. (promettere)

And the irregularities don't stop there! Just as I promised, the past absolute tense has *many* common irregular verb forms. The following pages allow you to work with some of the remaining irregular verbs.

Table 9-2 presents the conjugations of four very commonly used verbs in the past absolute: **avere, essere, dare,** and **stare.** Although I could technically place the verb **avere** into Table 9-1 because it follows the 1-3-3 pattern, I like to keep it near the other very irregular verbs with which I've grouped it. The other three verbs are irregular in all their persons, so the best way to deal with them is — you guessed it — to memorize them!

Table 9-2	Conjugations of Avere, Essere, Dare, and Stare			
Person	*avere* (to have)	*essere* (to be)	*dare* (to give)	*stare* (to stay, wait)
1st-person Sing. (io)	**ebbi**	**fui**	**diedi**	**stetti**
2nd-person Sing. (tu)	**avesti**	**fosti**	**desti**	**stesti**
3rd-person Sing. (lui, lei, Lei)	**ebbe**	**fu**	**diede**	**stette**
1st-person Pl. (noi)	**avemmo**	**fummo**	**demmo**	**stemmo**
2nd-person Pl. (voi)	**aveste**	**foste**	**deste**	**steste**
3rd-person Pl. (loro)	**ebbero**	**furono**	**diedero**	**stettero**

Here are some example conjugations of these four verbs:

- ✔ Teodora **ebbe** un ruolo importante a Costantinopoli nel VI secolo. (*Teodora had/held an important role in 6th-century Constantinople.*)

- ✔ *Il fu Mattia Pascal* **fu** un romanzo di Pirandello del 1904. (*The Late Mattia Pascal was a novel by Pirandello, written in 1904.*)

- ✔ Carlo Goldoni **diede** al mondo teatrale un patrimonio ricco. (*Carlo Goldoni gave the world of theater a rich patrimony.*)

- ✔ Don Abbondio **stette** ad **aspettare** Renzo e Lucia. (*Don Abbondio stayed and waited for Renzo and Lucia.*)

Some other irregular verbs are derived from Latin stems when in the past absolute. Note the similarities between the verbs in Table 9-3 (**bere, dire, fare,** and **tradurre**) — all the endings for each person are the same! The verbs in Table 9-3 share the same irregular stems with the Italian imperfect (at least, most of the persons of most of the verbs; see Chapter 8) and follow a 1-3-3 pattern.

Table 9-3	Conjugations of Bere, Dire, Fare, and Tradurre			
Person	*bere* (to drink)	*dire* (to say)	*fare* (to do, to make)	*tradurre* (to translate)
1st-person Sing. (io)	**bevvi**	**dissi**	**feci**	**tradussi**
2nd-person Sing. (tu)	**bevesti**	**dicesti**	**facesti**	**traducesti**
3rd-person Sing. (lui, lei, Lei)	**bevve**	**disse**	**fece**	**tradusse**
1st-person Pl. (noi)	**bevemmo**	**dicemmo**	**facemmo**	**traducemmo**
2nd-person Pl. (voi)	**beveste**	**diceste**	**faceste**	**traduceste**
3rd-person Pl. (loro)	**bevvero**	**dissero**	**fecero**	**tradussero**

Here are some example conjugations of these four verbs:

- Renzo **bevve** tutto il fiasco e ne **ordinò** un altro. (*Renzo drank the whole flask and ordered another.*)

- "Nonna, che occhi grandi che hai!" **disse** Cappuccetto Rosso. (*"Grandma, what big eyes you have!" said Little Red Riding Hood.*)

- "Allora, dopo gli occhi, gli **fece** il naso, ma il naso appena fatto, **cominciò** a crescere." (*"Then, after the eyes, he made his nose, but as soon as the nose was done, it began to grow."*)

- **Traducemmo** Ovidio in classe. (*We translated Ovid in class.*)

In the following exercise, you put the irregular verbs from Tables 9-2 and 9-3 into practice. Translate the different verbs into English, as I do in the example that follows, making sure to add the appropriate subjects:

Q. diedi _____

A. *I gave*

31. dissi _____

32. furono _____

33. ebbe _____

34. bevvi _____

35. tradusse _____

36. desti _____

37. fece _____

38. diceste _____

39. stemmo _____

40. fosti _____

Time for a bit of Italian culture. For this exercise, write complete sentences based on the information provided, conjugating the verbs in bold into the past absolute along the way. You can use regular or irregular verbs in these sentences. Follow my example:

Q. Cristoforo Colombo/**leggere**/*Il Milione* di Marco Polo.

A. Cristoforo Colombo **lesse** *Il Milione* di Marco Polo. (*Christopher Columbus read The Million by Marco Polo.*)

41. Veronica Franco e Vittoria Colonna/**scrivere**/poesie.

_____

42. Artemisia Gentileschi/**dipingere**/la Giuditta più di una volta.

_____

43. Dante /**nascere**/nel 1265 a Firenze.

_____

44. Il Vesuvio/**erompere**/nel 79 dopo Cristo.

_____

45. Vivaldi e Verdi/**essere**/compositori.

_____

Alternating the Past Absolute with the Imperfect

The past absolute (passato remoto) tense often alternates with the imperfect (imperfetto, which I cover in Chapter 8) in the Italian language. It's very common, in literature especially, to come across a sentence that contains both tenses. (The same sort of alternating pattern is also common with the imperfect and the recent past [passato prossimo], which you can practice in Chapter 14.)

In short, you use the past absolute to describe events completed in the not-so-recent past. You use the imperfetto, the descriptive past tense, to describe ongoing and habitual actions in the past; to describe physical and emotional states of being; or to discuss the weather. Note the use of the two tenses in the following examples, taken from "Andreuccio da Perugia," a novella in Boccaccio's *Decameron*:

"I due gli **dissero** che **ci doveva essere** ancora l'anello." (*The two said to him that the ring had to be there still.*)

"**Faceva** molto caldo e Andreuccio, appena **rimase** solo, **si levò** gli abiti . . ." (*It was very hot and as soon as he was alone, Andreuccio took off his clothes.*)

"Mentre **piangeva** su questi pensieri, **sentì** della gente **camminare** nella chiesa." (*While he was crying over these worries, he heard some people walking in the church.*)

For this "absolutely" perfect practice session, place the correct form of the past absolute in the blanks provided and then translate the sentences. I've adapted these exercises from *I tre porcellini* (*The Three Little Pigs*). Here's another example, though, from Boccaccio:

Q. Andreuccio _____ subito che era pronto a fare come i due dicevano. (rispondere)

A. Andreuccio **rispose** subito che era pronto a fare come i due dicevano. *Andreuccio quickly responded that he was ready to do what the two men said.*

46. C'erano una volta tre porcellini che _____ di partire per costruirsi la propria casa. (decidere)

_____

47. Lungo la strada il primo porcellino _____ un uomo che portava la paglia. (incontrare)

_____

48. I tre porcellini _____ a chiave nella casa di mattoni. (chiudersi)

_____

49. I tre porcellini _____ di gioia perchè pensavano di essere al sicuro. (esultare)

_____

50. Il giorno seguente, i tre porcellini _____ all'alba. (svegliarsi)

_____

Answer Key

1 Romeo e Giulietta **si amarono** così tanto che **morirono** per il loro amore. (*Romeo and Juliet loved each other so much that they died for their love.*)

2 Quando **finì** la Seconda Guerra Mondiale in Italia? Nel 1945. (*When did World War II end in Italy? In 1945.*)

3 Dove **morì** Dante? A Ravenna. (*Where did Dante die? In Ravenna.*)

4 Perchè **andaste** in Argentina? (*Why did you (pl.) go to Argentina?*)

5 Nonna, è vero che tu **studiasti** all'Università di Roma? (*Grandma, is it true that you studied at the University of Rome?*)

6 Noi **credemmo** a quello che diceva lui. (*We believed what he was saying.*)

7 I greci **si stabilirono** in Magna Grecia 2,500 anni fa. (*The Greeks settled in Magna Grecia 2,500 years ago.*)

8 **Dovetti** tornare in Italia per vendere la casa dei nonni. (*I had to return to Italy to sell my grandparents' house.*)

9 Ricciolidoro **mangiò** tutta la pappa degli orsi. (*Goldilocks ate all of the bears' porridge.*)

10 Quando **partirono** i primi immigranti? (*When did the first immigrants leave?*)

11 Tu, Amanda, **scrivesti** lettere d'amore. (*You, Amanda, wrote love letters.*)

12 Io e Caterina **scrivemmo** lettere d'amore. (*Caterina and I wrote love letters.*)

13 Samanta e Antonio **scrissero** lettere d'amore. (*Samantha and Antonio wrote love letters.*)

14 Io **accesi** il suo cuore. (*I lit up his/her heart.*)

15 Tu, Jacopo, **accendesti** il suo cuore. (*You, Jake, lit up her/his heart.*)

16 Emma e Carla **accesero** il suo cuore. (*Emma and Carla lit up his/her heart.*)

17 Tu, Dani, **conoscesti** Claudio 26 anni fa? (*You, Dani, met Claudio 26 years ago?*)

18 Alessandro **conobbe** Claudio 26 anni fa. (*Alessandro met Claudio 26 years ago.*)

19 Tu e tuo marito **conosceste** Claudio 26 anni fa. (*You and your husband met Claudio 26 years ago.*)

20 Maristella e Rosaria **conobbero** Claudio 26 anni fa. (*Maristella and Rosaria met Claudio 26 years ago.*)

21 **Vinsi** la gara di poesia. (*I won the poetry competition.*)

22 Dove **metteste** la barca l'anno scorso? (*Where did you (pl.) put the boat last year?*)

23 **Scegliesti** bene quando **sposasti** Robert. (*You chose well when you married Robert.*)

24 **Ruppero** le relazioni diplomatiche. (*They broke off diplomatic relations.*)

25 **Rimase** a bocca aperta. (*He was very surprised.*)

26   **Vedemmo** Il Colosseo per la prima volta nel 1976. (*We saw the Colosseum for the first time in 1976.*)

27   Io **conobbi** Claudio molti anni fa. (*I met Claudio many years ago.*)

28   Leopardi **scrisse:** "**Vissero** i fiori." (*Leopardi wrote: "The flowers lived."*)

29   Geppetto **seppe** che Pinocchio era davvero vivo. (*Geppetto found out that Pinocchio was really alive.*)

30   Pinocchio **promise** di essere un bravo ragazzo. (*Pinocchio promised to be a good boy.*)

31   **dissi** *I said*

32   **furono** *they were*

33   **ebbe** *he/she/You had*

34   **bevvi** *I drank*

35   **tradusse** *he/she/You translated*

36   **desti** *you (sing.) gave*

37   **fece** *he/she/You did or made*

38   **diceste** *you (pl.) said*

39   **stemmo** *we stayed, we were*

40   **fosti** *you (sing.) were*

41   Veronica Franco e Vittoria Colonna **scrissero** poesie. (*Veronica Franco and Victoria Colonna wrote poetry.*)

42   Artemisia Gentileschi **dipinse** la Giuditta più di una volta. (*Artemisia Gentileschi painted Judith more than once.*)

43   Dante **nacque** nel 1265 a Firenze. (*Dante was born in Florence in 1265.*)

44   Il Vesuvio **eruppe** nel 79 dopo Cristo. (*Mount Vesuvius erupted in 79 A.D.*)

45   Vivaldi e Verdi **furono** compositori. (*Vivaldi and Verdi were composers.*)

46   C'erano una volta, tre porcellini che **decisero** di partire per costruirsi la propria casa. *Once upon a time, there were three little pigs who decided to leave to build their own house.*

47   Lungo la strada il primo porcellino **incontrò** un uomo che portava la paglia. *On the way the first little pig met a man who was carrying straw.*

48   I tre porcellini **si chiusero** a chiave nella casa di mattoni. *The three little pigs locked themselves in the house made of bricks.*

49   I tre porcellini **esultarono** di gioia perchè pensavano di essere al sicuro. *The three little pigs exalted with joy because they thought they were safe.*

50   Il giorno seguente i tre porcellini **si svegliarono** all'alba. *The following day the three little pigs got up at dawn.*

Chapter 10

Che Sarà Sarà: Looking Ahead with the Future Tense

*T*he future is not ours to see, hence the phrase "Che sarà sarà" (*Whatever will be, will be*). But you can certainly dream and make plans. You use the future tense to talk about events that will occur in the very near and not-so-near future. In this chapter, you discover how to form the future tense and how to combine it with other, more precise phrases that indicate time. In English, we simply put the words "am going to" or "will" in front of an unconjugated verb; Italian verbs, however, have very specific future endings, and the good news is they are the same endings for all kinds of verbs — **-are, -ere,** and **-ire** regular and irregular verbs!

Forming the Regular Future Tense

The regular future tense (as opposed to the hypothetical future tense, which I discuss in Chapter 16) is one of the easiest tenses to form. (Further into this chapter, you can see how to form some irregular future stems.) To form the regular future tense, follow these simple steps:

1. Take the infinitive of an **-are, -ere,** or **-ire** verb.

2. Drop the final **-e** only to form the future stem.

3. Add the future ending.

Okay, you have to pay attention to one exception: **-are** verbs require a slight modification. The **a** in the stem becomes an **e.** (The "Spelling Out **-are** Exceptions" section a bit later in this chapter presents greater detail on the spelling changes for **-are.**) The following list provides a few examples of the modified future stems, to which you add your endings:

▶ **-are:** The **parlare** stem is **parler-** (the **a** becomes **e** in **-are** verbs).

▶ **-ere:** The **prendere** stem is **prender-.**

▶ **-ire:** The **partire** stem is **partir-.**

The stems you create are the same stems you use for the conditional tense (see Chapter 11).

The following table shows the endings that you attach to these stems. Notice that the future ending is the same for **-are, -ere,** and **-ire** verbs.

Future Tense Endings	
io -**ò**	noi -**emo**
tu -**ai**	voi -**ete**
lui, lei, Lei -**à**	loro -**anno**

The following tables give you some examples of regular **-are, -ere,** and **-ire** verbs conjugated in the future tense.

parlare (*to speak*)	
io parler**ò**	noi parler**emo**
tu parler**ai**	voi parler**ete**
lui, lei, Lei parler**à**	loro parler**anno**
Parlerò col professore dopodomani. (*I'll talk with the professor the day after tomorrow.*)	

prendere (*to have or to take*)	
io prender**ò**	noi prender**emo**
tu prender**ai**	voi prender**ete**
lui, lei, Lei prender**à**	loro prender**anno**
Prenderemo una bella bistecca alla fiorentina! (*We're going to have a nice steak Florentine style!*)	

partire (*to leave*)	
io partir**ò**	noi partir**emo**
tu partir**ai**	voi partir**ete**
lui, lei, Lei partir**à**	loro partir**anno**
Maria **partirà** per gli Stati Uniti domenica. (*Mary will leave/will be leaving for the United States on Sunday.*)	

Translate the following future verbs and provide the appropriate subject pronoun(s) — you may have more than one possibility. Here's an example:

Q. partirai _____

A. partirai *you will leave*

1. venderai ___You will sell___

2. comprerò ___I will Buy___

3. camminerete ___You will walk___

4. vincerà ___She will win___

5. arriverete ___You will arrive___

6. scriveranno ___they will write___

7. dormirai ___you will sleep___

8. prenoteremo ___we'll reserve___

9. aprirà ___he'll open___

10. parleremo ___we'll talk___

Conjugate the following verbs into the future, using the subjects provided. Here's an example:

Q. Lei _____. (uscire) _go out_

A. Lei **uscirà.** (*She will write.*)

11. Giuseppe ___finirà___ il compito. (finire)

12. Riccardo e Emilia ___cammineranno___. (camminare)

13. La mamma ___si alzerà___. (alzarsi)

14. Mio padre ___prenoterà___ l'albergo. (prenotare)

15. Gigio ed io ___apriremo___ il negozio. (aprire)

16. Io ___prenderò___ un cono. (prendere)

17. Tu ___chiederai___ un aumento. (chiedere)

18. Mia sorella ed io ___partiremo___ il 22 maggio. (partire)

19. Lui ___si divertirà___. (divertirsi)

20. Voi ___dormirete___ come sassi. (dormire)

Spelling Out -are Exceptions

Okay, the previous section gets all the really simple stuff out of the way. As with all languages, you have to jump through a few hoops here and there (but you can't be too upset . . . not many languages have more hoops than English!). In this section, I cover the spelling changes that you need to make with verbs ending in **-care, -gare, -ciare,** and **-giare.**

Verbs ending in **-care** (for example, **cercare** [*to look for*] and **dimenticare** [*to forget*]) and **-gare** (**pagare,** *to pay*) add an **h** after the **c** or **g** in their future stems. This change allows the verbs to keep their hard "c" and hard "g" sounds. The following tables provide you with some examples of the change.

cercare (*to look for*)	
io cercherò	noi cercheremo
tu cercherai	voi cercherete
lui, lei, Lei cercherà	loro cercheranno
Loro **cercheranno** un albergo quando arriveranno a Roma. (*They'll look for a hotel when they get to Rome.*)	

pagare (*to pay*)	
io pagherò	noi pagheremo
tu pagherai	voi pagherete
lui, lei, Lei pagherà	loro pagheranno
Pagherà (Lei) in contanti o con la carta di credito? (*Will you* (formal) *be paying with cash or a credit card?*)	

Verbs ending in **-giare** and **-ciare**, like **mangiare** (*to eat*) and **cominciare** (*to begin*), drop their **i** in the future stem because you don't pronounce the **i**; it's there only to maintain the soft "g" and "c" sounds. Compare **manger,** with a verb like **studier,** which keeps and pronounces its **i.** You can see the future forms at work in the following tables.

mangiare (*to eat*)	
io mangerò	noi mangeremo
tu mangerai	voi mangerete
lui, lei, Lei mangerà	loro mangeranno

studiare (*to study*)	
io studierò	noi studieremo
tu studierai	voi studierete
lui, lei, Lei studierà	loro studieranno

Conjugate the following verbs into the future. Watch out for spelling changes! See what I mean in this example:

0. __Cercherai__ un nuovo appartamento? (cercare [tu])

A. **Cercherai** un nuovo appartamento? (*Are you going to look for a new apartment?*)

21. __Mangeremo__ dalla nonna domenica. (mangiare [noi])

22. Quando __comincerà__ la scuola? (cominciare)

23. Voi _studierate_ molto all'università. (studiare)

24. Non ti _dimenticherò_ mai! (dimenticare [io])

25. I bambini _giocheranno_ a calcio anche l'anno prossimo. (giocare)

26. Quando _nevicherà_? (nevicare)

27. Marco, _ti stancherai_ troppo! (stancarsi)

28. Io _viaggerò_ il mondo un giorno. (viaggiare)

29. Il babbo _pagherà_ con la carta di credito. (pagare)

30. Mamma e papà _litigheranno_! (litigare)

Working with Irregular Roots

More discussion of future-tense Italian verbs, more exceptions to pack into your brain! The changeup here is that some verbs have irregular roots in the future tense, meaning that their stems change with regard to the regular future stems in the previous sections (where you keep most of the infinitives). But don't worry: After you change the stems of the verbs, you use the same future endings as you do with regular verbs: **-ò, -ai, -à, -emo, -ete,** and **-anno.** You can put these verbs into practice in the exercises that follow the verb tables in this section.

Some commonly used verbs change their stems in the future tense by dropping the second-to-last vowel in the infinitives, as you can see in Table 10-1.

Table 10-1	Common Verbs with Future Stems That Drop a Vowel
Infinitive	*Future Stem*
andare (*to go*)	**andr-**
avere (*to have*)	**avr-**
cadere (*to fall*)	**cadr-**
dovere (*to have to or need to*)	**dovr-**
potere (*to be able to*)	**potr-**
sapere (*to know*)	**sapr-**
vedere (*to see*)	**vedr-**
vivere (*to live*)	**vivr-**

Other future stems of verbs take on a double **r,** as you can see in Table 10-2.

Table 10-2	Common Verbs with Future Stems That Have Double Rs
Infinitive	*Future Stem*
bere (*to drink*)	**berr-**
tenere (*to hold*)	**terr-**
rimanere (*to stay*)	**rimarr-**
ottenere (*to obtain*)	**otter-**
sostenere (*to sustain, to support*)	**sosterr-**
mantenere (*to maintain*)	**manterr-**
venire (*to come*)	**verr-**
volere (*to want*)	**vorr-**

You can group the verbs **dare, fare,** and **stare** together (and call them the Law Firm of **dare, fare,** and **stare** if you like) because even though they're **-are** verbs, they keep their final **a** (see Table 10-3). *Note:* The infinitive stem simply drops the final **e** and then takes the future ending.

Table 10-3	The Future Forms of Dare, Fare, and Stare
Infinitive	*Future Stem*
dare (*to give*)	**dar-**
fare (*to do or to make*)	**far-**
stare (*to be or to stay*)	**star-**

The verb **essere** (*to be*) is in a category all by itself! Its future stem becomes **sar-,** upon which you add the future endings. The following table shows you some examples.

esserre (to be)	
io sar**ò**	noi sar**emo**
tu sar**ai**	voi sar**ete**
lui, lei, Lei sar**à**	loro sar**anno**
Sarò contenta quando **finisco** questo lavoro. (*I'll be happy when I finish this job.*)	

Luisa, an American college student, is studying Art History in Ravenna this summer. Complete Luisa's e-mail to her mom by conjugating some of the irregular future verbs in Tables 10-1 through 10-3 and the **essere** verb table.

Cara Mamma,

31 *Vorrò* _____ (volere [io]) dirti tutto quello che 32 *farò* _____
(fare) nei prossimi giorni. Dopodomani 33 *Sarà* _____ (essere)
l'esame di Storia dell'Arte. La professoressa 34 *terrà* _____ (tenere)
l'esame in biblioteca. Dopo l'esame noi tutti 35 *andremo* _____ (andare)
alla spiaggia a Marina di Ravenna e 36 *daremo* _____ (dare) una bella
festa! La mia amica Marcella 37 *rimarrà* _____ (rimanere) in città
perchè domani sera 38 *verranno* _____ (venire) i suoi genitori. Alla festa
noi 39 *mangeremo* _____ (mangiare) il pesce alla griglia e
40 *berremo* _____ (bere [noi]) il buon vino bianco! Mamma, non
41 *potrò* _____ (potere [io]) mai dimenticare questa meravigliosa
esperienza! 42 *Studierò* _____ (studiare [io]) ancora l'italiano negli Stati
Uniti perchè un giorno io 43 *vivrò* _____ (vivere) qui per sempre! Tu
e papà 44 *dovrete* _____ (dovere) venire la prossima volta! Ci
45 *vedremo* _____ (vedere) molto presto!

Un bacio,

Luisa

Talking About the Future

"Let's forget about **domani**, let's forget about **domani**, let's forget about **domani**, cause **domani** never comes." Although this popular tune encourages you to forget about **domani** (*tomorrow*) and the future, the elements of the future are important frames of reference for your daily existence. You can use the phrases in Table 10-4 to speak in precise terms about the future and to put together all the ideas of this chapter in practice exercises.

Table 10-4	Common Expressions That Often Take the Future		
Phrase	*Translation*	*Phrase*	*Translation*
domani	*tomorrow*	fra qualche giorno	*in a few days*
domani mattina	*tomorrow morning*	fra qualche mese	*in a few months*
domani sera	*tomorrow evening*	fra qualche anno	*in a few years*
dopodomani	*the day after tomorrow*	fra tre giorni	*in three days*

(continued)

Table 10-4 *(continued)*

Phrase	Translation	Phrase	Translation
sabato prossimo	*next Saturday*	quando	*when*
domenica prossima	*next Sunday*	appena	*as soon as*
la settimana prossima	*next week*	se	*if*
il mese prossimo	*next month*	più tardi	*later*
l'anno prossimo	*next year*	entro giugno	*by June*
quest'estate	*this summer*	entro la fine del mese	*by the end of the month*
stasera	*this evening*		

Translate the following future-tense sentences into Italian. Here's an example:

Q. I'll study tomorrow!

A. **Studierò** domani!

46. Mom's going out with Aunt Francis tomorrow evening.

La Mamma uscirà con zia Francis domani sera

47. We're going to the zoo in three days.

Andremo allo zoo fra 3 giorni

48. My friends the Smith's will visit me in Sicily by June.

I miei amici i Smith visiteranno in Sicilia entro giugno

49. We're arriving in Venice in a few days.

arriveremo a Venezia fra pochi giorni

50. Are you (inf., sing.) going to sing at La Scala next month?

Canterai alla La Scala prossimo mese?

51. My roommate and I will attend the University of Florence next year.

Mia amica ed io frequenteremo l'università di Firenze

52. My mother will visit as soon as she receives her passport.

Mia Madre visiterà appena riceverà il passaporto

53. If it rains, we'll eat at home this evening.

Se pioverà, mangeremo a casa stasera

54. We will visit Pompeii next Saturday.

Visiteremo Pompeii la prossima domenica

55. They will see the film the day after tomorrow.

Vedranno il film dopo domani

PRACTICE

Un viaggio in Italia! (*A trip to Italy!*) Respond to the following sentences in Italian by using the future tense. Here, your answers are purely subjective. I provide an example response for each question in the Answer Key, but no copying!

Q. Andrete al mare o in montagna?

A. Andremo al mare. (*We're going to the beach.*)

56. Studierai o viaggerai in Italia nel futuro?

Will you study or HS vacation in Italy in the future

57. Quando partirete?

When will you (coll) leave?

58. A che ora arriverà il tuo aereo?

a what time does your plane arrive

59. Arriverà a Venezia o a Firenze la nonna?

will your grandmother arrive in Venice or Florence

60. Mangerete la pizza quando sarete a Napoli?

will you eat pizza when you visit Naples?

61. I ragazzi berranno il Chianti o la Vernaccia in Toscana?

will the boys drink Chianti or Vernaccia in Tuscany

62. Scierai a Cortina d'Ampezzo?

Will you ski Cortina d' Ampezzo

63. Pagherà in contanti o con la carta di credito tua moglie?

Will your wife pay with cash or credit card?

64. Andrete anche a Taormina?

Will you (coll) also go to Taormina

65. Dormiranno in una pensione o in un albergo i tuoi genitori?

will your parents sleep in a B+b or in a hotel?

Dal cartomante: *sì* o *no?* (*At the fortune teller's: yes or no?*) It would be nice to go to a fortune teller and receive answers about the unknown future. The following questions help you to practice asking and answering concrete and abstract questions. Translate the question I pose and then follow the yes or no answer with a full Italian sentence in response.

Here's an example:

Q. Uscirò con i miei amici domani sera?

A. *Am I going out with my friends tomorrow evening?*

A. Sì, **uscirai** con i tuoi amici domani sera. (*Note:* The tu isn't necessary in these responses.)

A. No, non **uscirai** con i tuoi amici domani sera.

66. Nevicherà domani? _Will it snow tomorrow?_

Sì, _nevicherà domani._

67. Venderò la mia casa entro giugno? _Will I sell my house by July_

No, _non venderò la tua casa entro giugno_

68. Visiterò l'Italia quest'anno? _Will I visit Italy this year?_

Sì, _visitai l'Itali quest'anno_

69. Mi divertirò in Italia? _Will I enjoy myself in Italy_

Sì, _ti diventirai in Italia_

70. Mi innamorerò subito durante il viaggio? _Will I fall in love stoneodana my trip_

No, _Non ti innamerai subito durante il viaggio_

71. Parlerò italiano tutti i giorni? _will I speak Italian all day_

Sì, _Parlarai italiano tutto il giorno_

72. I miei figli torneranno a vivere con me dopo l'università? _will my children come back + live with me after college_

No, _i suoi figli non torneranno a vivere con te_

73. Sono stanco/a di pulire! Mi aiuterà mio marito/mia moglie domani? _I'm tired of cleaning, will my husband helping me tomorrow_

Sì, _suo marito aiutera domani_

74. Comprerò una villa al Lago di Como fra qualche anno? _Will I buy a villa a Lago Como in a few year_

Sì, _compera una villa al lago di Como fra qualque_

75. Vincerò presto la lotteria? _Am I going to win the lottery soon?_

No, _vincerà presto la lotteria_

Answer Key

1   *you will/shall sell; you're going to sell*

2   *I will buy*

3   *you (pl.) will walk*

4   *he, she, you (form.) will win*

5   *you all will be arriving*

6   *they will write*

7   *you will sleep*

8   *we will reserve*

9   *he, she, you (form.) will open*

10   *we will speak*

11   Giuseppe **finirà** il compito. (*Giuseppe will finish his homework.*) *[handwritten: Giuseppe la finirà / Giuseppe finirà il compito]*

12   Riccardo e Emilia **cammineranno.** (*Riccardo and Emilia will walk.*) *[handwritten: Riccardo e Emilia cammineranno]*

13   La mamma **si alzerà.** (*Mom will get up.*) *[handwritten: La mamma si alzerà alle sette]*

14   Mio padre **prenoterà** l'albergo. (*My dad will reserve the hotel.*) *[handwritten: Mio padre prenoterà l'albergo.]*

15   Giorgio ed io **apriremo** il negozio. (*Giorgio and I will open the store.*) *[handwritten: Giorgio ed io apriremo il negozio]*

16   Io **prenderò** un cono. (*I will have a cone.*) *[handwritten: Prenderò un cono. Ne prenderò uno]*

17   Tu **chiederai** un aumento. (*You will ask for a raise.*) *[handwritten: Chiederai un aumento]*

18   Mia sorella ed io **partiremo** il 22 maggio. (*My sister and I will leave on May 22.*) *[handwritten: Mia sorella ed io partiremo il 22 di maggio]*

19   Lui **si divertirà.** (*He will have fun.*) *[handwritten: Si divertirà]*

20   Voi **dormirete** come sassi. (*You [pl.] will sleep like a log [Literally: like a stone].*) *[handwritten: Dormirete come sassi]*

21   **Mangeremo** dalla nonna domenica. (*We're eating at grandma's on Sunday.*) *[handwritten: Ci mangeremo domenica]*

22   Quando **comincerà** la scuola? (*When will school begin?*) *[handwritten: Quando comincerà la scuola?]*

23   Voi **studierete** molto all'università. (*You [pl.] will study a lot in college.*) *[handwritten: Studierete molto all'università]*

24   Non ti **dimenticherò** mai! (*I shall never forget you!*) *[handwritten: Non ti dimenticherò mai!]*

25   I bambini **giocheranno** a calcio anche l'anno prossimo. (*The children will be playing soccer next year, too.*) *[handwritten: I bambini giocheranno il calcio anche l'anno prossimo]*

26   Quando **nevicherà?** (*When will it snow?*) *[handwritten: Quando nevicherà?]*

27 Marco, **ti stancherai** troppo! (*Marco, you're going to get too tired!*)

28 Io **viaggerò** il mondo un giorno. (*I am going to travel the world some day.*)

29 Il babbo **pagherà** con la carta di credito. (*Daddy's going to pay with his credit card.*)

30 Mamma e papà **litigheranno!** (*Mom and dad will argue!*)

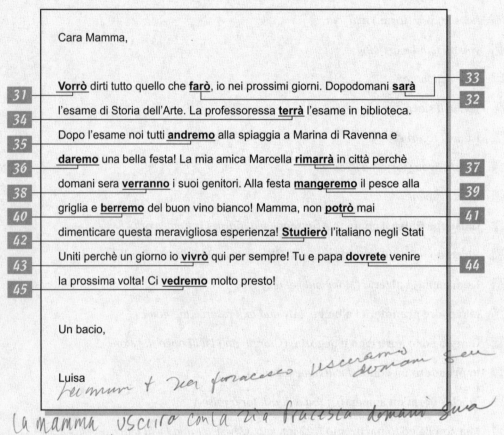

Cara Mamma,

31 **Vorrò** dirti tutto quello che **farò**, io nei prossimi giorni. Dopodomani **sarà** 33

32

34 l'esame di Storia dell'Arte. La professoressa **terrà** l'esame in biblioteca.

35 Dopo l'esame noi tutti **andremo** alla spiaggia a Marina di Ravenna e

36 **daremo** una bella festa! La mia amica Marcella **rimarrà** in città perchè 37

38 domani sera **verranno** i suoi genitori. Alla festa **mangeremo** il pesce alla 39

40 griglia e **berremo** del buon vino bianco! Mamma, non **potrò** mai 41

42 dimenticare questa meravigliosa esperienza! **Studierò** l'italiano negli Stati

43 Uniti perchè un giorno io **vivrò** qui per sempre! Tu e papa **dovrete** venire 44

45 la prossima volta! Ci **vedremo** molto presto!

Un bacio,

Luisa

46 La mamma **uscirà** con la zia Francesca domani sera.

47 **Andremo** allo zoo fra tre giorni.

48 I miei amici gli Smith **mi visiteranno** in Sicilia entro giugno.

49 **Arriveremo** a Venezia fra qualche giorno.

50 **Canterai** alla Scala il mese prossimo?

51 La mia compagna di stanza ed io **frequenteremo** l'Università di Firenze l'anno prossimo.

52 La mia mamma **visiterà** appena **riceverà** il suo passaporto.

53 Se **piove, mangeremo** a casa questa sera.

54 **Visiteremo** Pompeii sabato prossimo.

55 **Vedranno** il film dopo domani.

56 **Studierai** o **viaggerai** in Italia nel futuro? (*Will you be studying in or traveling to Italy in the future?*)

Viaggerò in Italia in futuro.

57 Quando **partirete**? (*When will you [pl.] leave?*)

Partiremo a luglio.

58 A che ora **arriverà** il tuo aereo? (*What time will your plane arrive?*)

Il mio aereo **arriverà** alle 10:20 di mattina.

59 **Arriverà** a Venezia o a Firenze la nonna? (*Will grandma be arriving in Venice or Florence?*)

Arriverà a Bologna!

60 **Mangerete** la pizza quando **sarete** a Napoli? (*Will you [pl.] eat pizza when you're in Naples?*)

Sì, **mangeremo** la pizza quando **saremo** a Napoli.

61 I ragazzi **berranno** il Chianti o la Vernaccia in Toscana? (*Will the guys drink Chianti or Vernaccia in Tuscany?*)

Berranno il Chianti.

62 **Scierai** a Cortina d'Ampezzo? (*Will you ski at Cortina d'Ampezzo?*)

No, non **scierò** a Cortina d'Ampezzo.

63 **Pagherà** in contanti o con la carta di credito tua moglie? (*Will your wife pay with a credit card or in cash?*)

Pagherà con la carta di credito.

64 **Andrete** anche a Taormina? (*Will you [pl.] also go to Taormina?*)

Sì, **andremo** a Taormina.

65 **Dormiranno** in una pensione o in un albergo i tuoi genitori? (*Will your parents sleep in a boarding house or a hotel?*)

Dormiranno in un albergo.

66 *Will it snow tomorrow?*

Sì, **nevicherà** domani sera.

67 *Am I going to sell my house by June?*

No, non **venderai** la tua casa entro giugno.

68 *Will I visit Italy this year?*

Sì, **visiterai** l'Italia quest'anno!

69 *Will I have fun in Italy?*

Sì, **ti divertirai** in Italia.

70 *Will I fall in love right away on the trip?*

No, non **ti innamorerai** subito durante il viaggio.

71 *Will I speak Italian every day?*

Sì, **parlerai** italiano tutti i giorni!

72 *Will my children come home and live with me after college?*

No, i tuoi figli non **torneranno** a vivere con te dopo l'università.

73 *I'm tired of cleaning! Will my husband/my wife help me clean tomorrow?*

Sì, tuo marito/tua moglie **ti aiuterà** a pulire.

74 *Am I going to buy a house at Lago di Como in a few years?*

Sì, fra qualche anno **comprerai** una casa a Lago di Como.

75 *Will I be winning the lottery soon?*

No, purtroppo, non **vincerai** presto la lotteria.

Chapter 11

Could-ing and Would-ing: The Conditional Tense

T he Italian conditional tense corresponds to saying *could, would,* or *should* in English. For example, the conditional tense allows you to focus on the finer, most important things in life, like "I would go to Italy in a heartbeat"; "I could never get tired of eating ice cream"; and "I should buy a Ferrari." The conditional is also the perfect tense for telling people what to do: "You should marry George," or "You could be a little nicer!" In this chapter, you practice conjugating the conditional by itself or with the present tense. I would tell you good luck, but you shouldn't need it!

Covering the Uses of the Conditional Tense

The conditional tense has a couple specific uses:

 ✔ **Asking a question.** When asking a question, the conditional is the polite way to go. "**Potrei provare** questi stivali?" (*Might I be able to try on these boots?*) "**Sarebbe** possibile **avere** un po' d'acqua, per favore?" (*Would it be possible to have some water, please?*)

 ✔ **Noting that one event is dependent upon (conditional to) another event occurring.** In this usage, the conditional often appears in the same sentence with the imperfect subjunctive (see Chapter 13) and with "if" sentences (see Chapter 21).

 But in this chapter, the conditional either exists by itself or is tied to another condition in the present tense or passato prossimo, as in this example: "Claudio **si sposerebbe** ma non **ha trovato** la donna giusta." (*Claudio would get married, but he hasn't found the right woman.*)

Forming the Regular Conditional

If you enjoy forming the regular future tense in Italian (see Chapter 10), you'll love forming the regular conditional tense because the two tenses use the exact same infinitive stems. (Remember that the **a** in the stem of **-are** verbs becomes an **e.**) And you add the same set of conditional endings for all three verb conjugations (**-are, -ere,** and **-ire** verbs) to the conditional stems.

The following table shows the conditional endings for the three verb conjugations.

Regular Conditional Tense Endings	
io **-ei**	noi **-emmo**
tu **-esti**	voi **-este**
lui, lei, Lei **-ebbe**	loro **-ebbero**

The following tables show some examples of regular **-are, -ere,** and **-ire** verbs conjugated in the conditional tense.

lavorare (*to work*)	
io lavorer**ei**	noi lavorer**emmo**
tu lavorer**esti**	voi lavorer**este**
lui, lei, Lei lavorer**ebbe**	loro lavorer**ebbero**
Lavorereste con me su questo progetto? (*Would you [all] work with me on this project?*)	

prendere (*to take or to have*)	
io prender**ei**	noi prender**emmo**
tu prender**esti**	voi prender**este**
lui, lei, Lei, prender**ebbe**	loro prender**ebbero**
Loro **prenderebbero** il gelato tutti i giorni! (*They would have ice cream every day!*)	

aprire (*to open*)	
io aprir**ei**	noi aprir**emmo**
tu aprir**esti**	voi aprir**este**
lui, lei, Lei aprir**ebbe**	loro aprir**ebbero**
Apriresti la finestra, per piacere? (*Would you open the window, please?*)	

Fill in this brief dialogue between two lovers by using the regular conditional conjugations. Here's an example to get you started:

Q. Lei: Mi _____ ogni sera? (telefonare)

Lui: Sì, ti _____ ogni sera. (telefonare)

A. Lei: Mi **telefoneresti** ogni sera? (*She: Would you phone me every night?*)

Lui: Sì, ti **telefonerei** ogni sera. (*He: Yes, I would phone you every night.*)

1. Lei: Tu mi _____ per sempre? (amare)

2. Lui: Sì, io ti _____ per sempre. (amare)

3. Lei: Tu _____ la mano sul fuoco? (mettere)

4. Lui: Sì, _____ la mano sul fuoco. (mettere)

5. Lei: Tu _____ con me per scoprire il mondo? (partire)

6. Lui: Amore, sì che _____ con te per scoprire il mondo. (partire [io])

7. Lei: _____ solo con me? (uscire [tu])

8. Lui: Sì, _____ solo con te. (uscire [io])

9. Lei: E quando mi _____? (sposare [tu])

10. Lui: Non ti _____ mai. (sposare [io])

Creating the Irregular Conditional

The irregular conditional tense and the spelling exceptions in the conditional tense use the same irregular stems as the irregular future tense verbs that I cover in Chapter 10. I include these stems again in Table 11-1 for your conjugating pleasure. *Note:* You use the regular conditional tense endings **-ei, -esti, -ebbe, -emmo, -este,** and **-ebbero.**

Table 11-1	Forming Irregular Conditional Verbs		
Infinitive	*Conditional Stem*	*Infinitive*	*Conditional Stem*
andare	andr-	venire	verr-
avere	avr-	volere	vorr-
cadere	cadr-	dare	dar-
dovere	dovr-	fare	far-
potere	potr-	stare	star-
sapere	sapr-	cercare	cercher-
vedere	vedr-	pagare	pagher-
vivere	vivr-	mangiare	manger-
bere	berr-	cominciare	comincer-
tenere	terr-	essere	sar-
rimanere	rimarr-		

Conjugate the following verbs into the conditional present tense and then translate. Some of these verbs should have irregular stems. Here's an example:

Q. Io _____ felice. (essere)

A. Io **sarei** felice. *I would be happy.*

11. Noi _____ una bistecca. (mangiare)

_____

12. Io _____ un po' di acqua. (volere)

_____

13. Loro _____ sopresi. (essere)

_____

14. Voi _____ il conto? (pagare)

_____

15. Tu _____ con me? (andare)

_____

16. Gianni _____ tutto. (dare)

_____

17. Anna Maria e Roberto _____ le vacanze in Portogallo. (fare)

_____

18. Tu e Domenico _____ a casa. (rimanere)

_____

19. MariaPaola ed io _____ il Campari — ora. (bere)

_____

20. Tu e Cristiano _____ il compito. (fare)

_____

21. Maria _____ tardi tutti i giorni. (alzarsi)

_____

22. Mi _____ conoscerlo. (piacere)

_____

23. Mi _____ un favore? (fare [tu])

_____

24. Tu _____ il nome di quella ragazza? (sapere)

_____

25. Non _____ di mangiare il gelato! (stancarsi [io])

_____

Imagine if you had all the money in the world! (You'd still be reading this book, right?) While you're still in dreamland, write five sentences, using the conditional tense, saying what you would do with all your money. Follow my cues and simply conjugate the verbs into the first-person singular of the conditional tense and then translate. I'll start with a personal example:

Q. _____ a Roma. (vivere)

A. **Vivrei** a Roma. *I would live in Rome.*

26. _____ un viaggio in Italia. (fare)

_____

27. _____ una villa ad Amalfi. (comprare)

_____

28. _____ i poveri. (aiutare)

_____

29. Non _____ più. (lavorare)

_____

30. _____ una casa in Florida a mia madre. (dare)

_____

Dovere, Potere, e Volere: Should, Could, and Would Like To in the Conditional

The irregular verbs **dovere** (*to have to, must*), **volere** (*to want, wish*), and **potere** (*to be able to, can*) always enrich a sentence (check out Table 11-1 for their conditional stems), and their use in the conditional tense is no exception. These verbs translate as *should* (**dovere**), *could* (**potere**), and *would like to* (**volere**).

Dovere, volere, and **potere** are often followed in the conditional by a second verb in the infinitive form:

    Dovrei studiare. (*I should study.*)

    Potrei dormire tutto il giorno. (*I could sleep all day.*)

    Vorrei sapere chi **ti credi** di **essere?** (*I'd like to know who you think you are?*)

The conditional is considered the polite tense, especially when combined with **dovere, potere,** and **volere.** Note the following three examples:

    Dovremmo spostarci? Diamo fastidio? (*Should we move (our spot)? Are we in the way?*)

    Vorrei un cappuccino, per favore. (*I'd like a cappuccino, please.*)

    Potresti darmi una mano, per piacere? (*Would you please give me a hand?*)

Conjugate the following verbs, using the present conditional tense, and then translate the sentences. Here's an example:

O. _____ stare zitta! (dovere [tu])

A. **Dovresti** stare zitta! *You should be quiet!*

31. Noi _____ divertirci di più. (dovere)

_____

32. Jenny e Lucy _____ dormire a casa nostra domani. (potere)

_____

33. Mamma, che cosa _____ servire per la festa? (volere)

_____

34. Tu e Patrizia _____ andare a cena senza i bambini. (potere)

_____

35. Tu _____ studiare di più questo semestre. (dovere)

_____

36. Giancarlo _____ mangiare, ma ha mal di denti. (dovere)

_____

37. Io _____ venire al cinema, ma non ho la macchina. (volere)

_____

38. Scusi, mi _____ dire l'ora? (potere [Lei])

_____

39. Anna Maria _____ lavorare di meno. (dovere)

_____

40. Noi _____ ordinare, per favore. (volere)

_____

Answer Key

1. Lei: Tu mi **ameresti** per sempre? (*Would you love me forever?*)

2. Lui: Sì, io ti **amerei** per sempre. (*Yes, I would love you forever.*)

3. Lei: Tu **metteresti** la mano sul fuoco? (*Are you willing to swear by it;* Literally: *Would you put your hand through fire to prove it?*)

4. Lui: Sì, **metterei** la mano sul fuoco. (*Yes, I'm willing to swear by it.*)

5. Lei: Tu **partiresti** con me per scoprire il mondo? (*Would you take off with me to explore the world?*)

6. Lui: Amore, sì che io **partirei** con te per scoprire il mondo. (*Yes, my love, I'd take off with you to explore the world.*)

7. Lei: **Usciresti** solo con me? (*Would you go out with me only?*)

8. Lui: Sì, **uscirei** solo con te. (*Yes, I would go out with you only.*)

9. Lei: E quando mi **sposeresti?** (*And when would you marry me?*)

10. Lui: Non ti **sposerei** mai. (*I would never marry you.*)

11. Noi **mangeremmo** una bistecca. *We would eat a steak.*

12. Io **vorrei** un po' di acqua. *I'd like some water.*

13. Loro **sarebbero** sorpresi. *They would be surprised.*

14. Voi **paghereste** il conto? *Would you pay the bill?*

15. Tu **andresti** con me? *Would you go with me?*

16. Gianni **darebbe** tutto. *Gianni would give everything.*

17. Anna Maria e Roberto **farebbero** le vacanze in Portogallo. *Anna Maria and Robert would take a vacation in Portugal.*

18. Tu e Domenico **rimarreste** a casa. *You and Domenico would stay home.*

19. MariaPaola ed io **berremmo** il Campari — ora. *Maria Paola and I would drink Campari — right now.*

20. Tu e Cristiano **fareste** il compito. *Cristiano and you would do your homework.*

21. Maria **si alzerebbe** tardi tutti i giorni. *Maria would get up late every day.*

22. Mi **piacerebbe** conoscerlo. *I'd like to meet him.*

23. Mi **faresti** un favore? *Would you do me a favor?*

24. Tu **sapresti** il nome di quella ragazza? *Would you know that girl's name?*

25. Non **mi stancherei** di mangiare il gelato! *I would never get tired of eating ice cream!*

26 **Farei** un viaggio in Italia! *I'd take a trip to Italy!*

27 **Comprerei** una villa ad Amalfi. *I'd buy a villa in Amalfi.*

28 **Aiuterei** i poveri. *I'd help the poor.*

29 Non **lavorerei** più. *I wouldn't work anymore.*

30 **Darei** una casa in Florida a mia madre. *I'd give my mom a house in Florida.*

31 Noi **dovremmo** divertirci di più. *We should have more fun.*

32 Jenny e Lucy **potrebbero** dormire a casa nostra domani. *Jenny and Lucy could sleep at our house tomorrow night.*

33 Mamma, che cosa **vorresti** servire per la festa? *Mom, what would you like to serve for the party?*

34 Tu e Patrizia **potreste** andare a cena senza i bambini. *Patrizia and you could go to dinner without the children.*

35 Tu **dovresti** studiare di più questo semestre. *You should study more this semester.*

36 Giancarlo **dovrebbe** mangiare, ma ha mal di denti. *Giancarlo should eat, but he has a toothache.*

37 Io **vorrei** venire al cinema, ma non ho la macchina. *I'd like to come to the movies, but I don't have a car.*

38 Scusi, mi **potrebbe** dire l'ora? *Excuse me, would you please tell me what time it is?*

39 Anna Maria **dovrebbe** lavorare di meno. *Anna Maria ought to work less.*

40 Noi **vorremmo** ordinare, per favore. *We would like to order, please.*

Chapter 12

Getting into the Present Subjunctive Mood

In This Chapter

▶ Putting together the present subjunctive

▶ Reining in spelling exceptions and irregular verbs

▶ Assimilating the many uses of the present subjunctive

*P*rior to this chapter, most of the exercises in this book have dealt with the *indicative mood,* which has present, past, imperfect, and past perfect tenses. You use the indicative mood when expressing certainty and objectivity (for example, "**Mangio** con Anna oggi" [*I'm eating with Anna today*] and "**So** che **sei** arrabbiato" [*I know that you're angry*]). But now the time has come to introduce a little uncertainty into your life with the *subjunctive mood.* The subjunctive expresses doubt, uncertainty, opinion, emotions — generally, all things *subjective* (for example, "Non **so** se Anna **mangi** con me oggi" [*I don't know if Anna is eating with me today*] and "**Penso** che tu **sia** arrabbiato" [*I think that you're angry*]).

In this chapter, I introduce you to the present subjunctive (or the congiuntivo presente). You find out how to form the present subjunctive, work with spelling exceptions and irregular forms, and make the subjunctive a valuable tool in your Italian arsenal. (You can check out Chapter 13 for the imperfect subjunctive. I also cover the two compound subjunctive tenses — the past subjunctive and the past perfect subjunctive — in Chapters 19 and 20, respectively.)

Forming the Present Subjunctive Mood

The formation of the subjunctive mood usually calls for a dependent clause, which you introduce with the word "che" (*that*). (I go into the different uses of the subjunctive and the verbs that usually require it in the following sections.) Notice the position of the subjunctive in the following sentence and what kind of verb I use in the main clause:

Credo che Emilia **dorma** poco. (*I think that Emilia sleeps little.*)

In this sentence, **credo** is in the present indicative tense, and **dorma** is in the present subjunctive tense. Note, also, that the subject in the main clause (io [*I*]) is different from the subject in the dependent clause (Emilia).

In English, I may say *I think Emilia sleeps little;* you sometimes omit the "that" in English, but you never omit it in Italian.

The following similarities can help you remember your subjunctive conjugations:

- ✔ The verb ending for **-are** verbs is the same for the first three persons (first-, second-, and third-person singular): **-i.**

- ✔ The verb ending for both **-ere** and **-ire** verbs in the first three persons is the same: **-a.**

- ✔ The verb endings for first-person plural (noi) and second-person plural (voi) verbs are the same for **-are, -ere,** and **-ire** verbs: **-iamo** and **-iate.**

- ✔ The verb ending for an **-are** verb in the third-person plural (loro) is **-ino,** and the ending for **-ere** and **-ire** verbs is **-ano.**

So, you can think that many present-subjunctive endings are almost the *opposites* of the present-indicative endings (see Chapters 2 and 3).

Here are some examples of the verb endings in action:

È importante che il nostro presidente **parli** con il vostro. (*It's important that our president speak with yours.*)

La scuola **esige** che tutti gli studenti **vengano** alla riunione. (*The school mandates that all of the students come to the meeting.*)

The personal pronoun is often superfluous and unnecessary in Italian because the person is inherent in the verb form. But in the present subjunctive, you use the same verb for all three first persons. Therefore, you should use the personal pronoun (io, tu, lui/lei/Lei) or subject (Gianni, for example) with the present subjunctive to avoid confusing your reader/listener.

È essenziale che io **capisca** questo congiuntivo. (*It's essential that I understand this subjunctive.*)

È bene che lei **capisca** sua nipote. (*It's a good thing that she understands her niece.*)

The following table shows the present subjunctive **-are** verb endings: **-i, -iamo, -iate,** and **-ino:**

parlare (*to speak*)	
che io parl**i**	che noi parl**iamo**
che tu parl**i**	che voi parl**iate**
che lui, lei, Lei parl**i**	che loro parl**ino**
Penso che voi **parliate** molto bene l'italiano! (*I think that you all speak Italian well!*)	

The following two tables show the present subjunctive **-ere** and **-ire** verb endings: **-a, -iamo, -iate,** and **-ano:**

vedere (*to see*)	
che io ved**a**	che noi ved**iamo**
che tu ved**a**	che voi ved**iate**
che lui, lei, Lei ved**a**	che loro ved**ano**
Speriamo che **vediate** questo film. (*We hope that you see this film.*)	

partire (to leave, to depart)	
che io part**a**	che noi part**iamo**
che tu part**a**	che voi part**iate**
che lui, lei, Lei part**a**	che loro part**ano**
I miei amici **sono** tristi che io **parta**. (*My friends are sad that I'm leaving.*)	

The following table shows the endings for **-ire(isc)** verbs in the present subjunctive:
-isca, -iamo, -iate, and **-iscano:**

capire (to understand)	
che io cap**isca**	che noi cap**iamo**
che tu cap**isca**	che voi cap**iate**
che lui, lei, Lei cap**isca**	che loro cap**iscano**
È importante che lui **mi capisca**. (*It's important that he undertand me.*)	

You conjugate reflexive verbs, such as **divertirsi,** just as you do any of the previous **-are, -ere, -ire,** and **-ire(isc)** verbs in the present subjunctive. The only difference is that you need to add the reflexive pronouns. (For more on reflexive verbs and pronouns, see Chapter 5.)

divertirsi (to have fun, to enjoy oneself, to have a good time)	
che io mi divert**a**	che noi ci divert**iamo**
che tu ti divert**a**	che voi vi divert**iate**
che lui, lei, Lei si divert**a**	che loro si divert**ano**
Quanto **sono** contenta che **vi divertiate!** (*I'm so happy that you're having a good time!*)	

For this exercise, conjugate the verbs in parentheses into the regular present subjunctive mood. This is a simple substitution exercise that should drive home the concepts of structure and conjugation. Try to establish a drill-like rhythm while you do them, and notice all the verbs and the expressions in the main clauses: **sperare** (*to hope*), **credere** (*to believe*), **È** importante (*It's important*), **sono** triste che (*I am sad that*). Follow my example:

Q. È importante che tu mi _____. (capire)

A. È importante che tu **mi capisca.** (*It's important that you understand me.*)

1. È importante che voi mi _____. (capire)

2. È importante che loro mi _____. (capire)

3. È importante che la mia ragazza mi _____. (capire)

4. È importante che noi _____. (capire)

5. È importante che tu _____. (finire)

6. È importante che io _____. (finire)

7. È importante che la bambina _____ a nuotare. (divertirsi)

8. È importante che voi _____ a nuotare! (divertirsi)

9. È importante che loro _____. (ascoltare)

10. Bisogna che loro _____. (partire)

11. (Io) Sono triste che tu _____. (partire)

12. (Io) Sono triste che lui _____. (partire)

13. La mamma è triste che voi _____. (partire)

14. Loro sono tristi che io _____. (partire)

15. Loro sperano che voi _____ il film. (vedere)

16. Loro sperano che la mamma _____ il film. (vedere)

17. Loro sperano che tu _____ il film. (vedere)

18. Loro sperano che il professore _____ l'italiano. (parlare)

19. Spero che Giancarlo _____ presto domani. (alzarsi)

20. I miei genitori sperano che io _____ presto domani. (alzarsi)

Mastering Spelling Exceptions and Irregular Forms within the Present Subjunctive

As with the indicative mood, the present subjunctive mood features verbs that undergo spelling changes and irregular verbs. Spelling exceptions are very common, but the good news is that the first three persons in the subjunctive (first-, second-, and third-person singular) are the exact same. Irregular verbs become easy to handle, too, after you learn their stems and structures. And the good thing about remembering the various exceptions to the present subjunctive? The io, tu, lei, Lei, and loro forms are the same as the Lei and Loro command (or imperative) forms (see Chapter 6).

One spelling exception calls for you to add an **h** to the end of the stems of **-care** and **-gare** verbs — such as **dimenticare** (*to forget*) and **pagare** (*to pay*) — before you add their subjunctive endings (see the previous section in this chapter for listings of regular endings). Doing so allows you keep the hard "c" and "g" sounds throughout, similar to the spelling exception you see in the present indicative tense (see Chapter 2). In the indicative, however, the spell change occurs only in the tu and noi persons; in the subjunctive, you add the **h** to all six persons.

È probabile che io **dimentichi** questo congiuntivo. (*It's probable that I'm going to forget this subjunctive.*)

È probabile che il nonno **paghi** la cena. (*It's probable that grandpa is paying for dinner.*)

Try a few exercises with verbs ending in **-care** and **-gare** now. Substitute the verb conjugations for the verbs in parentheses, just as you see in the example:

Q. È probabile che io _____ la cena. (pagare)

A. È probabile che io **paghi** la cena. (*It's probable that I'm paying for dinner.*)

21. È probabile che voi _____ la cena. (pagare)

22. È probabile che i nonni _____ il cane. (legare)

23. Non credo che tu _____ la verità. (cercare)

24. Non crede che io _____ la verità. (dimenticare)

25. Non voglio che il cane _____ la bambina. (leccare)

26. Sono contenta che Maria _____ a calcio (soccer). (giocare)

27. È bene che le ragazze _____ bene. (giocare)

28. Credo che John _____ il mondo. (girovagare)

29. È importante che voi _____ bene il cibo. (masticare)

30. Penso che loro _____ tutto! (negare)

Other verbs in the present subjunctive, like **cominciare** (*to begin*), **mangiare** (*to eat*), **lasciare** (*to leave*), and **svegliare** (*to wake*) — in other words, verbs that end in **-iare** — drop their **-i** before you add the subjunctive endings (see the previous section in this chapter for the endings). This is a functional change so you don't have to double up on the **-i** beginning of the endings. The following table shows the structure of **-iare** verbs.

cominciare (*to begin*)	
che io cominc**i**	che noi cominc**iamo**
che tu cominc**i**	che voi cominc**iate**
che lu, lei, Lei cominc**i**	che loro cominc**ino**
È ora che io **cominci** a **studiare**. (*It's time that I begin to study.*)	

The verbs in the following exercise all end in **-iare.** In the questions, I use the present indicative; in the responses, you should conjugate the verbs into the present subjunctive. During the exercise, you can begin to compare the differences in their use. Follow my example:

Q. A che ora comincia il film? (*What time does the film begin?*) Credo che _____ alle 7. (cominciare)

A. A che ora comincia il film? Credo che **cominci** alle 7. (*I think that it begins at 7:00.*)

31. A che ora mangiano i tuoi? (*What time does your family eat?*) Credo che _____ alle 7:30. (mangiare)

32. A che ora cominciano le prove? (*What time does rehearsal begin?*) Credo che _____ alle 5:00. (cominciare)

33. La mamma si dimentica di telefonare? (*Is mom going to forget to call?*) Sì, credo che lei _____ di telefonare. (dimenticarsi)

34. Svegli (tu) il babbo? (*Are you going to wake up dad?*) Sì, è ora che io lo (him) _____. (svegliare)

35. Dove lasciano i biglietti? (*Where are they going to leave the tickets?*) Credo che _____ li (them) con Anna. (lasciare)

The conjugations of the lei and loro imperative forms from Chapter 6 are very similar to the conjugations of irregular verbs in the present subjunctive. In fact, the conjugations are essentially the same. I put the main irregular forms in Table 12-1, though, so that you don't have to go back and forth too much while you work through the exercises in the rest of this chapter.

The three singular forms of each verb are the same, meaning that io, tu, lui/lei/Lei are all included in the first conjugation you see. For example, "**Pensa** che io **abbia**"; "**Pensa** che tu **abbia**"; "**Penso** che Lei **abbia**" (*He thinks that I have; He thinks that you have; I think that you* [form.] *have*).

Table 12-1	Irregular Present Tense Subjunctive Verbs	
Infinitive	*Conjugation*	*Example*
avere (*to have*)	**abbia, abbiamo, abbiate, abbiano**	Non **so** chi **abbia** il mio libro. (*I don't know who has my book.*)
andare (*to go*)	**vada, andiamo, andiate, vadano**	È bene che **vadano** via. (*It's a good thing that they're going away.*)
bere (*to drink*)	**beva, beviamo, beviate, bevano**	**Si dice** che lui **beva** troppo. (*They say he drinks too much.*)
dare (*to give*)	**dia, diamo, diate, diano**	**Vuoi** che gli **dia** una mano? (*Do you want for me to give him a hand?*)
dire (*to say*)	**dica, diciamo, diciate, dicano**	**Sembra** che **dicano** la verità. (*It seems like they're telling the truth.*)
dovere (*to have to*)	**deva (debba), dobbiamo, dobbiate, devano (debbano)**	Peccato che **dobbiate partire** così presto. (*It's too bad you have to leave so early.*)
essere (*to be*)	**sia, siamo, siate, siano**	**Voglio** che tu **sia** felice. (*I want for you to be happy.*)
fare (*to do, to make*)	**faccia, facciamo, facciate, facciano**	È ora che io **faccia** il footing. (*It's time for me to go jogging.*)
potere (*to be able to*)	**possa, possiamo, possiate, possano**	È strano che i miei amici **possano stare** fuori fino alle 3 di notte, e io no. (*It's strange that my friends can stay out until 3 in the morning, and I can't.*)
proporre (*to propose*)	**proponga, proponiamo, proponiate, propongano**	Cosa **vuoi** che io **ti proponga?** (*What would you like for me to suggest to you?*)

Infinitive	Conjugation	Example
rimanere (*to stay*)	rimanga, rimaniamo, rimaniate, rimangano	**Sperano** che io **rimanga** vicino a casa. (*They hope I'm going to stay close to home.*)
sapere (*to know*)	sappia, sappiamo, sappiate, sappiano	**Bisogna** che tu **sappia**. (*You need to know.*)
scegliere (*to choose*)	scelga, scegliamo, scegliate, scelgano	**Mi dispiace** che tu **scelga** un'università così lontana. (*I'm sorry that you're choosing a university so far away.*)
stare (*to be*)	stia, stiamo, stiate, stiano	**Immagino** che **stiano** ancora insieme. (*I guess they're still together.*)
uscire (*to go out*)	esca, usciamo, usciate, escano	Non **voglio** che tu **esca** senza il cappotto. (*I don't want for you to go out without a coat.*)
venire (*to come*)	venga, veniamo, veniate, vengano	Può **darsi** che **veniamo** in Italia. (*It's possible that we're coming to Italy.*)
volere (*to want*)	voglia, vogliamo, vogliate, vogliano	**Spero** che Emilia **voglia andare** alla spiaggia oggi. (*I hope that Emilia wants to go to the beach today.*)

The following exercise features two mothers talking about their hopes and fears for their children, and for themselves. Complete their conversation by conjugating the verbs in parentheses into the irregular present subjunctive (using Table 12-1 as a guide). Follow the example:

0. Mamma A: Non so dove _____ Fabio l'anno prossimo. (andare)

Mamma B: Io spero che Lorenzo _____ vicino a casa. (rimanere)

A. Mamma A: Non so dove **vada** Fabio l'anno prossimo. (*I don't know where Fabio is going next year.*)

Mamma B: Io spero che Lorenzo **rimanga** vicino a casa. (*I hope that Lorenzo stays close to home.*)

36. Mamma A: È bene che i ragazzi _____, ma non troppo. (uscire)

Mamma B: Non permettiamo che Lorenzo _____ mai. (uscire)

37. Mamma A: Voglio che Fabio _____ felice, qualunque cosa _____. (essere, fare)

Mamma B: Noi, invece, pensiamo che i nostri figli _____ solo studiare. (dovere)

38. Mamma A: Sì, va bene studiare, ma non credi che _____ necessario divertirsi un po'? (essere)

Mamma B: Credo che Lorenzo _____ divertirsi studiando. Abbiamo paura che _____ troppo se frequenta un'università lontana. (potere, bere)

39. Mamma A: Fabio beve un po' di birra, ma credo che ci _____ tutto quello che fa. Non credo che _____ molti segreti. (dire, avere)

    Mamma B: Sembra che Lorenzo _____ frequentare l'università molto lontano da noi. Ho paura che non _____ a casa per le vacanze. (volere, venire)

40. Mamma A: Spero soltanto che Fabio _____ scegliere bene, e che _____ bene all'università. (sapere, fare)

    Mamma B: Lorenzo vuole che noi gli _____ la nostra vecchia macchina, ma è improbabile che io gliela _____. (dare, dare)

For this exercise, imagine that you're on the beautiful Lipari Islands off the coast of Sicily. When you get your head out of the clouds, conjugate the irregular verbs in parentheses into the present subjunctive. Here's an example (the sentence remains basically the same for each verb, changing only in person, so all you have to worry about is the conjugation):

0. Dubito che Davide _____ in barca con noi. (venire)

A. Dubito che Davide **venga** in barca con noi. (*I doubt that David is coming on the boat with us.*)

41. Sono contenta che la nonna _____ in barca con noi. (venire)

42. Sono contenta che Giuditta e Ginevra _____ in barca con noi. (venire)

43. Sono contenta che tu e Gloria _____ in barca con noi. (venire)

44. Giancarlo spera che io _____ comprare il pesce fresco. (potere)

45. Giancarlo spera che Gianni e Marinella _____ venire a Vulcano. (potere)

46. Giancarlo spera che voi _____ portare anche i bambini. (potere)

47. È possibile che noi _____ il bagno nei fanghi termali (mud bath). (fare)

48. È possibile che Laura _____ il bagno nei fanghi termali. (fare)

49. È possibile che tu _____ il bagno nei fanghi termali? (fare)

50. È probabile che Lorenzo _____ una gita a Panarea. (proporre)

Making the Present Subjunctive a Valuable Tool

You have some options when it comes to using the present subjunctive. You can use it in different ways and in different expressions, all of which I present in this section. But first, some rules!

A subjunctive verb almost always appears in the dependent clause, generally introduced by the word "che" (*that*). Your verb in the main clause, on the other hand, has to be a verb or expression that requires the subjunctive.

For example, even though the word "che" separates the dependent and independent clauses in the following setences, the indicative always appears with the verb **sapere** (*to know*), and the subjunctive always goes with the verb **dubitare** (*to doubt*):

So che **sei** intelligente. (*I know that you are intelligent.*)

Dubito che tu **sia** intelligente. (*I doubt that you are intelligent.*)

The verbs in Table 12-2 all require that their accompanying verbs be in the subjunctive, because they express desires, wishes, commands, emotions, doubts, or disbeliefs. (This rule also applies to the subjunctive in Chapters 13, 19, and 20.) All these expressions should be followed by "che" and, in this chapter, the present subjunctive.

Table 12-2	Verbs Indicating a Desire, Wish, Command, Emotion, Doubt, or Belief		
Verb or Expression	*Translation*	*Verb or Expression*	*Translation*
augurarsi	to hope	non essere certo/a/i/e	to not be certain
avere l'impressione	to have the impression, the feeling, the idea	non essere sicuro/a/i/e	to not be certain
avere paura	to be afraid	non sapere	to not know
chiedere	to ask for	pensare	to think
credere	to believe, to think	permettere	to allow, to permit
desiderare	to desire	preferire	to prefer
dispiacere	to be sorry	pretendere	to demand, to expect
esigere	to demand	proibire(isc)	to forbid
essere contenta/o/i/e	to be happy	sperare	to hope
essere triste/i	to be sad	temere	to fear, to worry
immaginare	to imagine	volere	to want

For this exercise, conjugate the verbs in parentheses into the present subjunctive, using the verbs and expressions from Table 12-2 as a guide. Here's an example to get you started:

Q. Spero che mi _____ oggi. (telefonare [loro])

A. Spero che **mi telefonino** oggi. (*I hope that they call me today.*)

51. Permetti che tua figlia _____ con lui? (uscire)

52. Credo che _____ tardi — andiamo! (fare)

53. Diane desidera che Marc la _____ a teatro. (accompagnare)

54. Ho l'impressione che Guido non _____. (studiare)

55. Non siamo sicuri che _____ Berlusconi questa volta. (vincere)

56. Abbiamo paura che voi _____ arrabbiati. (essere)

57. Maria e Domenico pensano che lo zio John _____ in gamba. (essere)

58. La dogana proibisce che noi _____ fichi freschi negli Stati Uniti. (portare)

59. Ci dispiace che non _____. (capire [loro])

60. Anna e Robert vogliono che i figli _____ contenti. (essere)

61. Il professore pretende che io _____ la tesi il mese prossimo. (consegnare)

62. Temo che non ci _____ abbastanza vino rosso; vai a comprare altre due bottiglie di Barbaresco. (essere)

63. Preferisco che mia figlia _____ a calcio. (giocare)

64. Chiedo soltanto che non _____. (litigare [voi])

65. Non so chi _____ queste cose ridicole. (dire)

66. Mi auguro che tu _____ a trovarmi. (venire)

67. Anna, sei contenta che tuo figlio _____ per l'estate? (ritornare)

68. Mia madre esige che io _____ alla festa. (venire)

69. Giancarlo è triste che il suo capo gli _____ solo tre settimane di vacanza. (dare)

70. Immagino che _____ con l'alba. (partire [voi])

Ready for Round Two? Another instance when you use the subjunctive is when a verb in the main clause is an impersonal expression and the subject of the dependent clause is articulated:

> **È** importante **studiare.** (*It's important to study.*) In this example, no subject is articulated.

versus

> **È** importante che io **studi.** (*It's important that I study.*) In this example, the subject in the dependent clause is specified, so you use the subjunctive.

An *impersonal expression* has no specific subject and often translates as *one, you,* or *it.* Table 12-3 provides you with a list of common impersonal expressions. These impersonal expressions usually start with the third-person singular of the verb **essere** (*to be*): **È** (**È** bene che . . . [*It's a good thing that . . .*]). Not all impersonal expressions, however, require the subjunctive. For example, "È certo che . . ." (*It's certain that . . .*) expresses a certainty, so the clause to follow needs to be in the indicative — "È certo che lui **viene.**" (*It's certain that he's going to come.*) So, to recognize the need for impersonal expressions in the subjunctive, familiarize yourself with Table 12-3.

All the impersonal expressions you see in Table 12-3 can go before the second part (the part after "che") of the following sample sentence, which is why I provide you with only one example:

> **È** essenziale che lo **facciate.** (*It's essential that you* [pl.] *do it.*)

Table 12-3	Impersonal Expressions in Main Clauses
Expression	*Translation*
bisogna che	*it's necessary that/to have to/should*
è bene che	*it's good that*
è importante che	*it's important that*
è incredibile che	*it's incredible that*
è inutile che	*it's useless that, it's pointless that*
è male che	*it's bad that*
è meglio che	*it's better that*
è ora che	*it's time that*
è (im)possibile che	*it's (im)possible that*
è (im)probabile che	*it's (im)probable that, it's (un)likely that*
è strano che	*it's strange that*
pare che	*it seems that*
peccato che	*it's too bad that*
può darsi che	*it's possible that*
sembra che	*it seems that*

Here's a simple substitution exercise for the impersonal expressions you see in Table 12-3. I give you one impersonal expression in each problem, and you conjugate the verb that goes along with it into the present subjunctive. Here's an example to get you started:

Q. È strano che _____. (nevicare)

A. È strano che **nevichi.** (*It's strange that it's snowing.*)

71. È strano che _____ il bambino. (piangere)

72. È strano che _____ in ritardo il babbo. (essere)

73. È ora che _____. (partire [voi])

74. È ora che io _____. (studiare)

75. È ora che Maurizio _____. (sposarsi)

76. È probabile che io _____ Taormina. (andare)

77. È probabile che loro _____. (uscire)

78. È probabile che lui _____ l'università. (finire)

79. Sembra che la zia Carolina e lo zio Salvatore _____ un viaggio a maggio. (fare)

80. Sembra che Lorenzo _____ un bel libro. (leggere)

81. Sembra che tu e Paolo _____! (divertirsi)

82. È meglio che io _____ zitta. (stare)

83. È meglio che loro non _____ più partire all'alba. (volere)

84. È meglio che tu _____ i fatti tuoi! (fare)

85. È incredibile che Claudio e Rosaria si siano _____! (lasciarsi)

Nope, not time for the Answer Key just yet. You get to review a couple more categories of words and conditions that require the subjunctive tense! (Quite a useful tense, aye?) These areas include *conjunctions* (words connecting two different clauses) and indefinite forms ending in **-unque.** You don't use these constructions as frequently as the impersonal expressions (see Table 12-3) and the verbs and expressions in Table 12-2, but you should acquaint yourself with them anyway. Check out Table 12-4 for some conjunctions and Table 12-5 for some **-unque** words.

You attach the present subjunctive tense to the conjunctions and indefinite expressions, which will be in dependent clauses. Main clauses here should appear in the present indicative for the most part, but they can also be in the future tense (see Chapter 10). The order of the clauses doesn't matter, provided that you keep the subjunctive with its conjunction or **-unque** word.

Here's an example, using an **-unque** word, that illustrates that the clause position doesn't matter:

Dovunque tu **vada, ti amerò.** (*Wherever you go, I shall love you.*)

Ti amerò, dovunque tu **vada.** (*I shall love you, wherever you go.*)

Table 12-4	Sample Conjunctions
Conjunction	*Translation*
a meno che . . . non	*unless*
affinchè	*so that*
perchè	*so that*
di/in modo che	*so that*
benchè	*although*
sebbene	*although*
prima che	*before*
senza che	*without*
purchè	*provided that, on the condition that*
a patto che	*provided that, on the condition that*
a condizione che	*provided that, on the condition that*

Table 12-5	Sample -unque Words
-unque Word	*Translation*
chiunque	*whoever*
comunque	*however*
in qualunque modo	*however*
dovunque	*wherever*
qualunque cosa	*whatever*

In the following exercise, provide the present subjunctive form of the verbs in parentheses that go along with the phrases from Tables 12-4 and 12-5. Here's an example:

O. Vengo a cena, purchè io _____ offrire. (potere)

A. Vengo a cena, purchè io **possa** offrire. (*I'll come to dinner, provided I can treat.*)

86. Perchè tu _____, te lo spiego ancora una volta. (capire [io])

87. *Prima che il Gallo* _____ è un romanzo di Cesare Pavese. (cantare)

88. Lei non impara, sebbene _____. (studiare [lei])

89. Qualunque cosa _____, partiamo il primo agosto. (succedere)

90. Te lo spiego ancora una volta affinchè tu _____ d'accordo. (essere)

91. A condizione che io _____ offrire, vengo a cena. (potere)

92. In qualunque modo _____, per noi va bene. (fare [voi])

93. Andiamo in barca, a meno che non _____. (piovere)

94. Benchè _____ a dieta, non dimagrisce. (stare [lei])

95. Comunque _____, io ci vado lo stesso. (essere)

96. Te lo spiego ancora una volta in modo che tu _____. (capire)

97. Lui capisce, senza che io glielo _____. (dire)

98. Vengo in Puglia, a patto che io _____ portare la mia famiglia. (potere)

99. Può venire chiunque _____! (volere)

100. Do i soldi ad Emilia perchè lei _____ i biglietti per la gita scolastica.
(comprare)

Whew! If you've come this far in the chapter sequentially, you've successfully mastered
and used the present subjunctive: Congratulations! But before this trip into the subjunctive mood is complete, you should acknowledge a few less common, but still important
uses of the subjunctive. I list them here:

✔ In a relative clause:

- il/la/i/le più + adjective + che + subjunctive:

    Mary è la donna più gentile che io **conosca.** (*Mary is the nicest woman that I know.*)

- il/la/i/le meno + adjective + che + subjunctive:

    Questo **sarà** l'esercizio meno difficile che **facciate.** (*This is going to be the least difficult exercise that you do.*)

✔ With the adjectives unico/a/i che (*only*), solo/a/i/e (*only*), ultimo/a/i/e (*last*), and primo/a/i/e (*first*):

Laura è l'unica donna che **capisca** Francesco. (*Laura is the only woman who understands Francesco.*)

✔ With a negative expression, such as niente (*nothing*) or nessuno (*no one*):

- Non **c'è** niente che io **ti possa fare.** (*There's nothing that I can do for you.*)

- Non **c'è** nessuno che **parli** cinese in questo aereo? (*Isn't there anyone who speaks Chinese on this plane?*)

✔ In exclamations and blessings:

- Che Dio **ti benedica!** (*May God bless you!*)

- Dio **ci guardi!** (*Lord help us!*)

- Che **ti possa venire** un colpo! (*May you be struck by lightning!*)

Put the final uses of the present subjunctive into practice by conjugating the verbs I provide in the following sentences and then translating. Here's an example:

Q. Lecce è la città più bella che ci _____. (essere)

A. Lecce è la città più bella che ci **sia.** *Lecce is the most beautiful city that there is.*

101. Taormina è la città più romantica che tu _____ visitare. (potere)

_____

102. L'unico ristorante di pesce che _____ provare è la Trattoria Cubana. (dovere [loro])

_____

103. Maria è la sola donna che io _____. (amare)

_____

104. Non c'è nessuno che mi _____. (capire)

_____

105. Siete sicuri che questo è l'ultimo esercizio che voi _____ sul congiuntivo? (fare)

_____

Answer Key

1 È importante che voi **mi capiate.** (*It's important that you* (pl.) *understand me.*)

2 È importante che loro **mi capiscano.** (*It's important that they understand me.*)

3 È importante che la mia ragazza **mi capisca.** (*It's important that my girlfriend understands me.*)

4 È importante che noi **capiamo.** (*It's important that we understand.*)

5 È importante che tu **finisca.** (*It's important that you finish.*)

6 È importante che io **finisca.** (*It's important that I finish.*)

7 È importante che la bambina **si diverta** a nuotare. (*It's important that the baby have fun swimming.*)

8 È importante che voi **vi divertiate** a nuotare! (*It's important that you have fun swimming!*)

9 È importante che loro **ascoltino.** (*It's important that they listen.*)

10 Bisogna che loro **partano.** (*It's necessary that they leave/they need to leave.*)

11 Sono triste che tu **parta.** (*I'm sad that you're leaving.*)

12 Sono triste che lui **parta.** (*I'm sad that he's leaving.*)

13 La mamma è triste che voi **partiate.** (*Mom is sad that you all are leaving.*)

14 Loro sono tristi che io **parta.** (*They're sad that I'm leaving.*)

15 Loro sperano che voi **vediate** il film. (*They hope that you* (pl.) *see the movie.*)

16 Loro sperano che la mamma **veda** il film. (*They hope that mom sees the film.*)

17 Loro sperano che tu **veda** il film. (*They hope that you see the movie.*)

18 Loro sperano che il professore **parli** l'italiano. (*They hope that the professor speaks Italian.*)

19 Spero che Giancarlo **si alzi** presto domani. (*I hope that Giancarlo gets up early tomorrow.*)

20 I miei genitori sperano che io **mi alzi** presto domani. (*My parents hope that I get up early tomorrow.*)

21 È probabile che voi **paghiate** la cena. (*It's probable that you're* (pl.) *going to pay for dinner.*)

22 È probabile che i nonni **leghino** il cane. (*It's probable that grandma and grandpa are going to tie up the dog.*)

23 Non credo che tu **cerchi** la verità. (*I don't believe that you seek the truth.*)

24 Non crede che io **dimentichi** la verità. (*He doesn't think that I'm going to forget the truth.*)

25 Non voglio che il cane **lecchi** la bambina. (*I don't want for the dog to lick the baby.*)

26 Sono contenta che Maria **giochi** a calcio. (*I'm happy that Maria is playing soccer.*)

27 È bene che le ragazze **giochino** bene. (*It's a good thing that the girls are playing well.*)

28 Credo che John **girovaghi** il mondo. (*I think that John is wandering about the world.*)

29 È importante che voi **mastichiate** bene il cibo. (*It's important that you* (pl.) *chew your food well.*)

30 Penso che loro **neghino** tutto! (*I think that they're denying everything!*)

31 A che ora mangiano i tuoi? Credo che **mangino** alle 7:30. (*I believe they're eating at 7:30.*)

32 A che ora cominciano le prove? Credo che **comincino** alle 5:00. (*I believe they begin at 5:00.*)

33 La mamma si dimentica di telefonare? Sì, credo che lei **si dimentichi** di telefonare. (*Yes, I think she's going to forget to call.*)

34 Svegli il babbo? Sì, è ora che io lo **svegli.** (*Yes, it's time that I wake him.*)

35 Dove lasciano i biglietti? Credo che li **lascino** con Anna. (*I think they're leaving them with Anna.*)

36 Mamma A: È bene che i ragazzi **escano,** ma non troppo. (*It's a good thing that the kids go out, but not too much.*)

Mamma B: Non permettiamo che Lorenzo **esca** mai. (*We don't ever allow Lorenzo to go out.*)

37 Mamma A: Voglio che Fabio **sia** felice, qualunque cosa lui **faccia.** (*I want for Fabio to be happy, whatever he does.*)

Mamma B: Noi, invece, pensiamo che i nostri figli **debbano** solo studiare. (*We, instead, think that our children should only study.*)

38 Mamma A: Sì, va bene studiare, ma non credi che **sia** necessario divertirsi un po'? (*Yes, well, it's good to study, but don't you think that it's necessary to have a little bit of fun?*)

Mamma B: Credo che Lorenzo **possa** divertirsi studiando. Abbiamo paura che **beva** troppo se frequenta un'università lontana. (*I think that Lorenzo can have fun while studying. We're afraid he's going to drink too much if he attends a university that is far away.*)

39 Mamma A: Fabio beve un po' di birra, ma credo che **ci dica** tutto quello che fa. Non credo che **abbia** molti segreti. (*Fabio drinks a little bit of beer, but I believe that he tells us everything he does. I don't think he has many secrets.*)

Mamma B: Sembra che Lorenzo **voglia** frequentare l'università molto lontano da noi. Ho paura che non **venga** a casa per le vacanze. (*It seems like Lorenzo wishes to attend a university very far away from us. I'm afraid that he won't come home for vacation.*)

40 Mamma A: Spero soltanto che Fabio **sappia** scegliere bene, e che **faccia** bene all'università. (*All I hope is that Fabio knows how to choose well, and that he does well in college.*)

Mamma B: Lorenzo vuole che noi gli **diamo** la nostra vecchia macchina, ma è improbabile che io gliela **dia.** (*Lorenzo wants for us to give him our old car, but it's not likely that we're going to give it to him.*)

41 Sono contenta che la nonna **venga** in barca con noi. (*I'm happy that grandma is coming on the boat with us.*)

42 Sono contenta che Giuditta e Ginevra **vengano** in barca con noi. (*I'm happy that Giuditta and Ginevra are coming on the boat with us.*)

43 Sono contenta che tu e Gloria **veniate** in barca con noi. (*I'm happy that you and Gloria are coming on the boat with us.*)

44 Giancarlo spera che io **possa** comprare il pesce fresco. (*Giancarlo hopes that I can buy fresh fish.*)

45 Giancarlo spera che Gianni e Marinella **possano** venire a Vulcano. (*Giancarlo hopes that Gianni and Marinella can come to Vulcano.*)

46 Giancarlo spera che voi **possiate** portare anche i bambini. (*Giancarlo hopes that you can bring the children, too.*)

47 È possibile che noi **facciamo** il bagno nei fanghi termali. (*It's possible that we will take a mud bath.*)

48 È possibile che Laura **faccia** il bagno nei fanghi termali. (*It's possible that Laura is going to take a mud bath.*)

49 È possibile che tu **faccia** il bagno nei fanghi termali? (*Is it going to be possible for you to take a mud bath?*)

50 È probabile che Lorenzo **proponga** una gita a Panarea. (*It's probable that Lorenzo will propose a trip to Panarea.*)

51 Permetti che tua figlia **esca** con lui? (*Do you let your daughter go out with him?*)

52 Credo che **faccia** tardi — andiamo! (*I think that it's getting late — let's go!*)

53 Diane desidera che Marc **l'accompagni** a teatro. (*Diane wishes that Marc accompany her to the theater.*)

54 Ho l'impressione che Guido non **studi.** (*I have the impression that Guido doesn't study.*)

55 Non siamo sicuri che **vinca** Berlusconi questa volta. (*We're not certain that Berlusconi is going to win this time.*)

56 Abbiamo paura che voi **siate** arrabbiati. (*We're afraid that you're angry.*)

57 Maria e Domenico pensano che lo zio John **sia** in gamba. (*Mary and Domenick think that Uncle John is on the ball.*)

58 La dogana proibisce che **portiamo** fichi freschi negli Stati Uniti. (*Customs won't let us bring fresh figs into the United States.*)

59 Ci dispiace che non **capiscano.** (*We're sorry that they don't understand.*)

60 Anna e Robert vogliono che i figli **siano** contenti. (*Anna and Robert want their children to be happy.*)

61 Il professore pretende che io **consegni** la tesi il mese prossimo. (*The professor is expecting me to turn in my thesis next month.*)

62 Temo che non **ci sia** abbastanza vino rosso; vai a comprare altre due bottiglie di Barbaresco. (*I'm worried that there isn't enough red wine; go buy another two bottles of Barbaresco.*)

63 Preferisco che mia figlia **giochi** a calcio. (*I prefer that my daughter play soccer.*)

64 Chiedo soltanto che non **litighiate**. (*I only ask that you not argue.*)

65 Non so chi **dica** queste cose ridicole. (*I don't know who says these ridiculous things.*)

66 Mi auguro che tu **venga** a trovarmi. (*I hope that you come visit me.*)

67 Anna, sei contenta che tuo figlio **ritorni** per l'estate? (*Anna, are you happy that your son is coming home for the summer?*)

68 Mia madre esige che io **venga** alla festa. (*My mom is demanding that I come to the party.*)

69 Giancarlo è triste che il suo capo gli **dia** solo tre settimane di vacanza. (*Giancarlo is sad that his boss is giving him only three weeks of vacation.*)

70 Immagino che **partiate** con l'alba. (*I imagine that you'll be leaving at dawn.*)

71 È strano che **pianga** il bambino. (*It's strange that the baby is crying.*)

72 È strano che il babbo **sia** in ritardo. (*It's strange that daddy's late.*)

73 È ora che **partiate**. (*It's time for you to leave.*)

74 È ora che io **studi**. (*It's time for me to study.*)

75 È ora che Maurizio **si sposi**. (*It's about time that Maurizio got married.*)

76 È probabile che io **vada** a Taormina. (*It's likely that I'll go to Taormina.*)

77 È probabile che loro **escano**. (*It's probable that they're going out.*)

78 È probabile che lui **finisca** l'università. (*It's probable that he's going to finish college.*)

79 Sembra che la zia Carolina e lo zio Salvatore **facciano** un viaggio a maggio. (*It seems that Aunt Caroline and Uncle Salvatore are taking a trip in May.*)

80 Sembra che Lorenzo **legga** un bel libro. (*It looks like Lorenzo is reading a nice book.*)

81 Sembra che tu e Paolo **vi divertiate**! (*It seems like you and Paul are having a good time!*)

82 È meglio che io **stia** zitta. (*It's better that I stay quiet./I should be quiet.*)

83 È meglio che loro non **vogliano** più all'alba. (*It's better that they're not leaving at dawn anymore.*)

84 È meglio che tu **faccia** i fatti tuoi! (*It's better if you mind your own business!*)

85 È incredibile che Claudio e Rosaria si siano lasciati! (*It's incredible that Claudio and Rosaria have left each other!*)

86 Perchè tu **capisca**, te lo spiego ancora una volta. (*So that you understand, I'll explain it to you one more time.*)

87 *Prima che il Gallo **Canti*** è un romanzo di Cesare Pavese. (*Before the Cock Crows is a novel by Cesare Pavese.*)

88 Lei non impara, sebbene **studi.** (*She doesn't learn, even though she studies.*)

89 Qualunque cosa **succeda,** partiamo il primo agosto. (*Whatever happens, we're leaving August 1.*)

90 Te lo spiego ancora una volta affinchè tu **sia** d'accordo. (*I'll explain it to you again so that you agree.*)

91 A condizione che io **possa** offrire, vengo a cena. (*Provided that I can treat, I'll come to dinner.*)

92 In qualunque modo **facciate,** per noi va bene. (*However you do it, for us it's fine.*)

93 Andiamo in barca, a meno che non **piova.** (*We're going in the boat, unless it rains.*)

94 Benchè **stia** a dieta, non dimagrisce. (*Even though she's on a diet, she doesn't lose weight.*)

95 Comunque **sia,** io ci vado io stesso. (*However it is, I'll go anyway.*)

96 Te lo spiego ancora una volta in modo che tu **capisca.** (*I'll explain it to you again so that you understand.*)

97 Lui capisce, senza che io glielo **dica.** (*He understands, without my telling him.*)

98 Vengo in Puglia, a patto che io **possa** portare la mia famiglia. (*I'll come to Puglia, provided that I can bring my family.*)

99 Può venire chiunque **voglia!** (*Anyone who wants can come!*)

100 **Do** i soldi ad Emilia perchè lei **compri** i biglietti per la gita scolastica. (*I'm giving Emilia the money so that she can buy the tickets for the class trip.*)

101 Taormina è la città più romantica che tu **possa** visitare. *Taormina is the most romantic city you can visit.*

102 L'unico ristorante di pesce che **debbano** provare è la Trattoria Cubana. *The only fish restaurant they should try is the Trattoria Cubana.*

103 Maria è la sola donna che io **ami.** *Maria is the only woman that I love.*

104 Non c'è nessuno che **mi capisca.** *There's no one who understands me.*

105 Siete sicuri che questo è l'ultimo esercizio che voi **facciate** sul congiuntivo? *Are you sure that this is the last exercise on the subjunctive you're going to do?*

Chapter 13

I'd Like for You to Understand the Imperfect Subjunctive

In This Chapter
▶ Forming the imperfect subjunctive tense
▶ Pitting the imperfect subjunctive against the present subjunctive
▶ Incorporating irregular verbs

*T*he imperfect subjunctive is a construction that tries to hide in subordinate or dependent clauses. It lets all the terms that require the subjunctive make the introductions (*I was hoping that you/he/she/we/they . . .*; *we were wishing that . . .*; *I would like that you . . .* — the imperfect subjunctive would follow the ellipsis in each case). The main caveat of the imperfect subjunctive? The verb in the main clause has (in most cases) to be in the conditional (see Chapter 11) or imperfect (see Chapter 8).

In this chapter, I help you get a feel for the imperfect subjunctive by comparing it to the present subjunctive you discover in Chapter 12. I explain when to use the imperfect subjunctive, how to conjugate it and form sentences around it, and how to incorporate irregular verbs into the mix. I also provide plenty of practice exercises where you conjugate both regular and irregular verbs.

It's a very good idea to get comfortable with the present indicative (Chapters 2 and 3), the present subjunctive and the terms that require it, the conditional tense, and the imperfect tense before you go any further in this chapter.

Making the Imperfect Subjunctive Work for You

Before you can jump into forming sentences with the imperfect subjunctive, you first have to find out how to conjugate it. The 1st-, 2nd-, and 3rd-person singular and plural conjugations for **-are, -ere,** and **-ire** verbs look very similar:

-are endings: **-assi, -assi, -asse, -assimo, -aste, -assero**

-ere endings: **-essi, -essi, -esse, -essimo, -este, -essero**

-ire endings: **-issi, -issi, -isse, -issimo, -iste, -issero**

Repeat these endings a few times to yourself, using a quick pace or a tune, so that you begin to memorize them!

Here are some examples that show the different endings in action:

- ✔ **Vorrebbero** che **mangiassimo** da loro. (*They'd like for us to eat at their place.*)
- ✔ **Pensavo** che tu **avessi** fame. (*I thought that you were hungry.*)
- ✔ **Ero** felice che Domenico **venisse** in Italia. (*I was happy that Domenico was coming to Italy.*)
- ✔ **Era** bene che **studiaste.** (*It was good that you* (pl.) *studied.*)

    This last example is an *impersonal construction,* which means that it doesn't specify a subject.

The following tables show you the conjugations of the **-are, -ere,** and **-ire** verbs in the imperfect subjunctive tense. You'll notice the word "che" (*that, like*), which precedes the verb in the imperfect subjunctive in these constructions.

parlare (*to speak*)	
che io parl**assi**	che noi parl**assimo**
che tu parl**assi**	che voi parl**aste**
che lui, lei, Lei parl**asse**	che loro parl**assero**
Vorrei che tu **parlassi** con tuo padre. (*I would like for you to speak to your father.*)	

leggere (*to read*)	
che io legg**essi**	che noi legg**essimo**
che tu legg**essi**	che voi legg**este**
che lui, lei, Lei legg**esse**	che loro legg**essero**
Rudi **era** contento che **leggessimo** il suo libro. (*Rudi was happy that we were reading his book.*)	

capire (*to understand*)	
che io cap**issi**	che noi cap**issimo**
che tu cap**issi**	che voi cap**iste**
che lui, lei, Lei cap**isse**	che loro cap**issero**
Sembrava che tu **capissi** quello che **diceva** quel signore. (*It seemed like you understood what that man was saying.*)	

For this exercise, practice the three verb endings by conjugating the verbs in parentheses into the imperfect subjunctive tense. Here's an example of a reflexive verb (for which you need to add a reflexive pronoun; see Chapter 5):

Q. Non volevamo che la bambina _____. (svegliarsi)

A. Non volevamo che la bambina **si svegliasse.** (*We didn't want the baby to wake up.*)

1. Quanto ero contenta che voi _____! (divertirsi)

2. Speravamo che i miei genitori _____ il nuovo film di Tornatore. (vedere)

3. Era importante che lui mi _____. (capire)

4. Non credevo che Teresa _____ con Giancarlo. (litigare)

5. Sarebbe una buon'idea che tu _____ una bistecca alla fiorentina. (ordinare)

6. Vorrei che i miei figli _____! (sposarsi)

7. Domenico sperava che John _____ vicino a casa. (restare)

8. Sarebbe ora che voi _____ la bocca! (chiudere)

9. Marco era l'uomo più gentile che io _____. (conoscere)

10. Preferirei che _____ a San Gimignano. (mangiare)

11. Avevate paura che non _____ venire? (potere [noi])

12. Benchè io _____, non imparavo nulla. (studiare)

13. Ti seguirei, dovunque tu _____. (andare)

14. Non c'era nessuno che mi _____. (parlare)

15. Volevano che io _____ tutte le informazioni. (fornire)

Forming the Imperfect Subjunctive to Wish, Doubt, and Express

Finding out how to form the imperfect subjunctive is important if you want to express doubts, desires, and wants. Any of the verbs and constructions that require the present subjunctive in Chapter 12 also associate with the imperfect subjunctive. The tense of the verb in the main clause determines whether you use the present subjunctive or the imperfect subjunctive in the dependent clause. For example, if the verb in the main clause requires the subjunctive and is in the present tense, you use the present subjunctive (see Chapter 12) or the past subjunctive (see Chapter 19) in the dependent clause. If the verb in the main clause requires the subjunctive and is in the conditional (see Chapter 11), the imperfect (see Chapter 8), or the past subjunctive (see Chapter 19), you need to use the imperfect subjunctive in the dependent clause.

You usually use the imperfect subjunctive in dependent or subordinate clauses, introduced by the conjunction "che" (*that, like*). The verbs in the main clauses of these constructions are usually in one of two tenses: the conditional — in the sentence "**Vorrei** che tu **stessi** zitto" (*I'd like for you to be quiet*), **vorrei** is in the conditional, and **stessi** is in the imperfect subjunctive — or the imperfect, as previously stated — in the sentence "**Speravo** che **arrivassero** in tempo" (*I was hoping that they'd arrive in time*), **speravo** is in the imperfect, and **arrivassero** is in the imperfect subjunctive.

The following examples show the difference between using the present subjunctive and the imperfect subjunctive:

> ✔ **Credo** che lui **sia** intelligente. (*I think that he's intelligent.*)
>
> ✔ **Credevo** che lui **fosse** intelligente. (*I thought that he was intelligent.*)

Here's an easy-to-access rundown of construction of the imperfect subjunctive:

subject + verb in conditional or imperfect + che + imperfect subjunctive

In Chapter 12, you see all the many different uses of the present subjunctive tense. In that chapter, I also create a working list of verbs and expressions, which appear in the main clause of a sentence, that require the present subjunctive in the dependent clause. Such a list will come in handy when working on the imperfect subjunctive. The same verbs and expressions in the main clause of a sentence tell you that the imperfect subjunctive is necessary, so you can refer to Chapter 12 as necessary.

You can compare the tenses and the inner workings of the imperfect subjunctive in Table 13-1.

Table 13-1	Using the Correct Subjunctive Dependent Clause	
Independent Clause	*Dependent Clause*	*Example*
Present indicative	Present subjunctive	**Credo** che lui **sia** onesto. (*I believe that he is honest.*)
Present indicative	Past subjunctive	**Credo** che lui **sia stato** onesto. (*I think that he was honest.*)
Future	Present subjunctive	**Vorrai** che lui **sia** onesto! (*You're going to want him to be honest!*)
Imperative	Present subjunctive	**Digli** che **sia** onesto! (*Tell him to be honest!*)
Imperfect	Imperfect subjunctive	**Credevo** che lui **fosse** onesto. (*I thought that he was honest.*)
Conditional	Imperfect subjunctive	**Crederei** che lui **fosse** onesto. (*I would believe that he was honest.*)
Past conditional	Imperfect subjunctive	**Avrei creduto** che lui **fosse** onesto. (*I would've thought that he was honest.*)
Present perfect	Imperfect subjunctive	**Ho creduto** che lui **fosse** onesto. (*I believed that he was honest.*)
Past absolute	Imperfect subjunctive	**Credetti** che lui **fosse** onesto. (*I thought he was honest.*)

Don't worry too much about all the different verb tenses that require the imperfect subjunctive. For the exercises in this chapter, I focus on the more common uses of the imperfect subjunctive (with the conditional and imperfect tenses). However, it's a good idea for you to be able to recognize all the tenses I mention in Table 13-1.

You also use the imperfect subjunctive with the "se" (*if*) sentences in Chapter 21.

One of the best ways to understand the imperfect subjunctive tense is to take an exercise that you've already done in the present subjunctive and alter it. The repetition helps you to memorize and to make connections, and it reminds you that the language keeps building upon itself. For the following exercise, I steal some sample sentences from a set of practice exercises in Chapter 12. First, I rewrote them here in their entirety, and second, I altered the tense of the verbs in the main clauses. Now it's up to you to conjugate the verbs in the dependent clauses into the imperfect subjunctive tense and then translate both sentences. Follow my cue in this example:

Q. È importante che tu mi capisca. Era importante che tu mi _____. (capire)

A. È importante che tu mi capisca. Era importante che tu mi **capissi.**

It is important that you understand me.

It was important that you understand me.

16. È importante che voi mi capiate. Era importante che voi mi _____. (capire)

_____

_____

17. Loro sono tristi che io parta. Loro erano tristi che io _____. (partire)

_____

_____

18. Spero che Giancarlo si alzi presto domani. Speravo che Giancarlo _____ presto. (alzarsi)

_____

_____

19. Io credo che loro parlino italiano. Credevo che loro _____ l'italiano. (parlare)

_____

_____

20. Non voglio che il cane lecchi la bambina. Non vorrei che il cane _____ la bambina. (leccare)

_____

_____

21. È importante che le ragazze giochino bene. Sarebbe importante che le ragazze _____ bene. (giocare)

_____

_____

22. Credo che Anna abbia i biglietti. Credevo che Anna _____ i biglietti. (avere)

_____

_____

23. È bene che i ragazzi escano, ma non troppo. Sarebbe bene che i ragazzi _____, ma non troppo. (uscire)

_____

_____

24. Vuoi che io venga a casa tua? Vorresti che io _____ a casa tua? (venire)

_____

_____

25. Abbiamo l'impressione che voi vi amiate. Avevamo l'impressione che voi vi _____. (amarsi)

_____

_____

26. È strano che la bambina pianga. Era strano che la bambina _____. (piangere)

_____

_____

27. È ora che Maurizio si sposi. Sarebbe ora che Maurizio si _____. (sposarsi)

_____

_____

28. Andiamo a Ravenna purchè ci fermiamo a Pompeii. Andremmo a Ravenna purchè ci _____ a Pompeii. (fermarsi)

_____

_____

29. Maria è la sola donna che io ami. Maria era la sola donna che io _____. (amare)

_____

_____

30. Non c'è nessuno che mi capisca. Non c'era nessuno che mi _____. (capire)

_____

_____

Regulating Irregular Imperfect Subjunctives

Okay, so not every part of the imperfect subjunctive is as simple and beautiful as it seems, judging from the previous parts of this chapter! You have to deal with some irregular verbs in the imperfect subjunctive. What this means is that you need to change the stems of the verbs before you add the imperfect subjunctive endings. The good news is that you have only a few irregular verbs to worry about. The following are some of the most frequently used irregular verbs, along with their irregular stems:

- ✔ **bere** (*to drink*) → **bev-**
- ✔ **dare** (*to give*) → **d-**
- ✔ **dire** (*to say*) → **dic-**
- ✔ **essere** (*to be*) → **fossi, fossi, fosse** . . .
- ✔ **fare** (*to do, to make*) → **fac-**
- ✔ **stare** (*to be, to stay*) → **stessi, stessi, stesse** . . .
- ✔ **tradurre** (*to translate*) → **traduc-**
- ✔ **proporre** (*to propose*) → **propon-**

Many of these forms share the same irregular stem with the imperfect tense (which you can find in Chapter 8).

The following tables contain the conjugations of **bere** and **tradurre**. You can flip to Appendix C to see how the others conjugate — in the imperfect subjunctive and all the other tenses.

bere (*to drink*)	
io bev**essi**	noi bev**essimo**
tu bev**essi**	voi bev**este**
lui, lei, Lei bev**esse**	loro bev**essero**
Non **sapevo** che cosa **bevessero.** (*I didn't know what they were drinking.*)	

tradurre (*to translate*)	
io traduc**essi**	noi traduc**essimo**
tu traduc**essi**	voi traduc**este**
lui, lei, Lei traduc**esse**	loro traduc**essero**
Il professore **voleva** che noi **traducessimo** la poesia. (*The professor wanted us to translate the poem.*)	

Bere, dare, dire, fare, stare, tradurre, and **proporre** all follow the **-essi, -essi, -esse, -essimo, -este, -essero** ending pattern. **Essere** goes by **-ossi, -ossi, -osse, -ossimo, -oste, -ossero.**

Put your newfound knowledge of irregular verbs to the test. Conjugate the following verbs in parentheses into the imperfect subjunctive form. Here's an example to get you started:

0. Quanto vorrei che tu _____ qua! (essere)

A. Quanto vorrei che tu **fossi** qua! (*How I wish you were here!*)

31. Vorremmo che voi _____ il viaggio con noi. (fare)

32. Sembrava che Luigi _____ la verità. (dire)

33. Benchè io _____ il compito, non ho fatto bene all'esame. (fare)

34. Chiunque _____ al telefono, non rispondevo. (essere)

35. Vorrei che Emilia _____ più acqua. Sarebbe meglio che noi tutti _____ più acqua. (bere, bere)

36. Non sapevo che tu _____ dall'italiano all'inglese! (tradurre)

37. Mi auguravo che _____ una bella vacanza. (essere)

38. Non sapevamo cosa _____ Patrizia. (fare)

39. Era strano che _____ tutti insieme! (stare [noi])

40. Vorrei che tu _____ qui! (essere)

Answer Key

1 Quanto ero contenta che voi **vi divertiste!** (*I was so happy that you* (pl.) *had a good time!*)

2 Speravamo che i miei genitori **vedessero** il nuovo film di Tornatore. (*We hoped that my parents would see Tornatore's new film.*)

3 Era importante che lui mi **capisse.** (*It was important that he understand me.*)

4 Non credevo che Teresa **litigasse** con Giancarlo. (*I didn't think that Teresa fought with Giancarlo.*)

5 Sarebbe una buon'idea che tu **ordinassi** una bistecca alla fiorentina. (*It would be a good idea if you ordered a steak Florentine-style.*)

6 Vorrei che i miei figli **si sposassero!** (*I would like for my children to get married.*)

7 Domenico sperava che John **restasse** vicino a casa. (*Domenico hoped that John would stay close to home.*)

8 Sarebbe ora che voi **chiudeste** la bocca! (*It's about time that you all shut your mouths!*)

9 Marco era l'uomo più gentile che io **conoscessi.** (*Marco was the nicest man I knew.*)

10 Preferirei che **mangiassimo** a San Gimignano. (*I'd prefer that we eat at San Gimignano.*)

11 Avevate paura che non **postessimo** venire? (*Were you afraid we couldn't come?*)

12 Benchè io **studiassi,** non imparavo nulla. (*Even though I studied, I didn't learn anything.*)

13 Ti seguirei, dovunque tu **andassi.** (*I would follow you wherever you went/I'd follow you wherever you should go.*)

14 Non c'era nessuno che mi **parlasse.** (*There was no one who was speaking to me.*)

15 Volevano che io **fornissi** tutte le informazioni. (*They wanted me to provide all the information.*)

16 È importante che voi mi capiate. Era importante che voi mi **capiste.** *It's important that you understand me. It was important that you understand me.*

17 Loro sono tristi che io parta. Loro erano tristi che io **partissi.** *They're sad I'm leaving. They were sad that I was leaving.*

18 Spero che Giancarlo si alzi presto domani. Speravo che Giancarlo **si alzasse** presto. *I hope that Giancarlo gets up early tomorrow. I was hoping that Giancarlo would get up early.*

19 Io credo che loro parlino italiano. Credevo che loro **parlassero** l'italiano. *I think that they speak Italian. I thought that they spoke Italian.*

20 Non voglio che il cane lecchi la bambina. Non vorrei che il cane **leccasse** la bambina. *I don't want the dog to lick the baby. I wouldn't want the dog to lick the baby.*

21 È importante che le ragazze giochino bene. Sarebbe importante che le ragazze **giocassero** bene. *It's important that the girls play well. It would be important that the girls play well.*

22 Credo che Anna abbia i biglietti. Credevo che Anna **avesse** i biglietti. *I think that Anna has the tickets. I thought that Anna had the tickets.*

23 È bene che i ragazzi escano, ma non troppo. Sarebbe bene che i ragazzi **uscissero,** ma non troppo. *It's a good thing that the kids go out, but not too much. It would be a good thing if the kids were to go out, but not too much.*

24 Vuoi che io venga a casa tua? Vorresti che io **venissi** a casa tua? *Do you want me to come to your house? Would you like for me to come to your house?*

25 Abbiamo l'impressione che voi vi amiate. Avevamo l'impressione che voi vi **amaste.** *We have the impression that you love each other. We had the feeling that you loved each other.*

26 È strano che la bambina pianga. Era strano che la bambina **piangesse.** *It's strange that the baby is crying. It was strange that the baby was crying.*

27 È ora che Maurizio si sposi. Sarebbe ora che Maurizio si **sposasse.** *It's time that Maurizio got married.* (I would translate this the same way in both tenses.)

28 Andiamo a Ravenna purchè ci fermiamo a Pompeii. Andremmo a Ravenna purchè ci **fermassimo** a Pompeii. *We'll go to Ravenna provided that we stop in Pompeii. We would go to Ravenna provided that we stop in Pompeii.*

29 Maria è la sola donna che io ami. Maria era la sola donna che io **amassi.** *Maria is the only woman that I love. Maria was the only woman that I loved.*

30 Non c'è nessuno che mi capisca. Non c'era nessuno che mi **capisse.** *There's no one who understands me. There was no one who understood me.*

31 Vorremmo che voi **faceste** il viaggio con noi. (*We'd like for you* (pl.) *to take the trip with us.*)

32 Sembrava che Luigi **dicesse** la verità. (*It seemed like Luigi was telling the truth.*)

33 Benchè io **facessi** il compito, non ho fatto bene all'esame. (*Even though I did my homework, I didn't do well on the exam.*)

34 Chiunque **fosse** al telefono, non rispondevo. (*Whoever it might have been on the phone, I wasn't answering.*)

35 Vorrei che Emilia **bevesse** più acqua. Sarebbe meglio che noi tutti **bevessimo** più acqua. (*I'd like for Emilia to drink more water. It would be better if we all drank more water.*)

36 Non sapevo che tu **traducessi** dall'italiano all'inglese! (*I didn't know that you translated from Italian to English!*)

37 Mi auguravo che **fosse** una bella vacanza. (*I was hoping that it would be a nice vacation.*)

38 Non sapevamo cosa **facesse** Patrizia. (*We didn't know what Patricia was doing.*)

39 Era strano che **stessimo** tutti insieme! (*It was strange that we were all together!*)

40 Vorrei che tu **fossi** qui! (*I'd like for you to be here!/I wish you were here!*)

Part III
Building Compound Tenses

In this part . . .

Y ou find the eight compound tenses that use **avere** (*to have*) and **essere** (*to be*) as auxiliary verbs. The tenses range from the present perfect, to the future perfect, to the past subjunctive. You also discover how to determine which of the two helping verbs to use and how to form past participles (without which no compound tense in Italian is complete).

Chapter 14

Starting with the Present Perfect

. . . .

In This Chapter

▶ Solving the puzzle of the present perfect tense

▶ Identifying when you need to use **essere** or **avere** to form the present perfect

▶ Discovering the uses of the present perfect

. . . .

The present (or simple) perfect tense, or the passato prossimo, is the tense that you use to refer to events that happened anywhere from 5 minutes ago to 5 to years ago (in other words, the recent past). It may seem odd to talk about the past with the "present" perfect tense, but it makes sense when you think of it as the passato prossimo, because prossimo means *near, neighbor,* and *next* (you can also compare this tense to the passato remoto, the past absolute, which discusses the remote or distant past; see Chapter 9).

The passato prossimo is the tense you use most frequently in everyday speech (and in e-mails and letters) to talk about what's happened in recent times. In this chapter, I help you keep an eye on recent events by forming, conjugating, and using the present perfect tense. Along the way, you find out which auxiliary verbs you need in different situations, and you find out how to make irregular past participles. Soon, you'll look back on this lesson with fondness, by using the passato prossimo!

Forming the Present Perfect Tense

The present perfect is a compound tense. You always need two parts to make it work: the helping (or *auxiliary*) verb and the past participle:

> **avere** (*to have*) or **essere** (*to be*) in the present tense + the past participle

I cover **avere** and **essere** in the present tense in Chapter 3, so flip back there if you need a refresher. I'll wait.

Forming the regular past participle of **-are, -ere,** and **-ire** verbs is quite simple. You keep the stem and the endings become, respectively, **-ato, -uto,** and **-ito,** as you can see in Table 14-1. (For irregular past participles, see Tables 14-2 and 14-3 later in the chapter.)

Table 14-1	Forming Regular Past Participles	
Regular Infinitive	*Stem*	*Past Participle*
-are, like **parlare** (*to speak*)	**parl-**	**parlato** (*spoken*)
-ere, like **vendere** (*to sell*)	**vend-**	**venduto** (*sold*)
-ire, like **capire** (*to understand*)	**cap-**	**capito** (*understood*)

Here a couple examples of past participles, showing the present perfect format:

Hai parlato con tuo padre? (*Did you speak with your father?*)

Sei venuto in treno? (*Did you come by train?*)

Before moving into the present perfect, and before worrying about which auxiliary verb (**essere** or **avere**) to use, you should practice forming Italian past participles. You'll be using these past participles for all the compound tenses in Part IV of this book. Transform the following verbs from their infinitive forms into regular past participles. (Irregular past participles come later in the chapter.) Follow my example:

0. mangiare _____

A. **mangiato**

1. studiare _____   8. cantare _____

2. ricevere _____   9. credere _____

3. arrivare _____   10. partire _____

4. ballare _____   11. dare _____

5. sentire _____   12. stare _____

6. ripetere _____   13. andare _____

7. preparare _____   14. ringraziare _____

Knowing When to Use Essere or Avere as Your Auxiliary Verb

The past participle is the second part of the present-perfect construction (see the previous section). The first part is the helping, or auxiliary, verb **essere** or **avere**. In Italian compound tenses like the passato prossimo, *transitive verbs* take the auxiliary verb **avere**, and *intransitive verbs* take the auxiliary verb **essere**.

The rules of transitive and intransitive verbs seem pretty straightforward, but you need to be able to distinguish between the verbs, which can be tricky. Here are a couple pointers to guide your way:

- **Transitive verbs almost always are followed by direct objects.** For example, the verb **mangiare** (*to eat*) is transitive. You can say "I eat/I ate" without following the verb with a direct object, but you know that you can also say, "I eat gnocchi/I ate gnocchi." The gnocchi, in this case, is the direct object, answering the question "Who?" or "What?"

- **Intransitive verbs don't take a direct object.** For example, "**Sono partita** alle 8:00 di matting." (*I left at 8:00 in the morning.*)

Over the years, I've noted that instead of thinking about direct objects, students prefer memorizing an initial list of intransitive verbs, to which they then add little by little. I call this list "La Casa di **Essere**" (*The House of* **Essere**). If you want to check out this list immediately, you can skip over the next section on transitive verbs (the ones that take **avere**).

However, I don't advise such a jump: You have a good reason to start with the transitive verbs. The past participle of intransitive verbs always ends in **-o,** but the past participle of intransitive verbs has to agree in number and gender, too.

Conjugating with avere

When you conjugate with the auxiliary verb **avere** (*to have;* conjugating with this auxiliary verb means you're dealing with transitive verbs), you follow this structure:

subject + **avere** in the present tense + the past participle of the transitive verb

Here's an example of a transitive verb in the passato prossimo:

Io (subject) + **ho** (**avere** in the present tense) + **mangiato** (past participle that ends in **-o**) + la torta di mele (direct object). This translates to *I ate apple pie.*

The following table shows the full conjugation of **mangiare.**

mangiare (*to eat*)	
io **ho** mang**iato**	noi **abbiamo** mang**iato**
tu **hai** mang**iato**	voi **avete** mang**iato**
lui, lei, Lei **ha** mang**iato**	loro **hanno** mang**iato**
Loro **hanno mangiato** gli gnocchi. (*They ate gnocchi.*)	

Conjugate the following transitive verbs in parentheses into the present perfect tense, including the proper form of **avere,** and then translate. As you can see from my example, you have various ways of translating the passato prossimo. In real life, how you translate it depends on the context in which it appears. In the Answer Key, I alternate the translations. Just remember that my translations are subjective (as yours will be).

0. Io _____. (mangiare)

A. Io **ho mangiato.** *I ate, I have eaten, I did eat.*

15. Tu _____. (studiare)

_____

16. Loro _____? (dormire)

_____

17. Noi _____ bene. (sciare)

_____

18. Lui _____ una telefonata. (ricevere)

_____

19. Voi _____ molto gelato. (mangiare)

_____

20. Io _____ tutto. (capire)

_____

21. Lei _____ a suo marito. (credere)

_____

22. Tu _____ quel film? (affittare)

_____

23. _____ il bambino. (baciare [loro])

_____

24. Marcella ed io _____ a lungo. (chiacchierare)

_____

25. Cosa _____ a scuola oggi? (disegnare [voi])

_____

Your friends the Lisi's are on a trip to Venice. The mother of the family, Luisa, is writing postcards to send back to friends and family in the United States. Help her out by conjugating the following verbs in parentheses into the present perfect tense and then translating — just in case her friends back home don't understand! Here's an example to get you started:

Q. Sabato e domenica, _____ Venezia. (visitare [noi])

A. Sabato e domenica, **abbiamo visitato** Venezia. *On Saturday and Sunday, we visited Venice.*

26. Diane e Mark _____ la Peggy Guggenheim Collection. (visitare)

_____

27. Susan ed io _____ da mangiare ai piccioni a Piazza San Marco. (dare)

_____

28. Bruno _____ una bellissima maschera veneziana. (comprare)

_____

29. Io _____ gli spaghetti al nero di seppia. (mangiare)

_____

30. Cara _____ degli stivali nuovi. (comprare)

_____

Conjugating with essere

You have now entered the "Casa di **Essere.**" All the verbs in this house are intransitive, which means they don't take a direct object, and you conjugate them with the auxiliary verb **essere.** You'll have much success with the passato prossimo if you can memorize the intransitive verbs in Table 14-2 that take **essere.** (Of course, these verbs aren't the only ones, but as you learn more verbs, you can add to the list.) Take a look at these verbs. Can you guess why I put them into the "Casa di **Essere?**" These verbs are all the kinds of things that you can do in a house: go in, come out, go up the stairs, come down the stairs, fall out a window, be born, die, arrive, leave, return, and so on.

Note that some of the past participles are *irregular,* which means they don't follow the regular **-ato, -uto, -ito** endings. And, as always, using these verbs is the best way to learn them. (All reflexive verbs take **essere** in the present perfect as well. You can find practice on these verbs in Chapter 15.)

Intransitive past participles undergo a slight change from the transitive verbs: A past participle must agree in gender and number with the subject of the sentence. So, for the three singular verb persons (io; tu; and lui, lei, Lei), the ending you attach is **-o** or **-a;** for the three plural persons (noi, voi, and loro), the ending you attach is **-i** or **-e.**

Here's the structure of an intransitive verb in the present perfect tense:

> subject + **essere** in the present tense + the past participle of the intransitive verb that ends in **-o** (masc. sing.), **-a** (fem. sing.), **-i** (masc. pl.), or **-e** (fem. pl.)

Take note of these examples that illustrate the structure of intransitive verbs in the present perfect:

> Amy **è andata** a New York. (*Amy went to New York.*)

> This past participle takes the feminine singular **-a** ending, to agree with Amy.

> Danny e Cathy **sono andati** in montagna. (*Danny and Cathy went to the mountains.*)

> When you have both genders, the past participle takes the masculine plural **-i** ending.

If the gender in a sentence is unspecified, the masculine ending takes precedence. This is maybe the only time that you'll find it useful to remember that Italy is traditionally a patriarchal country (in other words, men rule, but keep the gloating to a minimum, fellas).

Table 14-2	The House of To Be (Verbs Conjugated with Essere)		
Infinitive	*Singular Past Participle (Masc., Fem.)*	*Plural Past Participle (Masc., Fem.)*	*Translation*
essere (*to be*)	**stato, stata**	**stati, state**	*has/have been, were*
entrare (*to enter*)	**entrato, entrata**	**entrati, entrate**	*has/have entered, entered, did enter*
(ri)tornare (*to return*)	**tornato, tornata**	**tornati, tornate**	*has/have returned, returned, did return*
venire (*to come*)	**venuto, venuta**	**venuti, venute**	*has/have come, came, did come*

(continued)

Table 14-2 (continued)

Infinitive	Singular Past Participle (Masc., Fem.)	Plural Past Participle (Masc., Fem.)	Translation
arrivare (to arrive)	arrivato, arrivata	arrivati, arrivate	has/have arrived, arrived, did arrive
andare (to go)	andato, andata	andati, andate	has/have gone, went, did go
partire (to leave)	partito, partita	partiti, partite	has/have left, left, did leave
uscire (to go out)	uscito, uscita	usciti, uscite	has/have gone out, went out, did go out
salire (to go up stairs, to get on a train or bus, to get in the car)	salito, salita	saliti, salite	has/have gone up, went up, did go up
scendere (to go down stairs, to get off of a train or bus, to get out of a car)	sceso, scesa	scesi, scese	has/have gone down, went down, did go down, got off
stare (to be, to stay)	stato, stata	stati, state	was, were
rimanere (to stay, to remain)	rimasto, rimasta	rimasti, rimaste	has/have stayed, remained
restare (to stay)	restato, restata	restati, restate	has/have stayed, stayed, did stay
nascere (to be born)	nato, nata	nati, nate	was/were born
diventare (to become)	diventato, diventata	diventati, diventate	has/have become, became, did become
morire (to die)	morto, morta	morti, morte	has/have died, died, did die
cadere (to fall)	caduto, caduta	caduti, cadute	has/have fallen, fell, did fall

The following table shows an example of an intransitive verb conjugated in the present perfect. Notice how the past participles agree with the subjects.

uscire (to go out)	
io **sono** usc**ito/a**	noi **siamo** usc**iti/e**
tu **sei** usc**ito/a**	voi **siete** usc**iti/e**
lui, lei, Lei **è** usc**ito/a**	loro **sono** usc**iti/e**
Io (fem.) **sono uscita** con Giancarlo ieri sera. (I went out with Giancarlo last night.)	

Conjugate the following intransitive verbs in parentheses into the passato prossimo. Keep in mind that all these verbs take the auxiliary verb **essere** and that all the past participles must agree with the subjects. Here's an example for you:

Q. Maria _____ a letto tutto il giorno. (stare)

A. Maria è **stata** a letto tutto il giorno. (*Maria stayed in bed all day.*)

31. Dove _____ i tuoi genitori? (nascere)

32. Ieri Giancarlo _____ con Gianni. (uscire)

33. Noi _____ al cinema. (andare)

34. Chi _____? (morire)

35. Anna Maria ed io (fem.) _____ a casa ieri. (rimanere)

36. Cathy _____ magra! (diventare)

37. La Zia Fran e lo Zio Dick _____ sposati per molti anni. (stare)

38. Daniele _____ sul treno. (salire)

39. A che ora _____? (arrivare [voi])

40. Io (fem.) _____ in Italia per la prima volta nel 1976. (venire)

41. Pier Paolo Pasolini _____ un regista (director) famoso. (essere)

42. Anna Maria ed io _____! (cadere)

43. A che ora _____ a letto? (andare [tu])

44. Tu e il babbo _____ giusto in tempo. (partire)

45. I ragazzi _____ tardi. (ritornare)

Put all your skills together here to translate the following phrases that contain intransitive verbs in the present perfect into English. Note, as you do with the verbs in Table 14-2, that you may be able to use more than one possible translation. Here's an example:

Q. Mia madre è nata nel 1940.

A. *My mother was born in 1940.*

46. Domenico è venuto in America con suo padre.

_____

47. I bambini sono nati in Connecticut.

_____

48. A che ora è partito il treno?

_____

49. Come siete arrivati?

_____

50. La mamma è scesa dall'autobus.

_____

51. Riccardo, sei uscito ieri sera?

_____

52. Non sono diventata famosa.

_____

53. Siamo stati a casa.

_____

54. Jenny e Lucy sono andate a sciare.

_____

55. Maria Paola, sei uscita ieri sera?

_____

Incorporating irregular past participles that take avere

In the previous section, you encounter some irregular past participles in Table 14-2. You conjugate the verbs with regular and irregular past participles (intransitive verbs) in that table with **essere** (_to be_). In Table 14-3, I present a list of common irregular past participles that you conjugate with **avere** (_to have_). Most of these are **-ere** verbs.

Many past participles are also nouns. "Un sorriso," for example, is _a smile;_ "un permesso" is _a permit;_ "un dipinto" is _a painting;_ and "uno scritto" is _a writing_.

Table 14-3	Irregular Past Participles Conjugated with Avere		
Infinitive	_Past Participle_	_Infinitive_	_Past Participle_
leggere (_to read_)	**letto**	**uccidere** (_to kill_)	**ucciso**
scrivere (_to write_)	**scritto**	**piangere** (_to cry_)	**pianto**
fare (_to do, to make_)	**fatto**	**ridere** (_to laugh_)	**riso**
dire (_to say_)	**detto**	**sorridere** (_to smile_)	**sorriso**
rispondere (_to answer_)	**risposto**	**aprire** (_to open_)	**aperto**
chiedere (_to ask_)	**chiesto**	**offrire** (_to offer_)	**offerto**
vedere (_to see_)	**visto, veduto**	**spingere** (_to push_)	**spinto**
scegliere (_to choose_)	**scelto**	**dipingere** (_to paint_)	**dipinto**

Infinitive	Past Participle	Infinitive	Past Participle
vivere (*to live*)	**vissuto**	**stringere** (*to squeeze, to shake hands*)	**stretto**
bere (*to drink*)	**bevuto**	**corrompere** (*to corrupt*)	**corrotto**
ammettere (*to admit*)	**ammesso**	**rompere** (*to break*)	**rotto**
commettere (*to commit*)	**commesso**	**correggere** (*to correct*)	**corretto**
mettere (*to put*)	**messo**	**tradurre** (*to translate*)	**tradotto**
permettere (*to allow, to permit*)	**permesso**	**produrre** (*to produce*)	**prodotto**
promettere (*to promise*)	**promesso**	**comporre** (*to compose*)	**composto**
perdere (*to lose*)	**perso, perduto**	**disporre** (*to arrange*)	**disposto**
prendere (*to have, to take*)	**preso**	**offrire** (*to treat, to offer*)	**offerto**
spendere (*to spend*)	**speso**	**soffrire** (*to suffer*)	**sofferto**
decidere (*to decide*)	**deciso**	**sottrare** (*to subtract*)	**sottratto**
dividere (*to divide, to split*)	**diviso**	**detrarre** (*to detract*)	**detratto**

Two verbs have two interchangeable past participles. You can use either one, although the second is more common.

✔ **Perdere: perduto** and **perso**

✔ **Vedere: veduto** and **visto**

What have the Marotti's done in the last couple of days? In this exercise, put the irregular past participles from Table 14-3 into practice by conjugating the verbs in parentheses and adding the correct forms of **avere**. Here's an example:

O. Anna Maria _____ il film italiano *Respiro.* (vedere)

A. Anna Maria **ha veduto** il film italiano *Respiro.* (*Anna Maria saw the Italian film Respiro.*)

56. Maria _____ una gita scolastica a Washington D.C. (fare)

57. Daniel _____ una canzone rap alla chitarra. (comporre)

58. Daniel e Maria _____ i loro telefonini (cell phones). (perdere)

59. Tu e Robert _____ molto ieri. (ridere)

60. Giancarlo ed io _____ il suo tema d'italiano. (correggere)

61. Anna Maria, _____ il *New York Times* di ieri? (leggere)

62. Noi _____ un'e-mail all'università di Giancarlo, e così

_____ il problema. (scrivere, risolvere)

63. Robert _____ la cena a tutti. (offrire)

64. Io _____ che Maria poteva venire con noi. (dire)

65. Tutti _____ il freddo. (soffrire)

Surveying the Past for Uses of the Present Perfect

After you discover *how* to form the present perfect tense and get some practice with its structure, you should get a good grasp on *when* to use the tense. In this final section, you bring together what you discover in previous sections to master the uses of the passato prossimo. The following list breaks down the five main uses for you.

You use the present perfect tense

✔ **To describe an action begun and completed in the past.** (Compare this use with the imperfect tense's ongoing and habitual actions in the past in Chapter 8.)

Ieri **siamo andati** al cinema. (*We went to the movies yesterday.*)

✔ **To describe an action that interrupts an ongoing action in the past.** (In this case, the ongoing action is in the imperfect.)

Io **dormivo** quando **ho sentito** un rumore. (*I was sleeping when I heard a noise.*)

✔ **With the adverbs mai** (*ever/never*), **già** (*already*), **ancora** (*yet*), **and sempre** (*always*).

Always place these adverbs between the auxiliary verb (**essere** or **avere**) and past participle, like in the following five examples:

- **Hai** mai **provato** la zuppa inglese? (*Have you ever tried English trifle?*)

- No, non **ho** mai **provato** la zuppa inglese. (*No, I've never tried English trifle.*)

- **Sono** già **stati** in Italia John e Laurie? (*Have Laurie and John been to Italy yet?*)

- No, non **sono** ancora **stati** in Italia./Sì, **sono** già **stati** in Italia. (*No, they haven't yet been to Italy./Yes, they've already been to Italy.*)

✔ **In narratives, where it alternates with the imperfect and takes the place of the past absolute (the passato remoto) (see Chapters 8 and 9, respectively).**

Cappuccetto Rosso **raccoglieva** i fiori quando **ha visto** il lupo. (*Little Red Riding Hood was picking flowers when she saw the wolf.*)

✔ **With common expressions of time.**

You can see terms and phrases associated with this use in Table 14-4.

Table 14-4	Common Expressions of Time
Expression	*Example*
ieri (*yesterday*)	I miei genitori **sono tornati** ieri da St. Maarten. (*My parents got back from St. Maarten yesterday.*)
ieri sera (*last night, yesterday evening*)	Ieri sera **abbiamo visto** Cinema Paradiso. (*We saw Cinema Paradiso last night.*)
l'altro ieri (*the day before yesterday*)	I nonni **sono partiti** l'altro ieri per il Lago di Como. (*Our grandparents left for Lago di Como the day before yesterday.*)
fa (*ago*)	5 minuti fa (*5 minutes ago*), un'ora fa (*an hour ago*), 3 mesi fa (*3 months ago*), due anni fa (*2 years ago*), anni fa (*years ago*)
scorso/a/i/e (*last*)	l'anno scorso (*last year*), la settimana scorsa (*last week*), il mese scorso (*last month*), i giorni scorsi (*last few days*), le scorse settimane (*the past few weeks*)

This exercise simulates real life, in that you can use regular and irregular past participles and transitive and intransitive verbs all in the same dialogue. Answer the following personal questions that I present in the passato prossimo either affirmatively or negatively (also in the passato prossimo), according to my indications. Use complete sentences in your answers.

Answer in the io (first-person singular) form if I ask the question in the tu (second-person singular), and answer in the noi (first-person plural) form if I ask the question in the voi (second-person plural).

Here's an example to get you started:

Q. Sei mai stata in Sardegna? (No . . . ancora) (*Have you ever been to Sardegna?*)

A. No, non **sono ancora stata** in Sardegna. (*No, I haven't yet been to Sardegna.*)

66. Sei mai andato/a in Italia? (Sì . . . l'anno scorso)

_____

67. Hai mai mangiato la trippa? (No . . . mai)

_____

68. Avete mai visitato il paese di tuo nonno? (Sì . . . anni fa)

_____

69. Siete mai stati a Venezia per Carnevale? (No . . . ancora)

_____

70. Avete già visitato gli Uffizi a Firenze? (Sì . . . 3 volte)

_____

71. Hai mai provato la piadina in Emilia-Romagna? (No . . . ancora)

_____

72. Avete mai visto la Cappella Sistina? (No . . . mai)

_____

73. Avete già preso la pizza a Trastevere? (Sì . . . ieri sera!)

_____

74. Hai già imparato il passato prossimo? (Sì . . . oggi)

_____

75. Siete andati a letto tardi? (Sì . . . sempre)

_____

Complete the following dialogues by conjugating the infinitives in parentheses into the present perfect, using the appropriate tools from throughout the chapter (such as the proper auxiliary verbs and adverbs). Follow my example:

Q. Teresa: Che cosa _____? (dire)

Giancarlo: Non _____ niente! (dire)

A. Teresa: Che cosa **hai detto?** (*What did you say?*)

Giancarlo: Non **ho detto** niente! (*I didn't say anything!*)

76. Teresa: Che cosa _____ ieri sera? (fare [voi])

Maria: Tuo padre _____ con lo Zio Salvatore, ed io _____ a casa. (uscire, rimanere) _____ gli gnocchi per la festa. (fare [io]) Voi che cosa _____? (fare)

Teresa: _____ gli spaghetti alle vongole e _____ al computer. (preparare, lavorare) Giancaro ed Emilia _____ al cinema e quando _____, _____. (andare, tornare, cenare [noi])

77. Laurie: Jenny _____ a sciare con John ieri. (andare)

Lizzie: O, _____ la prima volta per Jenny? (essere)

Laurie: No, l'anno scorso Jenny _____ 3 o 4 volte: _____ brava! (sciare, diventare)

Lizzie: Anche noi _____ Sadie e Kobe quest'anno! (portare) _____ Lucy a sciare? (portare [voi] [mai])

Laurie: No, noi _____ Lucy nel piccolo asilo (daycare) per bambini, ma l'anno prossimo comincerà a sciare anche lei. (mettere)

78. Maria Paola: Noi _____ al nuovo ristorante di Nancy ieri sera. (mangiare)

Sandro: _____ bene? (mangiare [voi])

Maria Paola: Sì, molto. Per il primo, io _____ il pappardelle al granchio (crab), e David _____ una zuppa di pesce, e per secondo _____ una spigola (sea bass). (prendere, prendere, dividere [noi])

Sandro: Che cosa _____? (bere [voi])

Maria Paola: _____ una bottiglia di Pignoletto, un vino bianco frizzante. (ordinare [noi])

Sandro: _____ molto? (spendere [voi])

Maria Paola: Abbastanza.

Answer Key

1 studiare → **studiato** (*studied*)

2 ricevere → **ricevuto** (*received*)

3 arrivare → **arrivato** (*arrived*)

4 ballare → **ballato** (*danced*)

5 sentire → **sentito** (*heard, felt, tasted*)

6 ripetere → **ripetuto** (*repeated*)

7 preparare → **preparato** (*prepared*)

8 cantare → **cantato** (*sang*)

9 credere → **creduto** (*believed*)

10 partire → **partito** (*left*)

11 dare → **dato** (*gave*)

12 stare → **stato** (*stayed*)

13 andare → **andato** (*went*)

14 ringraziare → **ringraziato** (*thanked*)

15 Tu **hai studiato.** *You studied.*

16 Loro **hanno dormito?** *Did they sleep?*

17 Noi **abbiamo sciato** bene. *We skied well.*

18 Lui **ha ricevuto** una telefonata. *He received a phone call.*

19 Voi **avete mangiato** molto gelato. *You (pl.) ate a lot of ice cream.*

20 Io **ho capito** tutto. *I understood everything.*

21 Lei **ha creduto** a suo marito. *She believed her husband.*

22 Tu **hai affittato** quel film? *Did you rent that film?*

23 **Hanno baciato** il bambino. *They kissed the baby.*

24 Marcella ed io **abbiamo chiacchierato** a lungo. *Marcella and I chatted for a long time.*

25 Cosa **avete disegnato** a scuola oggi? *What did you (pl.) draw in school today?*

26 Diane e Marc **hanno visitato** la Peggy Guggenheim Collection. *Diane and Marc visited the Peggy Guggenheim Collection.*

27 Susan ed io **abbiamo dato** da mangiare ai piccioni a Piazza San Marco. *Susan and I fed the pigeons in Piazza San Marco.*

28 Bruno **ha comprato** una bellissima maschera veneziana. *Bruno bought a beautiful Venetian mask.*

29 Io **ho mangiato** gli spaghetti al nero di seppia. *I ate spaghetti in black squid sauce.*

30 Cara **ha comprato** degli stivali nuovi. *Cara bought some new boots.*

31 Dove **sono nati** i tuoi genitori? (*Where were your parents born?*)

32 Ieri Giancarlo **è uscito** con Gianni. (*Yesterday Giancarlo went out with Gianni.*)

33 Noi **siamo andati** al cinema. (*We went to the movies.*)

34 Chi **è morto?** (*Who died?*)

35 Anna Maria ed io **siamo rimaste** a casa ieri. (*Anna Maria and I stayed home yesterday.*)

36 Cathy **è diventata** magra! (*Cathy has become skinny!*)

37 La Zia Fran e lo Zio Dick **sono stati** sposati per molti anni. (*Aunt Fran and Uncle Dick were married for many years.*)

38 Daniele **è salito** sul treno. (*Daniel got on the train.*)

39 A che ora **siete arrivati?** (*At what time did you* (pl.) *arrive?*)

40 Io **sono venuta** in Italia per la prima volta nel 1976. (*I came to Italy for the first time in 1976.*)

41 Pier Paolo Pasolini **è stato** un regista famoso. (*Pier Paolo Pasolini was a famous director.*)

42 Anna Maria ed io **siamo cadute!** (*Anna Maria and I fell.*)

43 A che ora **sei andato** a letto? (*What time did you go to bed?*)

44 Tu e il babbo **siete partiti** giusto in tempo. (*You and daddy left right on time.*)

45 I ragazzi **sono ritornati** tardi. (*The kids got back late/The kids returned late/The kids have come back late.*)

46 *Domenico came to America with his father./Domenico has come to America with his father.*

47 *The children were born in Connecticut.*

48 *What time did the train leave?*

49 *How did you arrive?*

50 *Mom got off the bus./Mom has gotten off the bus.*

51 *Riccardo, did you go out last night?*

52 *I didn't become famous./I haven't become famous.*

53 *We stayed home./We did stay home.*

54 *Jenny and Lucy went skiing./Jenny and Lucy have gone skiing./Jenny and Lucy did go skiing.*

55 *Maria Paola, did you go out last night?*

56 Maria **ha fatto** una gita scolastica a Washington D.C. (*Maria took a class trip to Washington, D.C.*)

57 Daniel **ha composto** una canzone rap alla chitarra. (*Daniel composed a rap song on the guitar.*)

58 Daniel e Maria **hanno perso** i loro telefonini. (*Daniel and Maria lost their cell phones.*)

59 Tu e Robert **avete riso** molto ieri. (*You and Robert laughed a lot yesterday.*)

60 Giancarlo ed io **abbiamo corretto** il suo tema d'italiano. (*Giancarlo and I corrected his Italian essay.*)

61 Anna Maria, **hai letto** il *New York Times* di ieri? (*Anna Maria, did you read yesterday's New York Times?*)

62 Noi **abbiamo scritto** un'e-mail all'università di Giancarlo, e così **abbiamo risolto** il problema. (*We wrote an e-mail to Giancarlo's university, and so we resolved the problem.*)

63 Robert **ha offerto** la cena a tutti. (*Robert treated everyone to dinner.*)

64 Io **ho detto** che Maria poteva venire con noi. (*I said that Maria could come with us.*)

65 Tutti **hanno sofferto** il freddo. (*Everybody suffered from the cold.*)

66 Sì, **sono andata** in Italia l'anno scorso. (*Yes, I went to Italy last summer.*)

67 No, non **ho** mai **mangiato** la trippa. (*No, I've never eaten tripe.*)

68 Sì, **abbiamo visitato** il paese di mio nonno anni fa. (*Yes, we visited my grandfather's town years ago.*)

69 No, non **siamo** ancora **stati** a Venezia per Carnevale. (*No, we haven't yet been to Venice for Carnevale.*)

70 Sì, **abbiamo visitato** gli Uffizi tre volte. (*Yes, we've visited the Uffizi three times.*)

71 No, non **ho** ancora **provato** la piadina in Emilia-Romagna. (*No, I haven't yet tried the piadina in Emilia-Romagna.*)

72 No, non **abbiamo** mai **visitato** la Cappella Sistina. (*No, we've never visited the Sistine Chapel.*)

73 Sì, **abbiamo preso** la pizza a Trastevere ieri sera! (*Yes, we had pizza in Trastevere last night!*)

74 Sì, **ho imparato** il passato prossimo oggi. (*Yes, I learned the passato prossimo today.*)

75 Sì, **siamo** sempre **andati** a letto tardi. (*Yes, we always went to bed late.*)

76 Teresa: Che cosa **avete fatto** ieri sera? (*What did you (pl.) do last night?*)

Maria: Tuo padre **è uscito** con lo Zio Salvatore, ed io **sono rimasta** a casa. **Ho fatto** gli gnocchi per la festa. Voi che cosa **avete fatto?** (*Your father went out with Uncle Salvatore, and I stayed home. I made gnocchi for the party. What did you (pl.) do?*)

Teresa: **Ho preparato** gli spaghetti alle vongole e **ho lavorato** al computer. Giancaro ed Emilia **sono andati** al cinema e quando **sono tornati, abbiamo cenato.** (*I made spaghetti with clams and worked on the computer. Giancarlo and Emilia went to the movies, and when they returned we had supper.*)

77 Laurie: Jenny **è andata** a sciare con John ieri. (*Jenny went skiing with John yesterday.*)

Lizzie: O, **è stata** la prima volta per Jenny? (*Oh, was it the first time for Jenny?*)

Laurie: No, l'anno scorso Jenny **ha sciato** 3 o 4 volte: **è diventata** brava! (*No, last year Jenny skied 3 or 4 times: she got to be good!*)

Lizzie: Anche noi **abbiamo portato** Sadie e Kobe quest'anno! **Avete mai portato** Lucy a sciare? (*We, too, brought Sadie and Kobe this year! Have you* (pl.) *ever brought Lucy skiing?*)

Laurie: No, noi **abbiamo messo** Lucy nel piccolo asilo per bambini, ma l'anno prossimo comincerà a sciare anche lei. (*No, we put Lucy in the little day care for babies, but next year she'll start to ski, too.*)

78 Maria Paola: Noi **abbiamo mangiato** al nuovo ristorante di Nancy ieri sera. (*We ate at Nancy's new restaurant last night.*)

Sandro: **Avete mangiato** bene? (*Did you eat well?*)

Maria Paola: Sì, molto. Per il primo io **ho preso** le pappardelle al granchio, e David **ha preso** una zuppa di pesce, e per il secondo **abbiamo diviso** una spigola. (*Yes, very. For the pasta course I had pappardelle with crab, and David had a zuppa di pesce, and for the second course we shared a sea bass.*)

Sandro: Che cosa **avete bevuto?** (*What did you* (pl.) *drink?*)

Maria Paola: **Abbiamo ordinato** una bottiglia di Pignoletto, un vino bianco frizzante. (*We ordered a bottle of Pignoletto, a white effervescent wine.*)

Sandro: **Avete speso** molto? (*Did you* (pl.) *spend a lot?*)

Maria Paola: Abbastanza. (*Pretty much.*)

Chapter 15

What Time Did You Get Up Today? Reflexive Verbs in the Past

In This Chapter

▶ Addressing the past tense of reflexive verbs

▶ Examining the reciprocal form in the past

You probably got up too early! But did you brush your teeth or wash your face? How long did it take you to get dressed? What did you put on? Were you bored in class? Did you get angry with your boyfriend or girlfriend? By the time you're done with this chapter, you'll be able to ask and answer all these questions in the passato prossimo (the present perfect, a form of the past tense [I tend to use the terms interchangeably]), using reflexive pronouns and verbs.

In this chapter, you find out how to conjugate reflexive verbs and their reciprocal forms into the passato prossimo (in other words, the reflexive past). For detailed information on reflexive verbs (including a list of the more common ones) and for practice problems that feature these verbs in the present tense, check out Chapter 5. For information on forming the passato prossimo with verbs that take **essere** (*to be*) in compound tenses, see Chapter 14.

Forming the Passato Prossimo of Reflexive Verbs

To form the passato prossimo (present perfect) of a reflexive verb, you need three parts:

▶ A reflexive pronoun (mi, ti, si, ci, vi, or si)

▶ **Essere** (*to be*) in the present tense

▶ A past participle that agrees with the subject, ending in **-o** (masc. sing.), **-a** (fem. sing.), **-i** (masc. pl.), or **-e** (fem. pl.). (See Chapter 14 for more on gender/number agreement with verbs conjugated with **essere.**)

Here are some examples of these necessities in sentence form:

▶ **Mi sono svegliata** alle 6 di mattina. (*I woke up at 6 in the morning.*)

In this example, **Mi** is the reflexive pronoun.

▶ Julia **si è messa** i miei pantaloni. (*Julia wore my pants.*)

In this example, **è** is the form of **essere** in the present tense.

▶ Monica e Michelle **si sono perse** tornando a casa. (*Monica and Michelle got lost coming home.*)

In this example, **perse** is the past participle that agrees with the subject (it ends in **-e**).

The following three tables show the conjugations for **-arsi**, **-ersi**, and **-irsi** verbs in the reflexive past. The personal pronouns (io, tu, lui, lei, Lei, noi, voi, and loro) aren't necessary with reflexive verbs; you use them only when you have to specify the subject — for example, when you have to say "lui" (*he*) rather than "lei" (*she*). (For more rules for reflexive verbs, check out Chapter 5.)

You use **-o** and **-i** endings for males and **-a** and **-e** endings for females.

alzarsi (*to get up, to wake up*)	
(io) mi **sono** alzat**o/a**	(noi) ci **siamo** alzat**i/e**
(tu) ti **sei** alzat**o/a**	(voi) vi **siete** alzat**i/e**
(lui, lei, Lei) si è alzat**o/a**	(loro) si **sono** alzat**i/e**
A che ora **ti sei alzata?** (*What time did you* (f.) *get up?*)	

mettersi (*to put on, to wear*)	
mi **sono** mess**o/a**	ci **siamo** mess**i/e**
ti **sei** mess**o/a**	vi **siete** mess**i/e**
si è mess**o/a**	si **sono** mess**i/e**
Maria Luisa **si è messa** una bella gonna oggi. (*Maria Luisa wore a nice skirt today.*)	

divertirsi (*to have fun, to have a good time*)	
mi **sono** divertit**o/a**	ci **siamo** divertit**i/e**
ti **sei** divertit**o/a**	vi **siete** divertit**i/e**
si è divertit**o/a**	si **sono** divertit**i/e**
Quanto **ci siamo divertiti** alla festa! (*We had such a good time at the party!*)	

In this exercise, you gain some practice conjugating reflexive verbs into the past tense. Take the following verbs in parentheses and conjugate them into the past reflexive. Make sure you choose the appropriate reflexive pronoun and have your past participle agree with the subject. Here's an example to get you started:

Q. Mio padre _____ al cinema. (addormentarsi)

A. Mio padre **si è addormentato** al cinema. (*My dad fell asleep at the movies.*)

1. Ieri, Toby _____ il braccio. (rompersi)

2. _____ subito! (innamorarsi [io, f.])

3. Mio marito _____ a vivere negli Stati Uniti. (abituarsi)

4. I miei genitori _____ quando erano molto giovani. (sposarsi)

5. Dove _____ a mangiare? (fermarsi [voi])

6. Maria, _____ male? (farsi [tu])

7. _____ nel 1983. (laurearsi [io, f.])

8. Daniele _____ il compito. (dimenticarsi)

9. _____ tanto in Italia! (divertirsi [noi])

10. _____ con tuo figlio? (arrabbiarsi)

Time to get personal. Answer the following personal questions, using the same verbs that I provide in the questions. Your answers, of course, may vary from the ones I provide in the Answer Key, but your verb forms should be the same as mine (that is, in the past reflexive). Just follow my example (noting that men use the ending **-o** and women use the ending **-a**):

Q. In quanti minuti ti sei vestita/o oggi? (*How many minutes did it take you to get dressed today?*)

A. Mi sono vestita/o in 10 minuti oggi. (*I got dressed in 10 minutes.*)

11. A che ora ti sei svegliata/o oggi? (*At what time did you wake up today?*)

_____

12. Ti sei alzato/a subito? (*Did you get up right away?*)

_____

13. A che ora ti sei addormentato/a ieri sera? (*What time did you fall asleep last night?*)

_____

14. Come ti sei vestito/a, elegante o sportivo/a? (*How did you dress, elegantly or casually?*)

_____

15. Quante volte ti sei lavato/a i denti oggi? (*How many times did you brush your teeth today?*)

_____

Right Back at Ya: The Reciprocal Form in the Past Tense

The reciprocal form in the past tense uses the same verbs as the reciprocal form in the present (see Chapter 5 for an explanation of reciprocal verbs and a list of commonly used verbs). And as with the present reciprocal, you use only the plural forms of the verbs (ci, vi, si) because the reciprocal form implies more than one person participating in an action. You always translate the reciprocal form as *with each other* or *to each other.*

Note the difference between the verbs **scrivere** (*to write*) and **scriversi** (*to write to each other*):

Io **ho scritto** una lettera a Gianni. (*I wrote a letter to Gianni.*)

Gianni ed io **ci siamo scritti.** (*Gianni and I wrote to each other.*)

To form the reciprocal form of the past tense, you need three building blocks:

- A reflexive pronoun (ci, vi, or si)
- The plural form of **essere** (*to be*) in the present (**siamo, siete,** or **sono**)
- A past participle with a plural ending (**-e** for feminine subjects and **-i** for masculine subjects)

I highlight some examples of these building blocks in the following list:

- Monica ed io **ci siamo viste** a casa di Julia. (*Monica and I saw each other at Julia's house.*)

  In this example, **ci** is the reflexive pronoun.

- Dove **vi siete conosciuti** tu e tuo marito? (*Where did you and your husband meet?*)

  In this example, **siete** is the plural form of **essere** in the present tense.

- Jenny e Lucy **si sono lamentate** del caldo. (*Jenny and Lucy complained about the heat.*)

  In this example, **lamentate** is the past participle with a plural ending (a feminine **-e** ending).

When you use the reciprocal form in the past, you conjugate all verbs with **essere,** even if those verbs are transitive verbs that you usually conjugate with **avere** (*to have*) in the compound tenses.

The following table shows the conjugation of **scriversi** in the past reciprocal.

scriversi (*to write to each other*)	
ci **siamo** scritti/e	Gianni ed io **ci siamo scritti.**
vi **siete** scritti/e	(*Gianni and I wrote to each other.*)
si **sono** scritti/e	

For this exercise, try conjugating some other reciprocal verbs into the past tense. I'll put the translations in the Answer Key. Follow my example:

O. Mia madre e mio padre _____ 50 anni fa. (conoscersi)

A. Mia madre e mio padre **si sono conosciuti** 50 anni fa. (*My parents met each other 50 years ago.*)

16. Giancarlo ed io _____ molte e-mail. (mandarsi)

17. Tu (m.) e tua sorella _____ ? (salutarsi)

18. La mamma ed io (f.) _____ al telefono. (sentirsi)

19. Tu e Marco _____ a New York ieri sera? (incontrarsi)

20. Le mie cugine _____ per cena. (vedersi)

21. Liora e Teresa _____ delle cartoline.
(scriversi)

22. Domenico ed Enzo _____ la mano. (darsi)

23. Il babbo ed io (f.) _____ ogni sera.
(telefonarsi)

24. Tu (m.) e la signora Costa _____ ? (baciarsi)

25. Laura e Gigio _____ senza dire una parola.
(guardarsi)

Gianni and Marinella fell in love one day, and they want you to help tell their story.
Conjugate all the following verbs in parentheses into the reciprocal form of the past
tense and then translate. I start your tale off with an example:

0. Gianni e Marinella _____ per la prima volta all'aeroporto di Milano. (vedersi)

A. Gianni e Marinella **si sono visti** per la prima volta all'aeroporto di Milano. *Gianni and
Marinella saw each other for the first time at the airport in Milano.*

26. Quindici ore dopo, _____ all'aeroporto in
Perù. (rivedersi)

_____

27. _____ tutto il giorno in autobus andando a
Machu Pichu. (guardarsi)

_____

28. Finalmente, Gianni e Marinella _____.
(presentarsi)

_____

29. I due giovani _____: Lui era di Ravenna e lei
era della Sardegna. (parlarsi)

_____

30. Gianni e Marinella _____. (innamorarsi)

_____

31. Quando sono tornati in Italia, _____

e _____. (scriversi, telefonarsi)

_____

32. Alla fine, _____. (sposarsi)

_____

Answer Key

1 Ieri Toby **si è rotto** il braccio. (*Toby broke his arm yesterday.*)

2 **Mi sono innamorata** subito! (*I fell in love right away!*)

3 Mio marito **si è abituato** a vivere negli Stati Uniti. (*My husband has gotten used to living in the United States.*)

4 I miei genitori **si sono sposati** quando erano molto giovani. (*My parents got married when they were very young.*)

5 Dove **vi siete fermati** a mangiare? (*Where did you stop to eat?*)

6 Maria, **ti sei fatta** male? (*Maria, did you get hurt?*)

7 **Mi sono laureata** nel 1983. (*I graduated in 1983.*)

8 Daniele **si è dimenticato** il compito. (*Daniel forgot his homework.*)

9 **Ci siamo divertiti** tanto in Italia! (*We had so much fun in Italy!*)

10 **Ti sei arrabbiato/a** con tuo figlio? (*Did you get angry with your son?*)

11 **Mi sono svegliata** alle sei e mezzo oggi. (*I got up at 6:30 today.*)

12 No, non **mi sono alzata** subito. (*No, I didn't get up right away.*)

13 **Mi sono addormentata** alle undici ieri sera. (*I fell asleep last night at 11:00.*)

14 **Mi sono vestita** elegante. (*I dressed very elegantly.*)

15 **Mi sono lavata** i denti tre volte oggi. (*I brushed my teeth three times today.*)

16 Giancarlo ed io **ci siamo mandati** molte e-mail. (*Giancarlo and I sent each other many e-mails.*)

17 Tu e tua sorella **vi siete salutati?** (*Did you and your sister greet each other?*)

18 La mamma ed io **ci siamo sentite** al telefono. (*Mom and I spoke to each other on the phone.*)

19 Tu e Marco **vi siete incontrati** a New York ieri sera? (*Did you and Marco meet in New York last night?*)

20 Le mie cugine **si sono viste** per cena. (*My cousins saw each other for dinner.*)

21 Liora e Teresa **si sono scritte** delle cartoline. (*Liora and Teresa wrote each other postcards.*)

22 Domenico ed Enzo **si sono dati** la mano. (*Domenico and Enzo shook hands.*)

23 Il babbo ed io **ci siamo telefonati** ogni sera. (*Your father and I phoned each other every night.*)

24 Tu e la signora Costa **vi siete baciati?** (*Did you and Mrs. Costa kiss each other?*)

25 Laura e Gigio **si sono guardati** senza dire una parola. (*Laura and Gigio looked at each other without saying a word.*)

26　Quindici ore dopo, **si sono rivisti** all'aeroporto in Perù. *Fifteen hours later, they saw each other again at the airport in Peru.*

27　**Si sono guardati** tutto il giorno in autobus andando a Machu Pichu. *They kept looking at each other the whole bus ride to Machu Pichu.*

28　Finalmente, Gianni e Marinella **si sono presentati.** *Gianni and Marinella finally introduced themselves to each other.*

29　I due giovani **si sono parlati:** Lui era di Ravenna e lei era di Sardegna. *The two young people spoke: He was from Ravenna and she was from Sardegna.*

30　Gianni e Marinella **si sono innamorati.** *Gianni and Marinella fell in love with each other.*

31　Quando sono tornati in Italia, **si sono scritti** e **si sono telefonati.** *When they went back to Italy, they wrote to each other and phoned each other.*

32　Alla fine, **si sono sposati.** *At the end, they got married.*

Chapter 16

By Tomorrow, You'll Have Spoken of a Perfect (or Hypothetical) Future

. . . .

In This Chapter

▶ Combining the parts of the future perfect tense

▶ Reviewing the uses of the future perfect

▶ Switching gears to the hypothetical future

. . . .

The future can't exist in the past, can it? Sure it can, and not just in the *Back to the Future* movies. Although not the most common of compound Italian tenses, you need the future perfect (futuro anteriore) to talk about events that will happen as soon as (appena) or after (dopo) something else happens in the future. In other words, the future tense expresses future action that will take place before another action in the future takes place. It translates as *will have + participle*. You can use the tense to explain what you'll do by a certain time or date (like, "I'll have finished my homework before noon comes tommorrow"), and you can use it to talk about events that will already (già) have happened (like, "I will have already forgotten my goal when I go to bed"). In this chapter, you discover how to form the future perfect tense, how to put the tense into action, and how to incorporate the hypothetical future to round out your knowledge of events to come.

Forming the Future Perfect Tense (Futuro Anteriore)

You form the future perfect tense just like you form all the other compound tenses in Italian (see Chapters 14 and 15): You take the future form of the auxiliary verb **essere** (*to be*) or **avere** (*to have*), and then you add the past participle of the verb in question. You often need the adverbs "già" (*already*), "appena" (*as soon as*), and "entro" (*by*) when forming the future perfect.

You can see the form in action in these examples:

▸ Appena **avrò finito** di studiare, uscirò. (*As soon as I'm done studying, I'm going to go out.*)

▸ Entro quando **si sarà sposato**, Enzo capirà che è la donna sbagliata. (*By the time he gets married, Enzo will understand that she's the wrong woman.*)

The following tables show you how to conjugate **parlare** and **andare** in the future perfect tense. Use each as a model for conjugating all the other verbs in the future perfect, according to whether they take **avere** (as **parlare** does) or **essere** (like **andare**) as their helping verb. (See Chapters 14 and 15 for more detail on how to distinguish between the verbs that take **essere** or **avere** as their auxiliary verb and for how to form the past participle.)

parlare (*to speak*)	
io avrò parl**ato**	noi avr**emo** parl**ato**
tu avr**ai** parl**ato**	voi avr**ete** parl**ato**
lui, lei, Lei avr**à** parl**ato**	loro avr**anno** parl**ato**
Avranno già **parlato** col regista. (*They will have already spoken with the director.*)	

andare (*to go*)	
io sarò and**ato/a**	noi sar**emo** and**ati/e**
tu sar**ai** and**ato/a**	voi sar**ete** and**ati/e**
lui, lei, Lei sar**à** and**ato/a**	loro sar**anno** and**ati/e**
Per le undici Marco **sarà andato** a casa. (*Marco will have gone home by 11 o'clock.*)	

The past participles of verbs that take **essere** must agree in gender and in number with the subjects: **-o** (masc. sing.); **-a** (fem. sing.); **-i** (masc. pl.); and **-e** (fem. pl.) You can find more on this agreement in Chapters 14 and 15.

All reflexive verbs (see Chapters 5 and 15 for more) take **essere** as their auxiliary verb in all compound tenses. When conjugating a reflexive verb, make certain to always include the appropriate reflexive pronoun: mi, ti, si, ci, vi, or si. The following table shows the conjugation of **alzarsi,** an example of a reflexive verb in the future perfect.

alzarsi (*to get up*)	
mi sarò alz**ato/a**	ci sar**emo** alz**ati/e**
ti sar**ai** alz**ato/a**	vi sar**ete** alz**ati/e**
si sar**à** alz**ato/a**	si sar**anno** alz**ati/e**
Mi sarò alzata entro mezzogiorno! (*I'll have gotten up by noon!*)	

Create sentences from the following verbs and adverbs in the future perfect tense (keeping the tense, of course). Follow the yellow-brick example. (Make certain that you place the adverbs "appena" and "già" in between the helping verbs and the past participles when necessary.)

Q. io/laurearsi/nel 2007

A. **Mi sarò laureata** nel 2007. (*I will have graduated* [*from college*] *in 2007.*)

1. noi/partire/appena _____

2. loro/capire _____

3. voi/sedersi/già _____

4. lui/conoscere/mia nonna _____

5. tu (f.) uscire/già _____

Putting the Future Perfect to Use Now

The future perfect tense gives you the opportunity to discuss time, events in the future, goals, plans, deadlines, and everyone's favorite subject: procrastination.

You can use the future perfect tense to talk about an action that will already have taken place when another action in the future takes place. In this case, you use one verb in the future perfect (the event that will already have taken place) and another verb in the future (see Chapter 10):

Avranno già **mangiato** quando **arriveremo.** (*They will have already eaten when we get there.*)

You can also use the future perfect to describe an action that will have taken place at a certain time:

Per maggio **avrò finito** questo libro! (*I'll have finished this book by May!*)

Entro le 7 **sarò partita.** (*I'll have left by 7 o'clock.*)

Entro Capodanno **ci saremo sposati.** (*We'll have gotten married by New Year's.*)

You often combine the future perfect with the following expressions in subordinate clauses: "quando" (*when*), "appena" (*as soon as*), and "dopo che" (*after*). In these cases, you put the verb in the main clause in the future tense.

Note the following three examples:

<u>Quando</u> **saranno tornati** i miei, **butteremo** la pasta. (<u>*When*</u> *my parents return [will have returned], we'll throw the pasta in the water.*)

<u>Appena</u> **avrai sentito** i risultati, **prenderai** una decisione. (<u>*As soon as*</u> *you've heard the results, you'll make a decision.*)

La mamma **andrà** a messa <u>dopo che</u> **si sarà vestita.** (*Mom will go to church <u>after</u> she gets dressed [will have gotten dressed].*)

In the following exercise, conjugate the verbs in parentheses into the future perfect tense to get a perfect picture of how things will be in the future. Here's an example for you:

Q. Quando avrò trent'anni _____. (sposarsi)

A. Quando avrò trent'anni **mi sarò sposata.** (*When I'm 30 years old I'll be married.*)

6. Per domani pomeriggio, Belinda _____ i compiti. (finire)

7. Fra mezz'ora, Caterina e Tiffany _____. (partire)

8. Quando _____ l'albergo, Giuseppe ed io telefoneremo ai nonni. (trovare)

9. Rudi, appena _____ lavorerai? (laurearsi)

10. Visiteremo il Vaticano dopo che _____ la Fontana di Trevi. (visitare)

11. È tardi! La mamma _____ via! (andare)

12. Matteo frequenterà Yale dopo che _____.
   (diplomarsi)

13. Ti telefoneremo appena _____ a Padova.
   (arrivare)

14. A settembre, Emilia _____ 6 anni. (compiere)

15. Entro venerdì, gli studenti _____ gli esami
   finali. (dare)

Talking about the Hypothetical Future

A special use of the future tense (see Chapter 10 and the first section in this chapter for more) is called the *hypothetical future* (futuro ipotetico). You use the futuro ipotetico not to talk about events in the future, but to talk about probability and possibility in the present and past. Sound confusing? Just think to yourself: I'm not talking about the future, I'm talking about wondering in the present and past.

The faction of the hypothetical future that talks about probability in the present uses the future tense. In a question, you translate it as "What could it be? Who could it be? How many people may there be? How old could she be? How much might it cost?" And so on. In a declarative sentence, you can translate it as "It's probably the wind. It's probably dad. There are probably around 20 people. She's probably 40." And so on.

Dove **saranno?** (*Where could they be?*)

Boh! **Saranno** a letto! (*I don't know! They're probably in bed!*)

Master your understanding of the hypothetical future, with which you can express probability in the present, by translating the following brief exchanges into English. You might want to check out the future tense in Chapter 10 if it's not fresh in your mind. Follow the example:

Q. Lui: Sarà lontana Ferrara?

Lei: Saranno 33 chilometri.

A. He: How far do you think Ferrara is?

She: It's probably about 33 kilometers.

16. Lei: Cosa sarà quel rumore? _____

   Lui: Sarà il vento. _____

17. Lei: Dove saranno i bambini? _____

   Lui: Saranno ancora al cinema. _____

18. Lui: Quanto costerà quella Ducati? _____

   Lei: Costerà 30 mila dollari. _____

19. Lei: Ma quanti bambini avranno? _____

Lui: Non saranno mica tutti loro. _____

20. Lui: Quanti anni avrà la professoressa d'italiano? _____

Lei: Avrà quarant'anni. _____

REMEMBER

The faction of the hypothetical future that talks about probability in the past uses the future perfect tense (see the first section in this chapter). You can (roughly) translate sentences in this form as "They've probably missed the train. You probably ate too much. He probably didn't study!" And so on.

EXAMPLE

Bambino: Mamma, **mi fa** male lo stomaco! (*Mommy, my stomach hurts!*)

Mamma: **Avrai mangiato** troppo cioccolato! (*You probably ate too much chocolate!*)

PRACTICE

Conjugate the following verbs in parentheses into the future perfect tense and then translate the sentences to talk about probability in the past (in other words, to talk in the hypothetical future). Here's an example to get you started:

O. Il Papa _____ già _____ via. (andare)

A. Il Papa **sarà** già **andato** via. *The Pope has probably already left.*

21. Che fine ha fatto Cristiano? _____. (sposarsi)

_____

22. La mamma e il babbo _____? (uscire)

_____

23. Quel vestito è ridicolo! Quanto lo _____? (pagare [tu])

_____

24. Voi _____ che io non accetto i compiti in ritardo. (capire)

_____

25. Cosa _____ quel rumore? (essere)

_____

Answer Key

1 **Saremo** appena **partiti.** (*We'll have just left.*)

2 **Avranno capito.** (*They'll have understood.*)

3 **Vi sarete** già **seduti.** (*You will already be seated.*)

4 Lui **avrà conosciuto** mia nonna. (*He will have met my grandmother.*)

5 Tu **sarai** già **uscita.** (*You'll already have gone out.*)

6 Per domani pomeriggio, Belinda **avrà finito** i compiti. (*For tomorrow afternoon, Belinda will have finished her homework.*)

7 Fra mezz'ora, Caterina e Tiffany **saranno partite.** (*In a half hour, Caterina and Tiffany will have left.*)

8 Quando **avremo trovato** l'albergo, Giuseppe ed io telefoneremo ai nonni. (*When we've found the hotel, Giuseppe and I will call our grandparents.*)

9 Rudi, appena **ti sarai laureato** lavorerai? (*Rudi, will you work as soon as you've graduated?*)

10 Visiteremo il Vaticano cena dopo che **avremo visitato** la Fontana di Trevi. (*We'll visit the Vatican after we've visited the Fountain of Trevi.*)

11 È tardi! La mamma **sarà andata** via! (*It's late! Mom will have left!*)

12 Matteo frequenterà Yale dopo che **si sarà diplomato.** (*Matteo will go to Yale after he graduates.*)

13 Ti telefoneremo appena **saremo arrivati** a Padova. (*We'll call you as soon as we arrive in Padua.*)

14 A settembre, Emilia **avrà compiuto** 6 anni. (*In September, Emilia will be 6 years old.*)

15 Entro venerdì, gli studenti **avranno dato** gli esami finali. (*By Friday, the students will have taken their final exams.*)

16 *She: What could that noise be? He: It must be the wind.*

17 *She: Where could the children be? He: They're probably still at the movies.*

18 *He: How much do you think that Ducati costs? She: It probably costs 30,000 dollars.*

19 *She: How many children could they possibly have? He: They're probably not all theirs.*

20 *He: How old do you think the Italian professor is? She: She's probably around 40.*

21 Che fine ha fatto Cristiano? **Si sarà sposato.** *Whatever happened to Cristiano? He probably got married.*

22 La mamma e il babbo **saranno usciti?** *Could mom and dad have gone out?*

23 Quel vestito è ridicolo! Quanto lo **avrai pagato?** *That dress is ridiculous! How much could you have paid for it?*

24 Voi **avrete capito** che io non accetto i compiti in ritardo. *You all have probably understood that I will not accept late homework.*

25 Cosa **sarà stato** quel rumore? *What could that noise have been?*

Chapter 17

Second Guessing Your Actions with the Past Conditional

. . . .

In This Chapter

▶ Combining the pieces of the past conditional

▶ Putting the past conditional to use

▶ Utilizing **dovere, potere,** and **volere** in the past conditional

. . . .

*I*n Italian, you use the past conditional tense (condizionale passato) to indicate what you would, could, or should have done, said, eaten, and so on. Unlike the present conditional tense, which implies the possibility that action could still take place (see Chapter 11 for more on the present conditional), the past conditional generally forecloses possibility, implying that "it's too late now!"

You very often see the past conditional in conjunction with the past perfect subjunctive (trapassato congiuntivo; see Chapter 20) and with "if" sentences (frasi ipotetiche; see Chapter 21) — for example, "Se io **avessi saputo, avrei telefonato.**" (*If I had known, I would've called.*) The past conditional, however, can stand very well on its own and sometimes with the present perfect tense (passato prossimo; see Chapters 14 and 15), the imperfect tense (imperfetto; see Chapter 8), and with gerunds (see Chapter 23). This chapter provides you with examples and exercises of all the past conditional possibilities.

Forming the Past Conditional (Condizionale Passato)

The past conditional tense is very easy to form in Italian. Like most compound tenses, you precede the verb in question with the auxiliary verb **essere** (*to be*) or **avere** (*to have*). In Chapter 14, I talk about distinguishing between verbs that take **essere** and verbs that take **avere** in the compound tenses. To form the past conditional, you put the auxiliary verb into the present conditional tense (see Chapter 11) and add the past participle (see Chapter 14).

Here are a couple examples of this construction:

Cosa **avresti** (auxiliary verb) **fatto** (past participle) tu? (*What would you have done?*)

Sarei (auxiliary verb) **andata** (past participle) via. (*I would've gone away.*)

The following tables show example conjugations for the verbs **parlare, uscire,** and **fermarsi.**

parlare (*to speak*)	
io avr**ei** parl**ato**	noi avr**emmo** parl**ato**
tu avr**esti** parl**ato**	voi avr**este** parl**ato**
lui, lei, Lei avr**ebbe** parl**ato**	loro avr**ebbero** parl**ato**
Io **avrei parlato** con lui, ma **avevo** paura. (*I would've spoken with him, but I was afraid.*)	

uscire (*to go out*)	
io sar**ei** usc**ita/o**	noi sar**emmo** usc**ite/i**
tu sar**esti** usc**ita/o**	voi sar**este** usc**ite/i**
lui, lei, Lei sar**ebbe** usc**ita/o**	loro sar**ebbero** usc**ite/i**
Tu **saresti uscita** con lui? (*Would you have gone out with him?*)	

The past participles of verbs conjugated with **essere** must always agree in gender (masculine [masc.] or feminine [fem.]) and number (singular [sing.] or plural [pl.]) with the subjects of the sentences — hence the four possibilities of past participle endings (see Chapter 14).

fermarsi (*to stop*)	
mi sar**ei** ferm**ata/o**	ci sar**emmo** ferm**ate/i**
ti sar**esti** ferm**ata/o**	vi sar**este** ferm**ate/i**
si sar**ebbe** ferm**ata/o**	si sar**ebbero** ferm**ate/i**
Abbiamo detto che **ci saremmo fermati** tornando da Venezia. (*We said that we would stop by on the way back from Venice.*)	

Fermarsi is a reflexive verb, so it takes the reflexive pronouns that you see in the previous table. For more on conjugating reflexive verbs, see Chapter 5.

Conjugate the following verbs in parentheses into the conditional past tense, adding the correct form of **essere** or **avere** along the way. You may not necessarily form complete sentences. For example, you could say, "Io **mi sarei alzata** . . . ma/se . . ." and mean "*I would've gotten up . . . but/if . . .*" and then follow with something else, but you could also say (as you may in English), "Io **mi sarei alzata.**" (*I would've gotten up.*)

The verb **avere** takes **avere** as its auxiliary verb, and the verb **essere** takes **essere** as its auxiliary verb.

Follow my example for this exercise:

Q. Io _____ . . . (alzarsi)

A. Io **mi sarei alzato/a** . . . (*I would've gotten up . . .*)

1. Guglielmo _____ il . . . (fare)

2. Giancarlo ed io _____ . . . (sposarsi)

3. Tu e Stefano _____ . . . (giocare)

4. Stefania e Michele _____ . . . (divertirsi)

5. Tu _____ . . . (partire)

6. Io _____ . . . (chiedere)

7. Davide _____ pronto . . . (essere)

8. Noi _____ . . . (mangiare)

9. Voi _____ . . . (nascondersi)

10. Casanova _____ . . . (sedurre)

Using the Past Conditional to Play Woulda, Coulda, Shoulda

You use the past conditional in Italian in many of the same situations when you would use it in English (heck, "you would use it" is in the present conditional, so the conditional is all over the place; see Chapter 11 for more on the present conditional).

The following is a list of the past conditional's common uses:

✔ You can use the past conditional to identify what you would/could/should have done if something hadn't prevented you from doing it. You use the word "ma" (*but*) to indicate that something stood in your way.

Avrei studiato, ma **ero** stanca. (*I would've studied, but I was tired.*); **Saremmo andati** al cinema, ma non **avevamo** soldi. (*We would've gone to the movies, but we didn't have any money.*)

✔ You can use the past conditional tense to ask for or offer an opinion.

Che cosa **avresti fatto** a posto mio? (*What would you have done in my place?*)

✔ Another use of the past conditional appears with verbs and expressions of knowing, believing, and saying, such as **sapere** (*to know*), **capire** (*to understand*), **dire** (*to say*), **promettere** (*to promise*), and **scrivere** (*to write*), to name a few. These uses of the past conditional translate into the present conditional in English.

Era chiaro che non **sarebbero andati** d'accordo. (*It was clear that they wouldn't get along.*); **Hai detto** che **avresti studiato**! (*You said that you would study!*); **Ho detto** che **avrei chiamato**, e invece non **ho chiamato**. (*I said that I would call, and instead I didn't call.*)

The following practice exercise combines the different uses of the past conditional I present in this section to describe the plot of *La Locandiera* (*The Innkeeper*), a comedy by 18th-century playwrite Carlo Goldoni. In each of the following sentences, conjugate the verb I provide into the past conditional tense and then translate the sentence. Follow my lead with this example:

Q. Mirandolina ha promesso al padre che _____ Fabrizio. (sposare)

A. Mirandolina ha promesso al padre che **avrebbe sposato** Fabrizio. *Mirandolina promised her father that she would marry Fabrizio.*

11. Il Cavaliere (The Knight) ha detto che non _____. (innamorarsi)

12. Il Marchese (The Marquis) _____ la mano di
Mirandolina, ma era troppo nobile. (chiedere)

_____

13. Mirandolina ha detto che _____ il regalo dal
Conte (the Count). (accettare)

_____

14. Mirandolina ha promesso che _____ cascare
il Cavaliere. (fare)

_____

15. Il Cavaliere, il Marchese, il Conte, e Fabrizio _____.
(dichiararsi)

_____

16. Mirandolina ha detto a Fabrizio che lei _____
il Cavaliere. (servire)

_____

17. Il Cavaliere _____ via prima, ma si è
innamorato di Mirandolina. (andare)

_____

18. Io _____ di più ieri sera, ma mi sono
addormentata! (leggere)

_____

Expressing Responsibilities, Desires, and Abilities in the Past Conditional

You often use the verbs **dovere** (*to have to*), **volere** (*to want to*), and **potere** (*to be able to*) in the past conditional tense to express the following, respectively:

- ✔ "I (you, he, we, they) should've . . ."
- ✔ "I would've liked to . . ."
- ✔ "I could've . . ."

You can also express negative connotations such as "I shouldn't have . . ." and "Couldn't I have . . . ?"

To use **dovere, volere,** and **potere** in the past conditional, you first decide whether you should use the conditional of the auxiliary verb **essere** or **avere,** and then you add the past participle — **dovuto, voluto,** or **potuto** — to the auxiliary verb. Both of these forms precede the action verb in the sentence:

> **Avrei dovuto prendere** gli spiedini di seppia! (*I should've gotten the squid kebobs!*)
>
> **Sarei dovuta partire** prima. (*I should've left earlier.*)

Use the **avere** conditional when the infinitive that follows the past participle (**dovuto, voluto,** or **potuto**) generally takes **avere,** and use **essere** when the infinitive that follows the past participle is an intransitive verb (in other words, a verb that takes **essere**).

(See Chapter 14 and the section "Forming the Past Conditional [Condizionale Passato]" earlier in this chapter for more on using **essere** or **avere**.)

Note the following examples of **avere**:

Avresti dovuto provare di più. (*You should've tried harder/rehearsed more.*)

Avrei voluto studiare la sociologia. (*I would've liked to study sociology.*)

Il babbo **avrebbe potuto telefonare.** (*Dad could've called.*)

Note the following examples of **essere**:

Saresti dovuto/a partire prima! (*You should've left earlier.*)

Sarei voluto/a diventare veterinaria. (*I would've liked to become a veterinarian.*)

Il babbo **sarebbe potuto divertirsi** di più. (*Dad could've had more fun.*)

The land of regrets and recriminations! In this exercise, everybody is complaining about what they should or shouldn't have done; could or couldn't have done; or would have liked to or wouldn't have liked to have done. Check your comprehension of the past conditional by translating the sentences from English to Italian. Use **dovere, volere,** and **potere** as your past participles. Here's an example to get you going:

Q. I could've eaten the whole cake!

A. **Avrei potuto mangiare** l'intera torta!

19. They should've told me the truth.

_____

20. We would've liked to sleep.

_____

21. You (sing.) could've telephoned.

_____

22. I shouldn't have gotten angry.

_____

23. Would you (pl.) have liked to see Ischia?

_____

24. Nikki couldn't have done better (di meglio)!

_____

25. They should've studied.

_____

Answer Key

1 Guglielmo **avrebbe fatto** il . . . (*Guglielmo would have done . . .*)

2 Giancarlo ed io **ci saremmo sposati** . . . (*Giancarlo and I would've gotten married . . .*)

3 Tu e Stefano **avreste giocato** . . . (*You and Stefano would've played . . .*)

4 Stefania e Michele **si sarebbero divertiti** . . . (*Stefania and Michele would've had fun . . .*)

5 Tu **saresti partito** . . . (*You would've left . . .*)

6 Io **avrei chiesto** . . . (*I would've asked . . .*)

7 Davide **sarebbe stato** pronto . . . (*David would've been ready . . .*)

8 Noi **avremmo mangiato** . . . (*We would've eaten . . .*)

9 Voi **vi sareste nascosti** . . . (*You (pl.) would've hidden . . .*)

10 Casanova **avrebbe sedotto** . . . (*Casanova would've seduced . . .*)

11 Il Cavaliere ha detto che non **si sarebbe innamorato.** *The Knight said that he wouldn't fall in love.*

12 Il Marchese **avrebbe chiesto** la mano di Mirandolina, ma era troppo nobile. *The Marquis would've asked for Mirandolina's hand, but he was too noble.*

13 Mirandolina ha detto che **avrebbe accettato** il regalo dal Conte. *Mirandolina said that she would accept the Count's gift.*

14 Mirandolina ha promesso che **avrebbe fatto** cascare il Cavaliere. *Mirandolina promised that she would make the Knight fall (for her).*

15 Il Cavaliere, il Marchese, il Conte, e Fabrizio **si sarebbero dichiarati.** *The Knight, the Marquis, the Count, and Fabrizio would've declared themselves.*

16 Mirandolina ha detto a Fabrizio che lei **avrebbe servito** il Cavaliere. *Mirandolina told Fabrizio that she would serve the Knight.*

17 Il Cavaliere **sarebbe andato** via prima, ma si è innamorato di Mirandolina. *The Knight would've left sooner, but he fell in love with Mirandolina.*

18 Io **avrei letto** di più ieri sera, ma mi sono addormentata! *I would've read more last night, but I fell asleep!*

19 **Avrebbero dovuto dirmi** la verità.

20 **Avremmo voluto dormire.**

21 **Avresti potuto telefonare.**

22 Non **sarei dovuta arrabbiarmi.**

23 Voi **avreste voluto vedere** Ischia?

24 Nikki non **avrebbe potuto fare** di meglio!

25 **Avrebbero dovuto studiare.**

Chapter 18

Reminiscing about the Past Perfect

In This Chapter
▶ Creating the past perfect tense (trapassato prossimo)
▶ Using the past perfect tense

The trapassato prossimo tense, or the past perfect and pluperfect, corresponds to the following English construction: had + a past participle. For example, you often say *had eaten, had left, had finished, had married* (and had divorced), and *had enjoyed* Italian until I started this rambling (okay, I'll stop).

You often use the past perfect tense to describe an activity done prior to another activity that also has taken place — "Siccome non **avevo studiato, ho fatto** finta di **essere** malata" (*Since I hadn't studied, I pretended I was sick*). You often find past perfect verbs accompanied by the adverbs "già" (*already*), "non . . . ancora" (*not yet*), and "appena" (*just*): "Quando **siamo arrivati** alla stazione, il treno **era** già **partito**." (*When we got to the station, the train had already left.*) Some other common uses of the trapassato prossimo include use with the imperfect subjunctive (Chapter 13) and past perfect subjunctive (Chapter 20), and use in fairy tales and literature.

In this chapter, you find out how to form the past perfect tense and how to use the tense like a pro to create your own Italian fairy tales!

Implementing the Past Perfect Tense

You form the trapassato prossimo like the other compound tenses in Italian: You combine the imperfect of **avere** (*to have*) or **essere** (*to be*) with the past participle of the verb in question. (For an explanation of when to use **essere** and when to use **avere** for your auxiliary verb, and to find out how to form regular and irregular past participles, see Chapter 14.) A brief recap may suffice: When you have a transitive verb, your auxiliary verb will be **avere**; when you have an intransitive verb or any reflexive verb, your auxiliary verb will be **essere** — and remember that when you have a reflexive verb, you need to add a reflexive pronoun (see Chapter 15).

A 6 anni, Daniel non **aveva** ancora **cominciato** a nuotare. (*When he was 6, Daniel hadn't yet begun to swim.*)

A 6 anni, Daniel **era** già **stato** in Italia. (*When he was 6, Daniel had already been to Italy.*)

A 6 anni, Daniel **si era** già **vestito** da solo. (*When he was 6, Daniel had already gotten dressed by himself.*)

When forming the past perfect in Italian, you often need to use the adverb "già" (*already*), which should be placed between the auxiliary verb and the past participle.

La mamma **aveva** già **preparato** tutto quando **siamo arrivati**. (*Mom had already prepared everything when we arrived.*)

The adverb "ancora" (*yet*) works in the same way:

> Luisa non **aveva** ancora **capito** che **doveva studiare**. (*Luisa hadn't yet understood that she needed to study.*)

As do the adverbs "mai" (*never*) — "Non **si era** mai **sposato** Donald" (*Donald hadn't ever gotten married*) — and "appena" (*just*) — "**Mi ero** appena **alzata** . . ." (*I had just gotten up . . .*)

The following tables show examples of a transitive verb (which takes **avere**), an intransitive verb (which takes **essere**), and a reflexive verb in the trapassato prossimo tense.

mangiare (*to eat*)	
io avev**o** mangi**ato**	noi avev**amo** mangi**ato**
tu avev**i** mangi**ato**	voi avev**ate** mangi**ato**
lui, lei, Lei avev**a** mangi**ato**	loro avev**ano** mangi**ato**
Abbiamo detto di no perchè **avevamo mangiato** a casa. (*We said no because we had eaten at home.*)	

partire (*to leave, to depart*)	
io er**o** part**ito/a**	noi er**avamo** part**iti/e**
tu er**i** part**ito/a**	voi er**avate** part**iti/e**
lui, lei, Lei er**a** part**ito/a**	loro er**ano** part**iti/e**
Quando **sono arrivata**, tu **eri** già **partita**. (*When I got there, you had already left.*)	

The past participles of verbs conjugated with **essere** (in any compound tense) must agree in number and gender with their subjects (see Chapters 14 and 15).

alzarsi (*to get up*)	
mi er**o** alz**ato/a**	ci er**avamo** alz**ati/e**
ti er**i** alz**ato/a**	vi er**avate** alz**ati/e**
si er**a** alz**ato/a**	si er**ano** alz**ati/e**
Quando **è suonata** la sveglia, Nicole e Mark **si erano** già **alzati**. (*When the alarm rang, Nicole and Mark had already gotten up.*)	

What kinds of things had you, your parents, your cousins, and other family members done by the time you were all grown up? And what kinds of things hadn't you done? Well, I give you my answers to these questions, up to the age of 30, in the following practice problems. Conjugate the verbs in parentheses into the past perfect tense, using the necessary helping verbs and adverbs (which I provide along with the verbs). Follow my example:

Q. A 30 anni, mia madre _____ tre bambini. (avere, già)

A. A 30 anni, mia madre **aveva già avuto** tre bambini. (*At the age of 30, my mom had already had three children.*)

1. A 30 anni, mio padre _____ per 14 anni. (lavorare, già)

2. A 30 anni, John non _____ Laurie. (conoscere, ancora)

3. A 30 anni, io _____ tre volte. (innamorarsi, già)

4. A 30 anni, mia sorella Anna Maria _____. (sposarsi, già)

5. A 30 anni, io non _____. (sposarsi, ancora)

6. A 30 anni, la mia amica Tommasina _____ la tesi. (scrivere, già)

7. A 30 anni, io _____ in Turchia. (andare, già)

8. A 30 anni, Giancarlo non _____ una sigaretta. (fumare, mai)

9. A 30 anni, i miei genitori _____ tre figli. (avere, già)

10. A 30 anni, non _____ in Spagna. (stare, ancora [noi])

You've gotten home about an hour too late! For this exercise, name some events that have already taken place by conjugating the verbs in parentheses into the past perfect tense (incorporating the proper adverbs when necessary). Follow the example:

Q. Quando sono arrivata a casa, la babysitter _____! (andare via)

A. Quando sono arrivata a casa, la babysitter **era andata via!** (*When I got home, the babysitter had left!*)

11. Quando sono arrivata a casa, Patrizia e Paul _____. (mangiare)

12. Quando sono arrivata a casa, mio marito _____. (telefonare)

13. Quando sono arrivata a casa, Emilia _____. (lavarsi)

14. Quando sono arrivata a casa, Vittoria e Carolina _____. (uscire)

15. Quando sono arrivata a casa, tutti _____. (andare a letto)

For this exercise, translate the following sentences from Italian to English. The sentences talk about the many reasons why one may not do something. The construction doesn't have to be as depressing as my example and exercise sentences, though. After all, you can say you had never had such a good time learning new things before this book!

Q. Non ti ho salutato perchè non ti avevo visto.

A. *I didn't say hi to you because I hadn't seen you.*

16. Non ti ho salutato perchè non ti avevo riconosciuto.

_____

17. Non ti ho salutato perchè non ti avevo sentito.

_____

18. Teresa non ha sposato Fabio perchè non lo aveva mai amato.

_____

19. Teresa non ha sposato Fabio perchè lei non aveva mai creduto al matrimonio.

_____

20. Teresa e Fabio non si sono sposati perchè non avevano mai avuto bambini.

_____

21. Non potevamo venire perchè il treno era già partito.

_____

22. Non eravamo ancora andati a letto, quando abbiamo sentito piangere la bambina.

_____

23. Ti ho chiesto di ripetere perchè non avevo capito la prima volta!

_____

The past perfect tense pops up very often in literature and in narratives describing past events. At times, the tense alternates with the imperfect tense (see Chapter 8) and the passato prossimo (present perfect; see Chapter 14). The following little story, for example, talks about two sweethearts, Giancarlo and Ines. Translate their story into English, paying attention to your trapassato prossimo (the imperfect of **essere** or **avere** + the past participle). Here's an example to start with:

Q. Giancarlo ed Ines si erano conosciuti tramite gli amici Laura e Gigio.

A. _Giancarlo and Ines had met through their friends Laura and Gigio._

24. Avevano parlato a lungo di politica.

_____

25. Ines aveva raccontato a Giancarlo della sua tesi di laurea.

_____

26. Avevano capito di avere molte cose in comune.

_____

27. Erano usciti insieme, e qualche settimana dopo si erano fidanzati.

_____

28. Erano andati a vivere insieme in un appartamento in centro.

_____

Answer Key

1 A 30 anni, mio padre **aveva già lavorato** per 14 anni. (*When he was 30 years old, my dad had already worked for 14 years.*)

2 A 30 anni, John non **aveva ancora conosciuto** Laurie. (*At 30, John hadn't yet met Laurie.*)

3 A 30 anni, io **mi ero già innamorata** tre volte. (*When I was 30, I had already fallen in love three times.*)

4 A 30 anni, mia sorella Anna Maria **si era già sposata.** (*When she was 30, my sister had already married.*)

5 A 30 anni, io non **mi ero ancora sposata.** (*At 30, I hadn't yet married.*)

6 A 30 anni, la mia amica Tommasina **aveva già scritto** la tesi. (*When she was 30 years old, my friend Tommasina had already written her thesis.*)

7 A 30 anni, io **ero già andata** in Turchia. (*At 30, I had already gone to Turkey.*)

8 A 30 anni, Giancarlo non **aveva mai fumato** una sigaretta. (*When he was 30 years old, Giancarlo hadn't ever smoked a cigarette.*)

9 A 30 anni, i miei genitori **avevano già avuto** tre figli. (*At the age of 30, my parents had already had three children.*)

10 A 30 anni, non **eravamo ancora stati** in Spagna. (*When we were 30, we hadn't yet been to Spain.*)

11 Quando sono arrivata a casa, Patrizia e Paul **avevano già mangiato.** (*When I got home, Patricia and Paul had already eaten.*)

12 Quando sono arrivata a casa, mio marito **aveva telefonato.** (*When I got home, my husband had called.*)

13 Quando sono arrivata a casa, Emilia **si era lavata.** (*When I got home, Emilia had already bathed.*)

14 Quando sono arrivata a casa, Vittoria e Carolina **erano uscite.** (*When I got home, Victoria and Caroline had gone out.*)

15 Quando sono arrivata a casa, tutti **erano andati** a letto. (*When I got home, everyone had gone to bed.*)

16 I didn't say hi to you because I hadn't recognized you.

17 I didn't greet you because I hadn't heard you.

18 Teresa didn't marry Fabio because she had never loved him.

19 Teresa didn't marry Fabio because she had never believed in marriage.

20 Teresa and Fabio didn't get married because they had never had children.

21 We couldn't come because the train had already left.

22 We hadn't yet gone to bed when we heard the baby cry.

23 *I asked you to repeat because I hadn't understood the first time!*

24 *They had spoken for a long time about politics.*

25 *Ines had told Giancarlo about her thesis.*

26 *They had understood that they had many things in common.*

27 *They had gone out together, and after a few weeks had gotten engaged.*

28 *They had gone to live together in an apartment in the center of town.*

Chapter 19

I Hope That You've Had Fun! The Past Subjunctive

In This Chapter
▶ Putting together the past subjunctive
▶ Discussing emotions, opinions, and doubts in the past subjunctive

*T*he subjunctive mood expresses *doubt, uncertainty, opinion, emotion* — all the things required for "subjective" thoughts (you know, things like, "I'm happy that you love Italian food," "I don't think that pasta is sitting too well," or "I think this book is great!"). I first introduce you to the subjunctive mood in Chapter 12, where I cover the mood in the present tense. However, there are times when you want or need to express doubt or uncertainty in the past tense, which is the job of the past subjunctive (for example, "It's probable that I loved Italian food before I ate that pasta and read this book"). In this chapter, I provide you with some stellar past subjunctive conjugation explanations, introduce you to the various uses of the tense, and present plenty of practice opportunities. Enjoy!

Forming the Past Subjunctive (Congiuntivo Passato)

If you have a handle on using the present subjunctive tense (see Chapter 12), you should find the past subjunctive to be a breeze. You follow the same format, except you express doubt, uncertainty, and so on about an action that occurred in the *past*.

The past subjunctive (or congiuntivo passato) is a compound tense. In most cases, you form the past subjunctive with the following parts:

> main clause + che (*that*) + present subjunctive of **avere** (*to have*) or **essere** (*to be*) + past participle

See Chapters 14 and 15 for the criteria on determining which verbs take **essere** and which verbs take **avere,** and also to find out how to form the past participle, or participio passato.

Just like with the present subjunctive, the past subjunctive appears in the dependent clause, usually introduced by "che". The verb in the main clause needs to be one of the verbs I list in Chapter 12 that denotes uncertainty, emotion, and so on.

> **Present subjunctive: Dubito** che loro **vengano.** (*I doubt that they're coming.*)
>
> **Past subjunctive: Dubito** che loro **siano venuti.** (*I doubt that they came.*)

You use the past subjunctive when the action in the dependent clause (the verb in the past subjunctive) happened before the action in the main clause. The verb in the main clause appears in the present tense (generally) or in the future or imperative tense (less frequently).

The following tables show three examples of the past subjunctive: a transitive verb (one that takes **avere;** see Chapter 14); an intransitive verb (one that takes **essere;** see Chapter 14); and a reflexive verb (which takes **essere;** see Chapter 15), respectively.

mangiare (to eat)	
che io **abbia** mang**iato**	che noi **abbiamo** mang**iato**
che tu **abbia** mang**iato**	che voi **abbiate** mang**iato**
che lui, lei, Lei **abbia** mang**iato**	che loro **abbiano** mang**iato**
Siamo contenti che **abbiate mangiato** bene! (*We're pleased that you ate well!*)	

arrivare (to arrive)	
che io **sia** arriv**ato/a**	che noi **siamo** arriv**ati/e**
che tu **sia** arriv**ato/a**	che voi **siate** arriv**ati/e**
che lui, lei, Lei **sia** arriv**ato/a**	che loro **siano** arriv**ati/e**
Benchè io **sia arrivata** in ritardo, **c'è** ancora da mangiare. (*Even though I arrived late, there's still some food left.*)	

vestirsi (to get dressed)	
che io mi **sia** vest**ito/a**	che noi ci **siamo** vest**iti/e**
che tu ti **sia** vest**ito/a**	che voi vi **siate** vest**iti/e**
che lui, lei, Lei si **sia** vest**ito/a**	che loro si **siano** vest**iti/e**
Come **si è vestito** Rudi per la festa? Non **so** come **si sia vestito**. (*How did Rudi dress for the party? I don't know what he wore.*)	

Conjugate the following verbs in parentheses into the past subjunctive, like I do in the example that follows:

Q. Sembra che _____. (partire [loro])

A. Sembra che **siano partiti.** (*It seems like they've left.*)

1. Sembra che la mamma _____ del freddo a Torino. (lamentarsi)

2. Sembra che voi _____ tardi. (alzarsi)

3. Non so se loro _____ a Napoli. (stare [mai])

4. Credo che _____ soltanto Capri ed Ischia. (visitare [loro])

5. È probabile che Emilia _____ queste parole a scuola. (imparare)

6. Cosa credi che _____? (succedere)

7. Mi dispiace che _____. (litigare [voi])

8. Mi dispiace che voi _____. (lasciarsi)

9. È bene che io finalmente _____. (capire)

10. Non mi pare che tu _____ così. (dire)

11. Non mi pare che tu _____ così. (fare)

12. Adriana e Rudi non sanno che io _____, vero? (arrivare)

13. Adriana e Rudi non sanno che io _____, vero? (telefonare)

14. È importante che Guglielmo _____ tanto. (impegnarsi)

15. Temo che gli avvocati _____ un errore. (commettere)

For this exercise, I ask questions in Italian by using the present perfect tense (see Chapters 14 and 15), and you answer in Italian by conjugating the verbs in parentheses into the past subjunctive. I lead you off with an example.

The adverbs of time — "già" (*already*), "mai" (*never, ever*), and "ancora" (*still, yet*) go between the auxiliary verb and the past participle. (For more on these adverbs of time, see Chapter 14.) Use these adverbs only where I specify in each problem.

0. Sono già partiti i tuoi? Sì, credo che _____. (partire [già])

A. Sì, credo che **siano già partiti.** (*Have your parents left already? Yes, I think they've already left.*)

16. Giancarlo ha preso i biglietti per il viaggio? No, non penso che _____ i biglietti. (prendere [ancora])

17. Anna e John hanno mai mangiato al Rustichello? No, non credo che _____ al Rustichello. (mangiare [mai])

18. Sono partiti tutti i treni? Sembra che _____. (partire)

19. Sono partite tutte le bambine? Sembra che _____. (partire)

20. A che ora si è svegliata Emilia? Dubito che _____ presto. (svegliarsi)

21. Ha nevicato? No, non credo che _____. (nevicare)

22. Sono tornati a casa i ragazzi? Sì, è bene che _____ perchè nevica forte. (tornare)

23. Cosa ha detto Rudi? Non so che cosa _____. (dire)

24. Cosa è successo alla fine tra Gianni e Marinella? Penso che _____. (sposarsi)

25. Quali città hanno visitato? L'unica città che _____ è Roma. (visitare [loro])

For this exercise, translate the following Italian sentences that feature the past subjunctive into English. Here's an example to get you started:

Q. Non so cosa sia successo.

A. *I don't know what happened.*

26. È importante che siano venuti alla festa.

_____

27. Mi auguro che tu abbia fatto il letto.

_____

28. Siete contenti che io abbia vinto?

_____

29. Temo che Mario abbia mangiato troppo!

_____

30. Anna e Robert pensano che Giancarlo abbia perso l'aereo!

_____

31. Benchè abbiano litigato molto, stanno ancora insieme.

_____

32. È bene che io abbia imparato a nuotare.

_____

33. Peccato che Fabio sia già partito.

_____

34. Lucy e Jenny credono che tu abbia fatto quella telefonata?

_____

35. Sebbene io abbia mangiato una pizza intera, ho ancora fame.

_____

36. Laurie è la donna più intelligente che io abbia mai conosciuto.

_____

37. Speriamo che vi siate divertiti!

_____

38. La madre è felice che i suoi figli siano tornati a casa.

_____

39. Si dice che lui abbia assunto la moglie per il lavoro.

_____

40. È importante che Patty e Janet si siano trasferite in Italia con la loro zia Virginia.

_____

Answer Key

1 Sembra che la mamma **si sia lamentata** del freddo a Torino. (*It looks like mom complained about the cold in Torino.*)

2 Sembra che voi **vi siate alzati** tardi. (*It seems like you* (pl.) *got up late.*)

3 Non so se loro **siano mai stati** a Napoli. (*I don't know if they've ever been to Naples.*)

4 Credo che **abbiano visitato** soltanto Capri ed Ischia. (*I believe that they've only visited Capri and Ischia.*)

5 È probabile che Emilia **abbia imparato** queste parole a scuola. (*It's likely that Emilia learned these words at school.*)

6 Cosa credi che **sia successo?** (*What do you think happened?*)

7 Mi dispiace che **abbiate litigato.** (*I'm sorry that you* (pl.) *argued.*)

8 Mi dispiace che voi **vi siate lasciati.** (*I'm sorry that you left each other.*)

9 È bene che io finalmente **abbia capito.** (*It's a good thing that I finally understood.*)

10 Non mi pare che tu **abbia detto** così. (*It doesn't seem to me that you said so.*)

11 Non mi pare che tu **abbia fatto** così. (*It doesn't seem to me that you did that.*)

12 Adriana e Rudi non sanno che io **sia arrivata,** vero? (*Adriana and Rudi don't know that I've arrived, right?*)

13 Adriana e Rudi non sanno che io **abbia telefonato,** vero? (*Adriana and Rudi don't know that I phoned, right?*)

14 È importante che Guglielmo **si sia impegnato** tanto. (*It's important that Will worked so hard.*)

15 Temo che gli avvocati **abbiano commesso** un errore. (*I fear that the lawyers made an error.*)

16 No, non penso che **abbia ancora preso** i biglietti. (*No, I don't think that he's gotten the tickets yet.*)

17 No, non credo che **abbiano mai mangiato** al Rustichello. (*No, I don't think that they've ever eaten at the Rustichello.*)

18 Sembra che **siano partiti.** (*It looks like they've left.*)

19 Sembra che **siano partite.** (*It looks like they've left.*)

20 Dubito che **si sia svegliata** presto. (*I doubt that she woke up early.*)

21 No, non credo che **abbia nevicato.** (*No, I don't believe that it snowed.*)

22 Sì, è bene che **siano tornati** perchè nevica forte. (*Yes, it's a good thing that they came back because it's snowing hard.*)

23 Non so che cosa **abbia detto.** (*I don't know what he said.*)

24 Penso che **si siano sposati.** (*I think that they got married.*)

25 L'unica città che **abbiano visitato** è Roma. (*The only city that they visited is Rome.*)

26 *It's important that they came to the party.*

27 *I hope that you made the bed.*

28 *Are you happy that I won?*

29 *I'm worried that Mario ate too much!*

30 *Anna and Robert think that Giancarlo missed the plane.*

31 *Even though they fought a lot, they're still together.*

32 *It's a good thing I learned how to swim.*

33 *Too bad that Fabio has already left.*

34 *Do Lucy and Jenny think that you made that call?*

35 *Even though I ate a whole pizza, I'm still hungry.*

36 *Laurie is the smartest woman I've ever met.*

37 *We hope that you've had a good time!*

38 *The mother is happy that her children have returned home.*

39 *They say that he hired his own wife for the job.*

40 *It's important that Patty and Janet moved to Italy with their Aunt Virginia.*

Chapter 20

Wrapping Up the Subjunctive with the Past Perfect

The time has come to close out the subjunctive saga with the past perfect subjunctive tense (which, for the rest of the chapter, I'll refer to as the shorter, more common trapassato congiuntivo, or trapassato). There are four subjunctive tenses in Italian, and this is the last one. It's different from the other subjunctive tenses because it refers to a specific time and generally translates as *had eaten* or *had jumped*. But like the other three tenses in the subjunctive (the present subjunctive from Chapter 12, the imperfect subjunctive from Chapter 13, and the past subjunctive from Chapter 19), the trapassato is most often used in subordinate clauses, introduced by the conjunction "che" (*that*), along with all of those verbs and expressions that require the subjunctive (which you can review in Chapter 12); verbs that imply uncertainty and indeterminacy; as well as many impersonal expressions.

In this chapter, I show you how to form the trapassato and when to use it. I provide you with a handy refresher on how to form sentences by using all four subjunctive tenses. And, of course, I provide you with fascinating and informative practice exercises along the way.

Forming the Past Perfect Subjunctive (Trapassato)

The trapassato is a compound tense that you form by combining "che" (*that*) + the imperfect subjunctive (see Chapter 13) of **avere** (*to have*) or **essere** (*to be*) + the past participle of the verb in question. If you guessed that from the start, congratulations! You may have guessed it because you form the trapassato just like you form the other compound tenses in this part of the book. At the risk of repeating myself, you can find the distinctions between using **essere** and **avere** in compound tenses, plus how to form the past participle, in Chapter 14 (and in 15 for the reflexive verbs).

The following tables give you three examples: a transitive verb (one that takes **avere**; see Chapter 14), an intransitive verb (one that takes **essere**), and a reflexive verb (which takes **essere**; see Chapter 15) in the trapassato, respectively.

mangiare (*to eat*)	
che io **avessi** mangi**ato**	che noi **avessimo** mangi**ato**
che tu **avessi** mangi**ato**	che voi **aveste** mangi**ato**
che lui, lei, Lei **avesse** mangi**ato**	che loro **avessero** mangi**ato**
Scusate! Pensavo che **aveste** già **mangiato!** (*I'm sorry! I thought that you had already eaten!*)	

uscire (*to go out*)	
che io **fossi** usc**ito/a**	che noi **fossimo** usc**iti/e**
che tu **fossi** usc**ito/a**	che voi **foste** usc**iti/e**
che lui, lei, Lei **fosse** usc**ito/a**	che loro **fossero** usc**iti/e**
Tina e Gina **avrebbero voluto** che Lisa **fosse uscita** con loro. (*Tina and Gina would have liked for Lisa to go out with them.*)	

For the following reflexive verb, note that you must add the proper reflexive pronoun during conjugation (mi, ti, si, ci, vi, and si). For more on reflexive requirements, see Chapters 5 and 15.

comportarsi (*to behave*)	
che io mi **fossi** comport**ato/a**	che noi ci **fossimo** comport**ati/e**
che tu ti **fossi** comport**ato/a**	che voi vi **foste** comport**ati/e**
che lui, lei, Lei si **fosse** comport**ato/a**	che loro si **fossero** comport**ati/e**
Chi **avrebbe** mai **creduto** che Janine **si fosse comportata** in quel modo? (*Who would have ever believed that Janine would behave in that way?*)	

The trapassato usually occurs in a dependent clause, introduced most often by the word "che" (*that*). You use it to express an action that has been completed before the action in the main clause. For example,

> **Avrei preferito** che tu **ti fossi sposata** Gino. (*I would've preferred that you marry Gino.*)

The verb in the main clause must be in some specific tense:

✔ **Most frequently:** the past conditional (Chapter 17) or the past perfect (Chapter 18).

- Past conditional: **Sarebbe stato** meglio che tu non **avessi detto** nulla. (*It would've been better had you said nothing.*)

- Past perfect: Non **avevo** mai **creduto** che Paul **avesse detto** ciò ad Americo. (*I never believed that Paul said that to Americo.*)

✔ **Less frequently:** the imperfect (Chapter 8).

Mia madre **credeva** che io **fossi diventata** importante. (*My mom believed that I had become important.*)

✔ **And less frequently still:** the passato prossimo (Chapter 14).

Ci **era sembrato** che **foste** già **partiti.** (*It seemed to us that you had already left./We thought you'd already left.*)

You also use the trapassato frequently in "if" clauses (see Chapter 21). For a complete list of the verbs and expressions that require the subjunctive in the dependent clause, refer to Chapter 12.

My students always worry about knowing when to put what tense where. A good rule of thumb, at least with the trapassato, is that when you have a compound tense in the main or independent clause, you place the trapassato in the dependent clause. Of course, this rule of thumb isn't set in stone, as evidenced in the previous verb table showing the conjugation of **mangiare**: "**Pensavo** che **aveste** già **mangiato**." Practice, repetition, and context, be your guide!

For this first set of exercises, you simply conjugate the verb in parentheses. The beginning part of the sentence, or the main clause (the part before "che"), should stay the same throughout. Practice doing these problems aloud so that you begin to internalize the conjugations. Here's an example:

Q. Il cane, Toby, sarebbe stato contento che tu lo _____. (comprare)

Il cane, Toby, sarebbe stato contento che tu lo _____. (lavare)

A. Il cane, Toby, sarebbe stato contento che tu lo **avessi comprato.** (*The dog, Toby, would've been happy had you bought him.*)

Il cane, Toby, sarebbe stato contento che tu lo **avessi lavato.** (*The dog, Toby, would've been happy that you washed him.*)

1. Mia madre sarebbe stata contenta che io _____ in Connecticut. (vivere)

2. Mia madre sarebbe stata contenta che io _____ famosa. (diventare)

3. Mia madre sarebbe stata contenta che io _____ con Enzo. (sposarsi)

4. Mia madre sarebbe stata contenta che io _____ 5 figli. (avere)

5. Mia madre sarebbe stata contenta che io _____ felice. (essere)

6. Eravamo arrabbiati che tu _____. (già partire)

7. Eravamo arrabbiati che tu ci _____ quello. (dire)

8. Eravamo arrabbiati che tu _____ le chiavi. (perdere)

9. Eravamo arrabbiati che tu _____ di Julia. (innamorarsi)

10. Eravamo arrabbiati che tu _____ la casa in Italia. (vendere)

11. Avevo sperato che Gina e Gino _____ insieme. (rimanere)

12. Avevo sperato che Gina e Gino _____. (venire a trovarmi)

13. Avevo sperato che Gina e Gino _____ la casa. (prendere)

14. Avevo sperato che Gina e Gino _____ del problema. (parlare)

15. Avevo sperato che Gina e Gino _____. (divorziare)

For this exercise, translate the following sentences containing the trapassato from Italian into English. Here's an example:

0. I miei genitori avrebbero pensato che io avessi sbagliato.

A. *My parents would've thought that I made a mistake.*

16. Benchè avessimo studiato tutta la notte, abbiamo fatto male all'esame.

_____

17. Giancarlo era l'uomo più sano che io avessi mai conosciuto.

_____

18. Comunque avesse fatto Sandro, avrebbe fatto bene.

_____

19. Non c'era nessuno che mi avesse potuto aiutare.

_____

20. Era bene che Domenico e Salvatore avessero venduto la pasticceria.

_____

Sequencing Your Tenses in the Subjunctive

The best way to end this chapter on the trapassato (past perfect subjunctive) is to look at the tense in comparison with the other three subjunctive tenses: the present subjunctive (Chapter 12), the imperfect subjunctive (Chapter 13), and the past subjunctive (Chapter 19). Each tense follows a certain sequence when forming the subjunctive. For example, you can use the imperfect subjunctive **only** when the verb in the main clause is in either the conditional, conditional perfect, imperfect, or past perfect.

Table 20-1 presents all the different variations to keep in mind while you're in the subjunctive mood.

Table 20-1	Sequencing the Subjunctive
Main Clause + che	*Dependent Clause*
Present	Present subjunctive or past subjunctive
Future	Present subjunctive or past subjunctive
Imperative	Present subjunctive or past subjunctive
Conditional	Imperfect subjunctive or trapassato congiuntivo
Conditional perfect	Imperfect subjunctive or trapassato congiuntivo
Imperfect	Imperfect subjunctive or trapassato congiuntivo
Passato prossimo (present perfect)	Imperfect subjunctive or trapassato congiuntivo
Trapassato imperfetto (past perfect)	Imperfect subjunctive or trapassato congiuntivo
Passato remoto (past absolute)	Imperfect subjunctive or trapassato congiuntivo

The following two examples provide the present in the main clause and, respectively, the present subjunctive and the past subjunctive in the subordinate clause.

Non **so** dove **sia** Pietro. (*I don't know where Pietro is.*)

Non **so** dove **sia andato** Pietro. (*I don't know where Pietro went.*)

The following exercise allows you to bring together most of the subjunctive tenses. Conjugate each verb in parentheses in the tense that I indicate and then translate. Here's an example for you:

0. Pare che Compare e Comare _____ a cena. (venire [present subjunctive])

A. Pare che Compare e Comare **vengano** a cena. *It looks like Godfather and Godmother are coming to dinner.*

21. Non sapevamo cosa _____. (succedere [imperfect subjunctive])

_____

22. Penso che loro _____. (perdere [past subjunctive])

_____

23. Janine avrebbe voluto che Tony _____ a trovarla (to visit her). (andare [imperfect subjunctive])

_____

24. Sono contenta che tu _____ qui con me. (essere [present subjunctive])

_____

25. Sarebbe meglio che noi _____ il viaggio a giugno. (fare [imperfect subjunctive])

_____

26. I miei genitori sarebbero stati felici che mio fratello _____. (laurearsi [trapassato congiuntivo])

_____

27. Non c'è nessuno che _____ la strada? (conoscere [present subjunctive])

_____

28. Fai bene comunque tu _____. (fare [present subjunctive])

_____

29. Credevano che tu _____! (sparire [trapassato congiuntivo])

_____

30. Non sapevamo chi _____ le elezioni. (vincere [trapassato congiuntivo])

_____

Answer Key

1 Mia madre sarebbe stata contenta che io **avessi vissuto** in Connecticut. (*My mother would have been happy if I had lived in Connecticut.*)

2 Mia madre sarebbe stata contenta che io **fossi diventata** famosa. (*My mother would have been happy if I had become famous.*)

3 Mia madre sarebbe stata contenta che io **mi fossi sposata** con Enzo. (*My mother would have been happy if I had married Enzo.*)

4 Mia madre sarebbe stata contenta che io **avessi avuto** 5 figli. (*My mother would have been happy if I had had 5 children.*)

5 Mia madre sarebbe stata contenta che io **fossi stata** felice. (*My mother would have been happy if I had been happy.*)

6 Eravamo arrabbiati che tu **fossi già partito.** (*We were angry that you had already left.*)

7 Eravamo arrabbiati che tu ci **avessi detto** quello. (*We were angry that you had told us that.*)

8 Eravamo arrabbiati che tu **avessi perso** le chiavi. (*We were angry that you had lost the keys.*)

9 Eravamo arrabbiati che tu **ti fossi innamorato** di Julia. (*We were angry that you'd fallen in love with Julia.*)

10 Eravamo arrabbiati che tu **avessi venduto** la casa in Italia. (*We were angry that you'd sold the house in Italy.*)

11 Avevo sperato che Gina e Gino **fossero rimasti** insieme. (*I had hoped that Gina and Gino would have stayed together.*)

12 Avevo sperato che Gina e Gino **fossero venuti** a **trovarmi.** (*I had hoped that Gina and Gino would have come to visit me.*)

13 Avevo sperato che Gina e Gino **avessero preso** la casa. (*I had hoped that Gina and Gino would have taken the house.*)

14 Avevo sperato che Gina e Gino **avessero parlato** del problema. (*I had hoped that Gina and Gino would have spoken about the problem.*)

15 Avevo sperato che Gina e Gino **avessero divorziato.** (*I had hoped that Gina and Gino would have divorced.*)

16 *Even though we had studied all night, we did poorly on the exam.*

17 *Giancarlo was the sanest man I had ever met.*

18 *However Sandro would have done it, he would have done it well.*

19 *There was no one who could've helped me.*

20 *It was a good thing that Domenico and Salvatore had sold the bakery.*

21 Non sapevamo cosa **succedesse.** *We didn't know what was happening.*

22 Penso che loro **abbiano perso.** *I think that they lost.*

23 Janine avrebbe voluto che Tony **andasse** a trovarla. *Janine would've liked for Tony to visit her.*

24 Sono contenta che tu **sia** qui con me. *I'm happy you're here with me.*

25 Sarebbe meglio che noi **facessimo** il viaggio a giugno. *It would be better for us to take the trip in June.*

26 I miei genitori sarebbero stati felici che mio fratello **si fosse laureato.** *My parents would have been happy that my brother graduated.*

27 Non c'è nessuno che **conosca** la strada? *Isn't there anybody who knows the way?*

28 Fai bene comunque tu **faccia.** *You do well at whatever you do.*

29 Credevano che tu **fossi sparito!** *They thought you had disappeared!*

30 Non sapevamo chi **avesse vinto** le elezioni. *We didn't know who had won the elections.*

Part IV

Reviewing a Few Underappreciated Tenses and Forms

The 5th Wave   By Rich Tennant

It's amazing what happens when you learn a little of their language.

In this part . . .

Here, I bring together some of the most commonly used, yet underappreciated tenses and forms in Italian. Here, you discover hypothetical constructions throughout most of the tenses, with which you can form an "if" or "as if" clause. Similarly, I walk you through the impersonal si, which appears in all the tenses I've thus far presented. Finally, I present the gerunds and the progressive forms that you use with the gerunds.

Chapter 21

Hypothetically Speaking: "If" Clauses Throughout the Tenses

. . . .

In This Chapter
▶ Exploring the conditional realm of reality
▶ Looking into the hypothetical world of probability and possibility
▶ Discussing the impossible
▶ Setting apart "as if" statements

. . . .

*H*ypothetical sentences, in Italian known as *frasi ipotetiche con se,* translate into English as "If . . ." sentences. They cover a wide range of speech and include many of the tenses I cover in this book. Hypothetical constructions always have two parts: a dependent clause introduced by the word "se" (*if*), and the main or independent clause that refers to the result of whatever you postulate or hypothesize in the "if" clause. The verb tenses you use in both clauses depend on the type of hypothetical sentence you want to construct.

Italian features three types of hypothetical constructions: expressions of reality, probability, and impossibility. Each type uses specific verb tenses. And guess what? I cover all three in this chapter. I also cover the phrase "as if" and give you some exercises that bring together all the concepts in the chapter. (I'll keep referring to the tenses at hand so you can reference them in other chapters as you do the exercises in this chapter.)

Expressing Conditions within the Realm of Reality

The first type of hypothetical construction lies within the realm of fact, reality, or actuality. If I say, for example, "Se **mangio** il gelato, **ingrasso**" (*If I eat ice cream, I gain weight*), I express a fact or a reality in my life. Notice that I used the present tense in both the dependent clause (**mangio**) and independent clause (**ingrasso**). I gain weight if I eat ice cream — period! As in English, the order of your clauses doesn't matter; you can also say, "**Ingrasso** se **mangio** il gelato" (*I gain weight if I eat ice cream*). What matters is that you attach the word "se" to the dependent clause (the "if" statement that implies the condition, not the result).

The verb tenses that you use for the fact/reality hypothetical construction are precisely those tenses that allow you to speak with certainty, as I outline in Table 21-1.

Table 21-1	Hypothetical Constructions in Reality	
Se + Dependent Clause	*Independent Clause*	*Example*
Present indicative* (Chapters 2 and 3)	Present indicative*	Se **studi**, **impari**. (*If you study, you learn.*)
Present reflexive (Chapter 5)	Present	Se **ti alzi** presto domani, **ti porto** a scuola. (*If you get up early tomorrow, I'll bring you to school.*)
Present indicative*	Imperative (Chapter 6)	Se **hai** fame, **mangia**! (*If you're hungry, eat!*)
Present indicative*	Future	Se **ti innamori**, te ne **pentirai**.**(*If you fall in love, you will regret it.*)
Future (Chapter 10)	Future	Se **arriveranno** a luglio, **potremo andare** in Sardegna insieme. (*If they arrive in July, we can go to Sardegna together.*)
Present perfect (Chapter 14)	Present indicative*	Se Maria **ha telefonato**, significa che **ha** notizie. (*If Maria called, it means that she has news.*)
Present perfect	Present perfect	Se **hai studiato**, perchè non **hai passato** l'esame? (*If you studied, why did you fail the exam?*)
Imperfect (Chapter 8)	Imperfect	Se **avevamo** sete, **prendevamo** un'aranciata. (*If we were thirsty, we would get an orange soda.*)
Imperfect	Present perfect	Se Maria **voleva venire** alla festa, perchè non **è venuta**? (*If Maria wanted to come to the party, why didn't she come?*)

*Present indicative listings also include reflexive verbs
Both of these verbs are reflexive: **innamorarsi and **pentirsi**

All the examples in Table 21-1 denote, in some way or another, the certainty of something that's happening, that happened, didn't happen, or that will happen. You see no doubt implied in any of the examples.

You don't always combine the verb tenses from the dependent clause in the left column in Table 21-1 with the verb tenses directly opposite them in the right-hand column denoting the main (independent) clause. You can mix and match your possibilities of hypothetical constructions in the realm of reality, as I do in the following example list. It all depends on what you want to say!

✔ **Present perfect + future:** Se **hai fatto** tutto, non **dovrai preoccuparti**. (*If you've done everything, you'll not have to worry.*)

✔ **Present indicative + imperative:** Se **vuole sedersi, si sieda!** (*If you wish to sit, do sit down!*)

For the following exercise, conjugate the verbs in parentheses with respect to the requested verb tenses and persons in order to form hypothetical constructions in the realistic sense. Here's an example to get you started:

Q. Se _____ stanca, dormo. (essere [io, present])

A. Se **sono** stanca, dormo. (*If I'm tired, I sleep.*)

1. Mangio, se _____ fame. (avere [present])

2. Se hai freddo, _____! (coprirsi [tu, imperative])

3. Se _____ tempo, ci fermiamo a Roma per due settimane. (avere [noi, present])

4. Se _____ l'amore, avete tutto! (avere [voi, present])

5. Se lo _____, diglielo! (amare [tu, present])

6. Se nevicherà tanto, _____ a sciare! (andare [noi, future])

7. Se la mamma viene stasera, _____ al ristorante. (mangiare [noi, present])

8. Se _____ fretta, perchè non sei partito prima? (avere [tu, imperfect])

9. Se il babbo ha detto così, allora _____ vero. (essere [lui, lei, Lei; present])

10. Se non _____ alla festa, andiamo via subito! (divertirsi [noi, present])

11. Se lavoro, _____ i soldi. (guadagnare [io, present])

12. Se avete caldo, _____ l'aria condizionata! (accendere [voi, imperative])

13. Se devi domire allora non _____. (uscire [tu, imperative])

14. Se Claudio non voleva sposarsi perchè _____? (sposarsi [lui, present perfect])

15. Se andrò in Italia, _____ le Dolomiti. (visitare [io, future])

Examining Hypothetical Constructions of Probability (And Possibility)

The hypothetical condition of probability and possibility implies that an action is conditional. In other words, a sentence always translates into, roughly, "If such and such were to happen, this and that would happen." Probability constructions are much more straightforward and simple than reality constructions (see the previous section). They usually require two different tenses: the imperfect subjunctive (see Chapter 13) and the conditional (see Chapter 11):

se + imperfect subjunctive (congiuntivo imperfetto) + present conditional (il condizionale)

Se io **studiassi** [imperfect subjunctive], **farei** [present conditional] bene. (*If I were to study [If I studied], I would do well.*)

You can also reverse the order of the clauses, placing the independent first — it doesn't matter as long as the imperfect subjunctive is in the dependent or subordinate clause:

Uscirei [present conditional] se non **dovessi studiare** [imperfect subjunctive] questi verbi! (*I'd go out if I didn't have to study these verbs!*)

You may also use a second, less-common verb tense combination for probability constructions. This comes in handy when you wish to express a regret, after the fact. You're speaking from a present standpoint about the past (even though you use the imperfect subjunctive). For example, *If I were smart, I would have studied yesterday instead of going dancing* (Se io **fossi** intelligente, **avrei studiato** ieri invece di **andare** a **ballare**). Here's the structure:

se + imperfect subjunctive (congiuntivo imperfetto) + conditional perfect (condizionale passato)

Se io **fossi** in te, **sarei rimasta** a Tucson. (*If I were you, I would have stayed in Tucson.*)

I know of so many things I would do if I could, so I've gone ahead and made an exercise of them! In this exercise, I provide you with one part of the sentence (the "if" clause), and you complete the sentence by conjugating the verbs in parentheses into the conditional. Follow this up with a translation. Here's an example:

Q. Se io fossi te, non lo _____! (fare [io])

A. Se io fossi te, non lo **farei!** *If I were you, I wouldn't do it!*

16. Se io fossi il presidente degli Stati Uniti, _____ i poveri. (aiutare)

_____

17. Se io fossi bella, _____ felice. (essere)

_____

18. Se io mangiassi di meno, _____. (dimagrire)

_____

19. Se io andassi in Italia, _____ la Costa Amalfitana. (visitare)

_____

20. Se potessi comprare una casa nuova, la _____ in Puglia. (comprare)

_____

Help me with this next set of hypothetical constructions by conjugating the verbs in parentheses into the imperfect subjunctive; I'll give you the conditional. After you finish, translate your sentence. Here's an example to get you started:

Q. Se la mamma _____ più tempo, farebbe più cose. (avere)

A. Se la mamma **avesse** più tempo, farebbe più cose. *If Mom had more time, she would do more things.*

21. Se tu _____, faresti meglio! (studiare)

_____

22. Se i miei genitori _____ di più, noi tutti saremmo felici! (viaggiare)

_____

23. Se Claudio _____, sua mamma non sarebbe contenta! (sposarsi)

_____

24. Se io e te _____ più tempo insieme, potremmo fare tante cose. (passare)

_____

25. Se io _____ zitta, non avrei tutti questi problemi! (stare)

_____

Now that you can construct hypothetical probabilities, you should have some fun. Go online and read Cecco Angiolieri's 13th century poem "S'i fossi foco" (*If I were fire*). You can be proud of yourself for being able to read it and understand! (Try www. filosofico.net/poesiacecco8732135.htm.)

What-iffing the Impossible

The hypothetical construction that denotes impossibility suggests that whatever action you would've done in the past is no longer possible now, no matter your desires. I can demonstrate this by saying, for example, "Se io **avessi saputo** che **venivi, avrei fatto** una bistecca in più" (*If I had known you were coming, I would've made an extra steak*). In other words, it's now too late for me to have made the extra steak while I was cooking. Nothing keeps me from making a steak now, of course, but if I want to convey that, I don't need an *if* clause!

As you can see from the previous example, the hypothetical construction denoting impossibility is composed of two compound tenses. You form it by rendering the structure of the construction of probability into the past: the past perfect subjunctive (trapassato congiuntivo; see Chapter 20) and the past conditional (condizionale passato; see Chapter 17).

> se + past perfect subjunctive (trapassato congiuntivo) + past conditional (condizionale passato)
>
> Se Toby **avesse imparato** [present perfect subjunctive] ad obbederci, non **sarebbe** mai **scappato** [conditional perfect]. (*If Toby had learned to obey us, he would never have run away.*)

Alternatively, but less common, you may have the following structure. These come in handy with recriminations. For example, *If you hadn't spent all of your money having a good time, you would not find yourself in this situation now.* (Se tu non **avessi speso** tutti i tuoi soldi a **divertirti**, non **ti troveresti** ora in questa situazione.)

> se + present perfect subjunctive + conditional
>
> Se **mi avessi ascoltato** [present perfect subjunctive], non **saresti** [conditional] in questi guai ora. (*If you had listened to me, you wouldn't be in this trouble now.*)

Se **avessi sposato** [present perfect subjunctive] Enzo, ora **abiterei** [conditional] a Cortona. (*If I had married Enzo, I'd be living in Cortona now.*)

College life seems to be filled with "what ifs," don't you think? Transform the following hypothetical sentences of possibility into hypothetical sentences of impossibility by rewriting the imperfect subjunctive into the present perfect subjunctive and the conditional into the conditional perfect. You can then try your hand at translating! Here's an example taken from my own undergrad experience:

Q. Se io mi svegliassi alle 8:00 di mattina ogni giorno, imparerei il francese.

A. Se io **mi fossi svegliata** alle 8:00 di mattina ogni giorno, **avrei imparato** il francese. *If I had woken up at 8:00 every morning, I would've learned French.*

26. Se io studiassi a Firenze, imparerei l'italiano.

_____

_____

27. Se Lisa non perdesse tanto tempo a divertirsi, finirebbe l'università in 4 anni.

_____

_____

28. Se Doug non bevesse tanto, potrebbe laurearsi!

_____

_____

29. Se tu spendessi meno soldi, andresti in Messico per la vacanza di primavera.

_____

_____

30. Se i miei genitori non mi venissero a trovare a Barcellona, sarei triste.

_____

_____

Come Se: In a Category of Its Own

The phrase "come se" means *as if,* and it works somewhat differently than the other hypothetical constructions you see in previous sections in this chapter.

The imperfect subjunctive (imperfetto congiuntivo) and the present perfect subjunctive (trapassato congiuntivo) always follow the expression "come se," regardless of the tense in the main clause. Here's the structure:

> any tense that makes sense + come se + imperfect subjunctive or present perfect subjunctive

Here are a couple of examples:

Lui **tratta** la moglie come se **fosse** una bambina. (*He treats his wife as if she were a child.*)

Mi sono comportata come se non **fosse successo** niente. (*I acted as if nothing had happened.*)

Translate the following "come se" (*as if*) sentences into Italian, following the structure I present earlier in this section. Follow my cue:

Q. She eats as if she has never eaten before!

A. (Lei) **Mangia** come se non **avesse** mai **mangiato!**

31. Mom, why are you speaking with Teresa as if she were deaf (sorda)?

_____

32. You treated me as if I were an idiot!

_____

33. Everyone was looking at us as if we had done something strange.

_____

34. He acts as if he were the boss (padrone).

_____

35. We will continue with our lives as if nothing has happened.

_____

Putting It All Together

A good way to master the hypothetical is to bring together all the tenses that you use for the "if" constructions.

For this final exercise, I mix up the three different kinds of hypothetical sentences: reality, probability, and impossibility. Take a look at the bolded verb that I provide for you, and conjugate the verb in parentheses into the most logical or appropriate tense. Here's an example to get you started:

Q. Se **piove**, non _____. (uscire [io])

A. Se piove, non **esco**. (*If it rains, I'm not going out.*)

36. Se lui **mi amasse**, me lo _____. (dire [lui])

37. Se **avete** i soldi, perchè non _____ in Italia per un mese? (andare [voi])

38. Se io **avessi saputo** che eri a Ravenna, noi ti _____ alla nostra festa! (invitare)

39. Se i miei studenti _____ imparare, **imparerebbero!** (volere)

40. Se noi **vogliamo avere** tanti figli, _____ cominciare subito! (dovere)

41. Se **hai** bisogno, _____ mi! (chiamare [attach your imperative to the "mi!"])

42. Se mia sorella _____ infelice, **avrebbe divorziato!** (essere)

43. Se **parlassimo** di meno e **ascoltassimo** di più, _____ di più! (imparare)

44. Se i miei genitori _____ in Italia ad agosto, **potremmo** portarli al castello. (venire)

45. Se io _____ a Cortona, **mi sarei sposata** Enzo. (rimanere)

Answer Key

1 Mangio, se **ho** fame. (*I eat if I'm hungry.*)

2 Se hai freddo, **copriti!** (*If you're cold, cover yourself!*)

3 Se **abbiamo** tempo, ci fermiamo a Roma per due settimane. (*If we have time, we're going to stay in Rome for two weeks.*)

4 Se **avete** l'amore, avete tutto! (*If you have love, you have everything!*)

5 Se lo **ami,** diglielo! (*If you love him, tell him!*)

6 Se nevicherà tanto, **andremo** a sciare! (*If it snows a lot, we'll go skiing!*)

7 Se la mamma viene stasera, **mangiamo** al ristorante. (*If mom comes tonight, we'll eat at the restaurant.*)

8 Se **avevi** fretta, perchè non sei partito prima? (*If you were in a hurry, why didn't you leave earlier?*)

9 Se il babbo ha detto così, allora è vero. (*If that's what daddy said, then it's true.*)

10 Se non **ci divertiamo** alla festa, andiamo via subito! (*If we don't have fun at the party, we'll leave right away!*)

11 Se lavoro, **guadagno** i soldi. (*If I work, I earn money.*)

12 Se avete caldo, **accendete** l'aria condizionata! (*If you're (pl.) hot, turn on the air conditioner!*)

13 Se devi domire, allora non **uscire.** (*If you need to sleep, don't go out.*)

14 Se Claudio non voleva sposarsi perchè **si è sposato?** (*If Claudio didn't want to get married, why did he get married?*)

15 Se andrò in Italia, **visiterò** le Dolomiti. (*If I go to Italy, I'm going to visit the Dolomites.*)

16 Se io fossi il presidente degli Stati Uniti, **aiuterei** i poveri. *If I were the president of the United States, I'd help the poor.*

17 Se io fossi bella, **sarei** felice. *If I were beautiful, I'd be happy.*

18 Se io mangiassi di meno, **dimagrirei.** *If I ate less, I'd lose weight.*

19 Se io andassi in Italia, **visiterei** la Costa Amalfitana. *If I were to go to Italy, I would visit the Amalfi Coast.*

20 Se potessi comprare una casa nuova, la **comprerei** in Puglia. *If I could buy a new house, I'd buy it in Puglia.*

21 Se tu **studiassi,** faresti meglio! *If you studied, you'd do better!*

22 Se i miei genitori **viaggiassero** di più, noi tutti saremmo felici! *If my parents were to travel more, we would all be happy!*

23 Se Claudio **si sposasse,** sua mamma non sarebbe contenta! *If Claudio were to get married, his mom wouldn't be happy!*

24 Se io e te **passassimo** più tempo insieme, potremmo fare tante cose. *If you and I spent more time together, we could do many things.*

25 Se io **stessi** zitta, non avrei tutti questi problemi! *If I stayed quiet, I wouldn't have all of these problems!*

26 Se io **avessi studiato** a Firenze, **avrei imparato** l'italiano. *If I had studied in Florence, I would've learned Italian.*

27 Se Lisa non **avesse perso** il tempo a divertirsi, **avrebbe finito** l'università in 4 anni. *If Lisa hadn't wasted time having a good time, she could've finished college in 4 years.*

28 Se Doug non **avesse bevuto** tanto, **avrebbe potuto laurearsi/si sarebbe potuto laureare!** *If Doug hadn't drunk so much, he could've graduated!*

29 Se tu **avessi speso** meno soldi, **saresti andato** in Messico per la vacanza di primavera. *If you had spent less money, you could've gone to Mexico for Spring Break.*

30 Se i miei genitori non **fossero venuti** a trovarmi a Barcellona, **sarei stata** triste. *If my parents hadn't come to visit me in Barcelona, I would've been sad.*

31 Mamma, perchè **parli** con Teresa come se **fosse** sorda?

32 **Mi hai trattato** come se io **fossi** idiota!

33 Tutti **ci guardavano** come se **avessimo fatto** qualcosa di strano.

34 Lui **si comporta** come se **fosse** il padrone.

35 Noi **continueremo** con le nostre vite come se niente **fosse successo.**

36 Se lui mi amasse, me lo **direbbe.** (*If he loved me, he would tell me.*)

37 Se avete i soldi, perchè non **andate** in Italia per un mese? (*If you have the money, why don't you go to Italy for a month?*)

38 Se io avessi saputo che eri a Ravenna, noi ti **avremmo invitato** alla nostra festa! (*If I had known you were in Ravenna, we would have invited you to our party!*)

39 Se i miei studenti **volessero imparare,** imparerebbero! (*If my students wanted to learn, they would learn!*)

40 Se noi vogliamo avere tanti figli, **dobbiamo** cominciare subito! (*If we want to have lots of children, we need to start right away!*)

41 Se hai bisogno, **chiamami!** (*If you need help, call me!*)

42 Se mia sorella **fosse stata** infelice, avrebbe divorziato! (*If my sister had been unhappy, she would have gotten a divorce!*)

43 Se parlassimo di meno e ascoltassimo di più, **impareremmo** di più! (*If we spoke less and listened more, we would learn more!*)

44 Se i miei genitori **venissero** in Italia ad agosto, potremmo portarli al castello. (*If my parents were to come to Italy in August, we could bring them to the castle.*)

45 Se io **fossi rimasta** a Cortona, mi sarei sposata Enzo. (*If I had stayed in Cortona, I would have married Enzo.*)

Chapter 22

Putting a Personal Touch on the Impersonal and the Passive

In This Chapter

▶ Concentrating on the present tense of the impersonal "you"

▶ Branching out into all other tenses

▶ Actively studying the passive voice

"Come **si forma** il si impersonale?" (*How do you form the impersonal?*) "Quando **è** usata la forma passiva?" (*When is the passive voice used?*) Did you just notice that I used the impersonal "you" (si impersonale) in the first sentence and the passive voice in the second? Bravo/Brava! (*Good job!*) These constructions *are used* (**sono usate** — another example!) all the time in everyday language, so why do I wait until the end of the book to present them? Well, one reason is that you can carry the passive construction (costruzione passiva) and the impersonal "you" across most of the tenses. So, if you've reviewed the tenses I present earlier in this book, you know what the different tenses can do and mean when I refer to them. Another reason that I wait is that both constructions allow you to review the major concepts in Italian, but with a different perspective.

In this chapter, you discover how to form and use the impersonal "you" across many tenses, and you find out how to recognize and use the passive voice when appropriate.

Forming the Impersonal in the Present

How do you form the si impersonale, and what does it mean? It translates as the *impersonal "you, we, they, people."* The form is synonymous with the less common "one" — as in, how does *one* form the si impersonale? And as you can see, the subject is indefinite. More than in American English, however, people often use the impersonal "you" in Italian to talk about their everyday activities. For example, you often hear the question, "Quando **si parte?**" (*When are we leaving?*)

Now, on to the formation. To form the si impersonale, you take the word "si" (*one/you/we/people/they*) and add either

✔ The third-person singular form of a verb (and a singular direct object, if you have one).

✔ The third-person plural form of a verb (with a plural direct object).

si + third-person singular of a verb:

Come **si dice** "hi" in Italiano? (*How do you say "hi" in Italian?*)

Cosa **si mangia** stasera? (*What are we eating tonight?*)

Si mangia la pasta (singular direct object). (*We're eating pasta.*)

si + third-person plural of a verb:

> Cosa **si mangia** stasera? **Si mangiano** gli gnocchi (plural direct object). (*What are we eating tonight? We're eating gnocchi.*)
>
> Dove **si vendono** i francobolli (plural direct object) in Italia? (*Where can you buy stamps in Italy?*)

When you have to deal with reflexive verbs and the reciprocal form (I cover both in Chapter 5), you start with the impersonal pronoun "si," but you transform it miraculously into the word "ci" (ci doesn't translate, except as the impersonal "you"). At that point, you *add* the third-person reflexive pronoun "si" and then include the third-person singular. (You can't very well have one "si" right after the other, can you?)

Here's this construction broken down and compared with a sentence in the present indicative that has a specified subject:

> ci + si + **sveglia** presto in vacanza. (*You/they get up early on vacation.*) This is the impersonal "you" without a specified subject.
>
> I ragazzi **si svegliano** presto in vacanza. (*The kids get up early on vacation.*) This is the present indicative with a specified subject (i ragazzi — *the kids*).

Here are some examples of the reflexive construction in the si impersonale:

> **Ci si alza** presto in campagna. (*They get up early in the country.*)
>
> **Ci si vede** (from the reciprocal verb **vedersi**). (*See you around.*)
>
> **Ci si diverte** in Italia; **ci si diverte** a sciare. (*People have fun in Italy; skiing is fun.*)

Put the formation rules you've just gone over into practice by rewriting the following sentences that appear in the present indicative into the singular or plural form of the impersonal "you." Don't worry about these sentences translating precisely into English: Many times they don't! However, in Italian, the phrases are very common. Here's an example to get you started:

Q. Posso entrare? (*May I come in?*)

A. **Si può entrare?** (*May I/we/you/people/one come in?*)

> *Note:* Although you don't use a similar expression in English, **si può** can also translate as *Is it possible . . .?*

1. Andiamo al cinema stasera. _____

2. Compriamo qui i cornetti caldi (a breakfast pastry)?_____

3. Come mangiate in quel ristorante?_____

4. Dove mettiamo le valige? _____

5. Parlate l'italiano qui. _____

6. Non facciamo gli sconti! _____

7. Vi divertite a parlare l'italiano! _____

8. Sentiamoci presto. _____

9. Posso pagare con la carta di credito? _____

10. Nuotano a casa di Enrico stasera._____

Applying the Impersonal in Other Tenses

Technically, you can apply the si impersonale to any verb tense — and certainly any of the tenses I cover in this book. You simply take the word "si" + the verb, be it third-person singular or plural. (The only exception to this construction is the present perfect impersonal, which I discuss in a moment.) But, for the sake of brevity, you can look at the impersonal in only a few of the more common tenses in Table 22-1.

Table 22-1		Forming the Impersonal in Common Tenses	
Tense	*Infinitive*	*Example*	*Translation*
Imperfect (Chapter 8)	**parlare** (*to speak, to talk*)	**Si parlava** spesso al telefono.	*We used to speak often on the phone.*
		Si parlavano l'inglese e l'italiano a casa.	*We used to speak English and Italian at home.*
Future (Chapter 10)	**visitare** (*to visit*)	**Si visiterà** una vetreria.	*We're going to visit a glass-blowing factory.*
		Si visiteranno le vetrerie a Murano.	*We're going to visit the glass-blowing works in Murano.*
Subjunctive (Chapter 12)	**dire** (*to say, to tell*)	Non **so** come **si dica** "earnest".	*I don't know how to say "earnest".*
		È bene che **si dicano** le regole.	*It's a good thing that they articulate the rules.*

The present perfect (see Chapter 14) is similar to the normal construction of the impersonal, but it has its own set of quirky rules.

For the present perfect, always use the verb **essere** (*to be*) as your auxiliary verb, regardless of whether you're working with an **essere** verb (intransitive and reflexive) or **avere** (transitive [*to have*]) verb. Nonetheless, you still distinguish between the transitive and intransitive verbs!

Verbs that take **essere** have the following structure:

si + past participle ending in **-i.**

Si è andati a letto presto. (*Everyone went to bed early.*) (**Andare** is an intransitive verb that takes **essere.**)

Ci si è divertiti alla festa! (*We had fun at the party!*) (**Divertirsi** is a reflexive verb that takes **essere.**)

Verbs that take **avere** have a past participle that ends in **-o,** if the sentence identifies no object. If the sentence specifies a direct object, the past participle agrees with the direct object (**-o, -a, -i, -e**):

Si è parlato del più e del meno. (*We talked about this and that.*)

Si è preparata la cena. (*The dinner was prepared.*)

Si sono comprati gli stivali a Venezia. (*Boots were bought in Venice; We/they bought boots in Venice.*)

Si sono dette delle brutte cose. (*Ugly things were said; They said ugly things.*)

You've just returned from a semester in Florence, and you want to describe the things you did there. In this exercise, transform the sentences from the present tense impersonal into the present perfect (passato prossimo) or imperfect (imperfetto) forms of the impersonal (I indicate which tense to use). Remember to make all necessary changes. Here's an example:

Q. Si arriva il 2 gennaio. (passato prossimo)

A. **Si è arrivati** il 2 gennaio. *We arrived/The arrival date was (on) January 2nd.*

No subject is really specified with the si impersonale. And when you see the pronoun "ci," you know that the verb is reflexive.

11. Ci si iscrive all'università di Firenze. (passato prossimo)

_____

12. Si vedono tutte le gallerie d'arte. (passato prossimo)

_____

13. Si mangia spesso la pappa al pomodoro. (imperfetto)

_____

14. Si prende il gelato da Vivoli ogni sera. (imperfetto)

_____

15. Ci si innamora a Firenze. (passato prossimo)

_____

16. Si frequentano le lezioni di letteratura italiana. (imperfetto)

_____

17. Si parla italiano. (passato prossimo)

_____

18. Si fanno le gite in Toscana i finesettimana. (imperfetto)

_____

19. Si torna il primo luglio. (passato prossimo)

_____

20. Si comprano le giacche di pelle al mercato. (passato prossimo)

_____

Now you want to plan a long weekend to visit your friend Monica in Venice, and you need to ask her what you can do there. For each question, I provide a clue in parentheses as to how Monica should respond. You fill in the missing pieces of the si impersonale according to the cue (you may have to adjust the impersonal "you" to agree with the direct object). You'll be using the future in this exercise. I translate all the questions, but remember that you have more than one way to translate them. Here's an example:

Q. Dove si potrà dormire? (*Where can we sleep?*) (all'albergo Des Bains o a casa mia gratis)

A. **Si potrà dormire** all'albergo Des Bains o a casa mia gratis. (*You can sleep at the Des Bains Hotel or at my house free of charge.*)

21. Che cosa si mangerà? (*What can you eat there?*) (gli spaghetti al nero di seppia)

_____

22. Quali musei si visiteranno? (*What museums can we visit?*) (la Peggy Guggenheim Collection e la Galleria dell'Accademia)

_____

23. Che cosa si vedrà a Murano? (*What can be seen in Murano?*) (le vetrerie a Murano)

_____

24. Si farà un giro in gondola? (*Will we take a ride in a gondola?*) (un giro nella nostra propria gondola)

_____

25. Si visiterà anche il Palazzo Ducale? (*Are we also going to visit the Ducal Palace?*) (certo)

_____

Getting Proactive about the Passive Voice

The passive voice takes the action out of a sentence. For example, you can change the sentence "La bambina **apparecchia** la tavola" (*The little girl is setting the table*) to the passive form: "La tavola **è apparecchiata** dalla bambina." (*The table is set by the little girl.*)

The passive voice is very similar in meaning to the impersonal "you" (see the previous sections in this chapter). For example, when you ask the question "Scusi, **si parla** inglese?" (*Excuse me, is English spoken here?*) by using the impersonal "you," you may also say, "Scusi, l'inglese **è parlato** qui?" (*Excuse me, is English spoken here?*) In this particular case, the impersonal is the more common of the two, but many other cases call for the passive voice as the more common construction. For example, if you don't want to assign blame, you can use the passive voice as a tool. Science and medicine often use the passive voice in writings. After you understand how to form it — which is quite simple — you'll find yourself using it quite often in conversation (much to your English teacher's chagrin).

To form the passive voice in any tense — present, present perfect, past absolute, imperfect, future, conditional, present subjunctive, imperfect subjunctive, past subjunctive, . . . — you take the verb **essere** (*to be*) (in that particular tense) + the past participle of the verb. The past participle always agrees with the subject in number and gender. (You can review past participles in Chapter 14.) You can use only *transitive verbs* (verbs that usually take **avere** [*to have*] in compound tenses; see Chapter 14) in the passive voice. However, as part of the passive construction, transitive verbs take **essere.** Don't worry, this only sounds confusing!

Le poesie **sono pubblicate** dalla casa editrice Wiley. (*The poems are published by Wiley Publishing.*)

La cena **è preparata** dal babbo. (*Dinner is being prepared by dad.*)

With the passive voice, you reverse the order of a sentence in the indicative or subjunctive: The direct object becomes the subject, and the subject (person or thing doing the action), if articulated, is introduced by the preposition "da" (*by*) by itself or contracted with a definite article. Table 22-2 gives you a listing of definite articles and where they appear in passive constructions.

Table 22-2	Definite Articles That Introduce Subjects		
Singular Article	*Position in Sentence*	*Plural Article*	*Position in Sentence*
dal	In front of masc. nouns beginning with most consonants	dai	In front of masc. nouns beginning with most consonants
dallo	In front of masc. nouns beginning with z-, st-, sp-, gn-	dagli	In front of masc. nouns beginning with z-, st-, sp-, gn-, and also vowels
dall'	In front of masc. or fem. nouns beginning with a vowel	dalle	In front of fem. nouns
dalla	In front of fem. nouns beginning with a consonant		

Here are some examples of the passive voice across the tenses:

Present: Le pesche **sono vendute** solo a luglio e agosto. (*Peaches are sold only in July and August.*)

Past: Questo libro **fu scritto** nel 1906. (*This book was written in 1906.*)

Future: Emilia **sarà incontrata** alla stazione dalla nonna. (*Emilia will be met at the station by her grandmother.*)

For this exercise, rewrite the following sentences, transforming the active voice into the passive voice. Use the tense (present, present perfect, future, imperfect, past absolute, present subjunctive, past subjunctive, . . .) that appears in the active-voice sentence. If I specify a subject, remember to use the preposition "da" (*by*) or the proper definitive article. Here's an example:

Q. Cambiano le lenzuola (sheets) ogni giorno in questo albergo?

A. **Sono combiate** ogni giorno le lenzuola in questo albergo? (*Are the sheets changed everyday in this hotel?*)

Note: The verb **cambiano** appears in the present active voice, so I use the present passive voice in my sentence transformation.

26. I bambini fanno i letti a casa nostra. (present) (*The children make the beds in our house.*)

_____

27. Il babbo ha aperto la lettera misteriosa. (present perfect) (*The father opened the mysterious letter.*)

_____

28. Ariosto scrisse *L'Orlando Furioso*. (past absolute) (*Ariosto wrote Orlando Furioso.*)

_____

29. Gli spagnoli conquistarono le Americhe. (past absolute) (*The Spanish conquered the Americas.*)

_____

30. Ho distrutto la macchina. (present perfect) (*I destroyed the car.*)

_____

31. Benigni presenterà il premio. (future) (*Benigni will present the prize.*)

_____

32. Tutti mangiano la pasta. (present) (*Everyone eats pasta.*)

_____

33. Hanno ripetuto le mie parole. (present perfect) (*Everyone repeated my words.*)

_____

34. Il padre della sposa comprerà la loro nuova casa. (future) (*The bride's father will buy their new house.*)

_____

35. Quali città visitiamo? (present) (*What cities are we vitsiting?*)

_____

36. La matrigna odiava Biancaneve. (imperfect) (*The stepmother hated Snow White.*)

_____

37. Tutti gli animali la amavano. (imperfect) (*All the animals loved her.*)

_____

38. Ricciolidoro aveva mangiato tutta la pappa! (past perfect) (*Goldilocks had eaten all the porridge.*)

_____

39. Credo che abbiano venduto la loro villa in Sardegna. (past subjunctive) (*I think that they've sold their house in Sardegna.*)

_____

40. È importante che studino i verbi. (present subjunctive) (*It's important that they study the verbs.*)

_____

For this exercise, translate the following Italian sentences that appear in the passive voice into English sentences that appear in the passive voice. The sentences feature most of the tenses I cover in this book. Follow my example:

Q. Tu sarai sempre ricordato. (future)

A. *You will always be remembered.*

41. Sono contenta che Caterina sia stata accettata dalla Columbia University. (present/past subjunctive)

42. Ero contenta che i miei studenti fossero stati invitati in Italia dai loro pen-pal italiani. (imperfect/past perfect subjunctive)

43. Mi dispiace che Giuseppe sia criticato da Belinda. (present/past subjunctive)

44. Tutta la torta sarebbe stata mangiata (se noi non fossimo arrivati)! (conditional perfect/past perfect subjunctive)

45. Giancarlo sarebbe sempre amato da Teresa. (conditional)

46. Penso che Marinella sia stata lasciata a casa. (present/past subjunctive)

47. Siamo stati presentati da Gigio e Laura. (present perfect)

48. Questa casa è stata costruita da mio marito. (present perfect)

49. Le poesie sono lette ad alta voce. (present)

50. Sono fatti a mano i ravioli? (present)

Answer Key

1 **Si va** al cinema stasera. (*Tonight we're going to the movies.*)

2 **Si comprano** qui i cornetti caldi? (*Can you buy hot cornetti here?*)

3 Come **si mangia** in quel ristorante? (*How's the food in that restaurant?*)

4 Dove **si mettono** le valige? (*Where should the suitcases be placed?*)

5 **Si parla** l'italiano qui. (*Italian is spoken here.*)

6 Qui non **si fanno** gli sconti! (*We don't do discounts here!*)

7 **Ci si diverte** a **parlare** l'italiano! (*We have fun speaking Italian./It's fun to speak Italian.*)

8 **Ci si sente** presto. (*We'll talk soon.*)

9 **Si può pagare** con la carta di credito? (*May I pay with a credit card?*)

10 **Si nuota** a casa di Enrico stasera. (*We're going swimming at Enrico's tonight.*)

11 **Ci si è iscritti** all'università di Firenze. (*We all enrolled at the University of Florence.*)

12 **Si sono viste** tutte le gallerie d'arte. (*All of the art galleries were seen.*)

13 **Si mangiava** spesso la pappa al pomodoro. (*We would often eat pappa al pomodoro [Tuscan bread soup].*)

14 **Si prendeva** il gelato da Vivoli ogni sera. (*Every evening we would get an ice cream at Vivoli's.*)

15 **Ci si è innamorati** a Firenze. (*Everyone fell in love in Florence.*)

16 **Si frequentavano** le lezioni di letteratura italiana. (*I used to take classes in Italian literature.*)

17 **Si è parlato** italiano. (*We spoke Italian.*)

18 **Si facevano** le gite in Toscana i finesettimana. (*On the weekends we all would take trips in Tuscany.*)

19 **Si è tornati** a luglio. (*We returned in July.*)

20 **Si sono comprate** le giacche di pelle al mercato. (*Leather jackets were bought at the market.*)

21 **Si mangeranno** gli spaghetti al nero di seppia. (*We will eat spaghetti in black squid sauce.*)

22 **Si visiteranno** la Peggy Guggenheim Collection e la Galleria dell'Accademia. (*We'll be visiting the Peggy Guggenheim Collection and the Accademia.*)

23 **Si vedranno** le vetrerie a Murano. (*We'll see the glass-blowing factories in Murano.*)

24 **Si farà** un giro nella nostra propria gondola. (*We'll take a ride in our very own gondola.*)

25 Certo che **si visiterà** anche il Palazzo Ducale. (*Of course the Ducal Palace will also be visited!*)

26 I letti **sono fatti** dai bambini a casa nostra. (*The beds are made by the children in our house.*)

27 La lettera misteriosa **è stata aperta** dal babbo. (*The mysterious letter was opened by the father.*)

28 *L'Orlando Furioso* **fu scritto** da Ariosto. (*Orlando Furioso was written by Ariosto.*)

29 Le Americhe **furono conquistate** dagli spagnoli. (*The Americas were conquered by the Spanish.*)

30 La macchina **è stata distrutta** da me. (*The car was destroyed by me.*)

31 Il premio **sarà presentato** da Benigni. (*The prize will be awarded by Benigni.*)

32 La pasta **è mangiata** da tutti. (*Pasta is eaten by everybody.*)

33 Le mie parole **sono state ripetute.** (*My words were repeated.*)

34 La loro nuova casa **sarà comprata** dal padre della sposa. (*Their new house is going to be purchased by the bride's father.*)

35 Quali città **si visitano?** (*What cities will be visited?*)

36 Biancaneve **era odiata** dalla matrigna. (*Snow White was hated by her stepmother.*)

37 **Era amata** da tutti gli animali. (*She was loved by all of the animals.*)

38 Tutta la pappa **era stata mangiata** da Ricciolidoro! (*All of the porridge had been eaten by Goldilocks!*)

39 Credo che la loro villa in Sardegna **sia stata venduta.** (*I think that their villa in Sardegna was sold.*)

40 È importante che i verbi **siano studiati.** (*It's important that the verbs be studied.*)

41 *I'm happy that Caterina was accepted to Columbia University.*

42 *I was happy that my students were invited to Italy by their Italian pen-pals.*

43 *I'm sorry that Joseph was criticized by Belinda.*

44 *The whole cake would've been eaten (had we not arrived)!*

45 *Giancarlo would always be loved by Teresa.*

46 *I think that Marinella was left at home.*

47 *We were introduced by Gigio and Laura.*

48 *This house was built by my husband.*

49 *The poems are read aloud.*

50 *Are the ravioli homemade?*

Chapter 23

Progressing in Italian through Gerunds

In This Chapter

▶ Creating gerunds in the present tense

▶ Incorporating irregular gerunds into your constructions

▶ Taking on the past gerund form

▶ Concentrating on the now with the present progressive

▶ Utilizing the imperfect progressive form

Gerunds (words ending in "ing" in English) are very common in spoken and written Italian, much as they are in English. They give immediacy to a sentence or phrase and can express action. For example, you're *reading* this book, and you're really *enjoying* yourself! The Italian gerund (in the present) corresponds roughly to the English present participle ending in **-ing**: eating (**mangiando**), waking up (**svegliandosi**), going out (**uscendo**), and so on.

When you combine the verb **stare** (to be) + a gerund, you form what is called the *progressive,* which you use to describe things that are going on right at this moment or to describe things that were going on at a precise moment in the past. For example: "Cosa **stai facendo? Sto scrivendo** questa frase." (*What are you doing? I'm writing this sentence.*) In this chapter, you discover how to use Italian gerunds and form them in the present and past tenses. You also get to work with the irregular forms of gerunds. From there, you move on to the present and imperfect progressive forms. This chapter also builds on material from previous chapters. For example, you often combine a clause containing a gerund with a verb in another tense, like the present perfect or the future.

Forming Gerunds in the Present Tense

In many cases, you may need to use a gerund by itself, as with *present gerunds.* In this case, the subject is the same in both parts of your sentence. Notice that the gerunds in the following examples are in the subordinate clauses (the part of a sentence that can't stand on its own two legs):

Tornando a casa, **mi fermo** al mercato. (*On the way home/While returning home* [Literally: *Returning home*], *I'm going to stop at the market.*)

Essendo stanco, Josh **ha dormito** tutto il giorno. (*Being tired* [or *Because he was tired*], *Josh slept all day.*)

Gerunds that appear in the present tense are quite easy to form. You take the stem of **-are** verbs and add **-ando**; the stem of **-ere** verbs and add **-endo**; and the stem of **-ire** verbs and add **-endo**. The gerunds of reflexive verbs become **-andosi** (for **-arsi** verbs), **-endosi** (for **-ersi** verbs), and **-endosi** (for **-irsi** verbs).

-are → **parlare** → **parlando** (*speaking*) → **Parlando** con te, **ho perso** il treno. (*While I was talking to you, I missed the train.*)

-ere → **mettere** → **mettendo** (*putting*) → **Abbiamo rimasto** duecento dollari, **mettendo** a parte trecento per l'albergo. (*We have 200 dollars left, putting aside 300 for the hotel.*)

-ire → **partire** → **partendo** (*leaving*) → **Partendo** in orario, **sarò** da te alle 10:00. (*If I leave on time, I'll be there at 10:00.*)

-irsi (reflexive) → **alzarsi** → **alzandosi** (*getting up*) → **Alzandosi** presto, **riesco a produrre** di più. (*Getting up early, I can accomplish more.*)

When you have a reflexive (see Chapter 5), direct object (see Chapter 6), or indirect-object pronoun (see Chapters 6 and 7), you attach it to the end of the gerund (again, the subject in the main and dependent clauses is the same):

Vedendomi così in contemplazione, Angelina **mi chiese** . . . (*Seeing me that way in contemplation, Angelina asked me . . .*)

Essendosi alzati presto, i ragazzi **hanno fatto** una colazione abbondante. (*Having woken up early, the kids had an abundant breakfast.*)

Parlandogli a quattro occhi, **mi sono resa conto** che **era** un idiota. (*Speaking to him face to face, I realized he was an idiot.*)

For this first exercise, transform the following infinitives into the present gerund form and then translate. Here's an example:

Q. diventare

A. **diventando** *becoming*

1. andare _____

2. viaggiare _____

3. vedere _____

4. riflettere _____

5. lasciarsi _____ (this verb is reciprocal; see Chapter 5)

6. vestirsi _____

7. finire _____

8. avere _____

9. non sapere _____

10. morire _____

Now you can further practice the present gerund form by translating the following sentences into English. Start with this example:

Q. Vedendoti felice mi sento tranquilla.

A. *Seeing you happy makes me feel at ease.*

11. Morendo, le sue ultime parole sono state. . .

_____

12. Non sapendo il tuo indirizzo . . .

_____

13. Vestendosi rapidamente, Portia uscì di casa.

_____

14. Lasciandosi, hanno riscoperto la pace.

_____

15. Avendo mal di testa, Marco ha lasciato il lavoro.

_____

Working with Irregular Gerund Forms

Not every gerund construction is as easy as you see in the previous section, of course! You have to deal with some irregular gerund forms when writing and speaking in Italian. But even the irregular forms will come easily to you if you can master the irregular stems of the imperfect tense (the imperfetto; if you don't remember the stems, turn to Chapter 8).

Verbs that have irregular stems in the imperfect tense — such as **bere** (*to drink*), **dire** (*to say, to tell*), **fare** (*to do, to make*), **tradurre** (*to translate*), and so on — also have irregular stems when forming a gerund. However, after you isolate the irregular stem, you simply add the gerund ending. This goes for gerunds, period (whether they are in the present or past, or combined with **stare**):

- **Bere: Stai bevendo** troppo! (*You're drinking too much!*)
- **Dire: Sto dicendo** la verità! (*I'm telling the truth!*)
- **Fare:** La mamma **sta facendo** la spesa. (*Mom's doing the marketing.*)
- **Porre** (like **imporre** and **supporre**): **Ponendo** il problema del giorno, il professore **aspetta.** (*Posing the problem of the day, the professor waits.*)

You can practice working with some irregular gerunds in the following brief exercise. Transform the infinitives in parentheses into the correct gerund forms. Here's an example for you:

Q. _____ la sua volontà, il padre proibì alla figlia di uscire. (imporre)

A. **Imponendo** la sua volontà, il padre proibì alla figlia di uscire. (*Imposing his will, the father forbade his daughter to go out.*)

16. _____ una passeggiata in centro, ho visto Marco e Ermanna. (fare)

17. _____ che non venivi non ti ho aspettato. (supporre)

18. _____ la verità, ti sentirai meglio. (dire)

19. Non _____ l'acqua, il suo corpo si è disidratato. (bere)

20. _____ dal latino all'italiano abbiamo imparato molto. (tradurre)

Forming Gerunds in the Past Tense

The past gerund is a compound tense that you form by using the gerund of **essere** (**essendo;** *having*) or **avere** (**avendo;** *having*) plus the past participle. (See Chapter 14 to find out which verbs take **essere** and which verbs take **avere.**) Both past gerunds translate as "*having . . .*". It's understood that the subject in both the dependent and main clauses is the same.

Because reflexive verbs take **essere** in compound tenses (as you can learn all about in Chapter 15), you use **essendosi** + the past participle (see the previous sections to find out how to combine gerund endings and pronouns).

You can see from the following examples that there's no single way to translate the past gerund:

Avendo ballato tutta la notte, i ragazzi **erano stanchi.** (*Since they danced all night/ Because they danced all night/Having danced all night, the boys and girls were tired.*)

Essendo partiti presto, **siamo arrivati** in anticipo. (*Having left early, we arrived early;* this sentence can also mean *Because we left early/Given that we left early . . .*)

Essendosi innamorati all'improvviso, i due **erano confusi.** (*Because they fell in love quickly/Having fallen suddenly in love, both were confused.*)

Form the past gerund in the following exercise problems by conjugating the infinitives into the proper past gerund form. Follow my example:

O. _____ male, è rimasto a letto. (sentirsi [lui])

A. **Essendosi sentito** male, è rimasto a letto. (*Because he didn't feel well, he stayed in bed.*)

21. Alessandro, non _____, ha fatto una domanda. (capire)

22. _____ già a Taormina, Julia e Cole sono andati a Sircacusa. (stare)

23. _____ da Dartmouth, il padre voleva che anche la figlia frequentasse quell'università. (laurearsi)

24. _____ una bugia, Pinocchio non poteva guardare la Fata Turchina (the Blue Fairy). (dire)

25. Lei ha detto di no, _____ a lungo. (riflettere)

26. Isa è tornata ieri, _____ per 11 mesi in Italia. (stare)

27. _____ il suo matrimonio, Ben cominciò a rovinare anche la sua carriera. (distruggere)

28. _____ presto, ho fatto una passeggiata sulla spiaggia. (svegliarsi [io])

29. _____ med tutta la notte, Libby si addormentò all'esame. (studiare)

30. _____ il treno, Simona ed io abbiamo fatto l'autostop fino a Urbino. (perdere)

Putting Gerunds in the Present Progressive

The *present progressive* (or il progressivo presente) is a wonderful tense that you use to talk about something that's going on at the same time you're talking about it. In this way, the present progressive corresponds somewhat in meaning to the present indicative (with gerunds; see the section "Forming Gerunds in the Present Tense"), but the gerunds in the present progressive allow you to more specifically refer to an action in progress. For example, when you say "**Sto studiando**" in the present progressive, it means *I'm studying* (right now, at this moment); **Studio** in the present indicative can mean one of several things (*I do study, I am studying, I study*).

To form the present progressive, you use the present form of **stare** (*to be*) + the present gerund form of the verb in question.

The following table shows the conjugation of a verb in the present progressive and an example.

mangiare (*to eat*)	
io sto mangiando	noi stiamo mangiando
tu stai mangiando	voi state mangiando
lui, lei, Lei sta mangiando	loro stanno mangiando
Cosa **state mangiando?** (*What are you* (pl.) *eating?*)	

You're studying at the University of Florence this year. Tell me what you and your friends are doing right now (unless I don't want to know) by conjugating the verbs in parentheses into the present progressive form. Just follow the example:

Q. _____ al computer. (scrivere [io])

A. **Sto scrivendo** al computer. (*I'm writing on the computer.*)

31. La mia amica Amy _____ la lezione di letteratura. (seguire)

32. Oona _____ la tesi su Ungaretti. (scrivere)

33. I miei amici italiani Claudio e Maurizio _____ le compere. (fare)

34. Noi _____ presto ogni mattina! (alzarsi)

35. Nina, cosa _____? (bere)

36. Ti _____! (parlando [io])

37. Che cosa _____? (fare [voi])

38. _____ il tuo e-mail. (leggere [noi])

39. _____ moltissimo! (divertirsi [io])

40. Rosamaria _____ tutte le sere. (uscire)

Tune in to your sense of the now by translating the next few sentences from Italian into English. Here's an example:

Q. Giancarlo sta leggendo il giornale.

A. *Giancarlo is reading the newspaper.*

41. Sto facendo una passeggiata.

_____

42. Stiamo aiutando la mamma.

_____

43. Il babbo sta preparando la cena.

_____

44. Stai pulendo la tua camera?

_____

45. State parlando di me?

_____

46. A cosa stai pensando?

_____

47. Emilia e Libby stanno giocando bene.

_____

48. Nessuno mi sta ascoltando!

_____

49. Giancarlo sta costruendo una casa.

_____

50. Mi sto addormentando!

_____

What Were You Thinking?
The Imperfect Progressive

You use the *imperfect progressive* form to refer to an action or event that *was* in the process of happening. For example, you can say "Cosa **stavi facendo?**" (*What were you doing?*) when you want to query a guilty-looking child. You may also want to use the imperfect progressive to discuss an action or event that was in the process of happening when something else happened. For example, you can get more specific by saying "Cosa **stavi facendo** quando **ho telefonato?**" (*What were you doing when I called?*)

You form the imperfect progressive with the imperfect form of the verb **stare** (*to be;* see Chapter 8) + the past participle of the verb in question. (See Chapters 14 and 15 to review how to form regular and irregular past participles — they're the ones that end in **-ato, -uto,** and **-ito** when regular.)

The following table shows the imperfect progressive conjugation of the verb **dormire** and an example.

dormire (*to sleep*)	
io st**avo** dorm**endo**	noi st**avamo** dorm**endo**
tu st**avi** dorm**endo**	voi st**avate** dorm**endo**
lui, lei, Lei st**ava** dorm**endo**	loro st**avano** dorm**endo**
Stavo dormendo quando **ho sentito suonare** il telefono. (*I was sleeping when I heard the phone ring.*)	

In this exercise, talk about what everyone in your house was doing last night at 11:00 p.m. by conjugating the verbs I present (along with the subjects and sometimes objects) into the imperfect progressive, making complete sentences in the process. Here's an example:

Q. Io/studiare

A. Io **stavo studiando.** (*I was studying.*)

51. Toby/addormentarsi

_____

52. Giancarlo/lavorare

_____

53. I ragazzi/guardare la televisione

_____

54. Anna Maria ed io/fare programmi per la cena

_____

55. Io/lavarsi i denti

_____

Answer Key

1 **andando** *going*

2 **viaggiando** *travelling*

3 **vedendo** *seeing*

4 **riflettendo** *reflecting*

5 **lasciandosi** *leaving each other*

6 **vestendosi** *dressing him/herself*

7 **finendo** *finishing*

8 **avendo** *having*

9 **non sapendo** *not knowing*

10 **morendo** *dying*

11 *Dying, his last words were . . .*

12 *Not knowing your address . . .*

13 *Getting dressed quickly, Portia left the house.*

14 *Upon leaving each other, they rediscovered peace.*

15 *Because he had a headache, Marco left work.*

16 **Facendo** una passeggiata in centro, ho visto Marco e Ermanna. (*While taking a walk in the center of town, I saw Marco and Ermanna.*)

17 **Supponendo** che non venivi non ti ho aspettato. (*I supposed you weren't coming and didn't wait for you.*)

18 **Dicendo** la verità, ti sentirai meglio. (*In telling the truth, you'll feel better.*)

19 Non **bevendo** l'acqua, il suo corpo si è disidratato. (*By not drinking water, his/her body became dehydrated.*)

20 **Traducendo** dal latino all'italiano, abbiamo imparato molto. (*Translating from Latin to Italian, we learned much.*)

21 Alessandro, non **avendo capito,** ha fatto una domanda. (*Not having understood, Alexander asked a question.*)

22 **Essendo stati** già a Taormina, Julia e Cole sono andati a Sircacusa. (*Since they had already been to Taormina, Julia and Cole went to Syracuse.*)

23 **Essendosi laureato** da Dartmouth, il padre voleva che anche la figlia frequentasse quell'università. (*Having graduated from Dartmouth, the father wanted that his daughter also attend that college.*)

24 **Avendo detto** una bugia, Pinocchio non poteva guardare la Fata Turchina. (*Because he had told a lie, Pinocchio could not look at the Blue Fairy.*)

25 Lei ha detto di no, **avendo riflettuto** a lungo. (*She said no, after having reflected a while.*)

26 Isa è tornata ieri, **essendo stata** per 11 mesi in Italia. (*Isa returned yesterday, after being in Italy for 11 months.*)

27 **Avendo distrutto** il suo matrimonio, Ben cominciò a rovinare anche la sua carriera. (*Having destroyed his marriage, Ben began to ruin his career, too.*)

28 **Essendomi svegliata** presto, ho fatto una passeggiata sulla spiaggia. (*Since I had woken up early, I took a walk on the beach.*)

29 **Avendo studiato** tutta la notte, Libby si addormentò all'esame. (*After having studied all night, Libby fell asleep at the exam.*)

30 **Avendo perso** il treno, Simona ed io abbiamo fatto l'autostop fino a Urbino. (*Since we had missed the train, Simona and I hitchhiked to Urbino.*)

31 La mia amica Amy **sta seguendo** la lezione di letteratura. (*My friend Amy is taking a literature class.*)

32 Oona **sta scrivendo** la tesi su Ungaretti. (*Oona is writing her thesis on Ungaretti.*)

33 I miei amici italiani Claudio e Maurizio **stanno facendo** le compere. (*My Italian friends Claudio and Maurizio are shopping.*)

34 Noi **ci stiamo alzando** presto ogni mattina! (*We're getting up early every morning!*)

35 Nina, cosa **stai bevendo?** (*Nina, what are you drinking?*)

36 Ti **sto parlando!** (*I'm talking to you!*)

37 Che cosa **state facendo?** (*What are you* (pl.) *doing?*)

38 **Stiamo leggendo** la tua e-mail. (*We're reading your e-mail.*)

39 **Mi sto divertendo** moltissimo! (*I'm having a very good time!*)

40 Rosamaria **sta uscendo** tutte le sere. (*Rosamaria is going out every night.*)

41 *I'm taking a walk.*

42 *We're helping mom.*

43 *Dad's preparing dinner.*

44 *Are you cleaning your room?*

45 *Are you* (pl.) *talking about me?*

46 *What are you thinking about?*

47 *Emilia and Libby are playing well together.*

48 *No one's listening to me!*

49 *Giancarlo is building a house.*

50 *I'm falling asleep!*

51 Toby **si stava addormentando.** (*Toby was falling asleep.*)

52 Giancarlo **stava lavorando.** (*Giancarlo was working.*)

53 I ragazzi **stavano guardando** la televisione. (*The kids were watching TV.*)

54 Anna Maria ed io **stavamo facendo** programmi per la cena. (*Anna Maria and I were making plans for dinner.*)

55 Io **mi stavo lavando** i denti. (*I was brushing my teeth.*)

Part V
The Part of Tens

"Honey, can you look in the phrase book and tell me how 'scrambled' is pronounced in Italian?"

In this part . . .

The two chapters in this part contain lists of the ten most frequently used verbs and the ten Italian verbs most frequently mixed up.

Chapter 24

Ten Most Frequently Used Verbs

In This Chapter

▶ Mastering ten verbs you hear and use all the time

▶ Arming yourself with useful phrases containing these verbs

T his is it . . . don't get scared now. If you're serious about getting a solid grasp on the Italian language, you need to know how to conjugate and use the ten verbs I present in this chapter backward and forward. And as an added challenge, it just so happens that many of the ten most commonly used Italian verbs are irregular. Lucky you!

Some of the verbs I present in this chapter have multiple translations or meanings. In these cases, I provide the most common translation or meaning in parentheses and include an ellipsis to indicate that more translations/meanings exist.

Essere o Non Essere . . . (To Be or Not to Be . . .)

The verb **essere** (*to be*) is one of the most commonly used verbs in any language. You can use it to declare your physical state — "**Sono** bellissima" (*I'm gorgeous*) — your emotional state — "**Sono** felice" (*I'm happy*) — your nationality — "**Sono** greca" (*I'm Greek*) — or your location — "**Sono** a casa" (*I'm at home*). You can also use it to express sentiments such as "La mia macchina è veloce" (*My car is fast*), and you can use it to ask many questions:

Sei americano? (*Are you American?*)

È medico tuo padre? (*Is your dad a doctor?*)

Sono i tuoi, questi pantaloni? (*Are these pants yours?*)

You can find the conjugation of **essere** and many of its uses in Chapter 4; you can also combine it with all the compound tenses in Part III.

Avere (To Have)

Avere is a versatile verb. It can mean *to have,* as in "**Ho** una casa a Ravenna" (*I have a house in Ravenna*), and it can mean *to be* when combined with certain idiomatic constructions, such as in the following sentences:

Ho 29 anni. (*I'm 29 years old.*)

Ho freddo. (*I'm cold.*)

Ho fretta! (*I'm in a hurry!*)

For a more complete list of **avere's** many uses and for its conjugation, check out Chapter 4. And don't forget that **avere** is one of two auxiliary verbs you find in all the compound tenses in Part III.

Andare (To Go)

The verb **andare** (*to go*) can get you pretty far! You can "**andare** a piedi" (*go by foot*) or "in macchina" (*by car*). You can "**andare** al mercato" (*go to the market*). You can tell someone to go away and stop bothering you with the tu and Lei command forms: **Vai via**, **Vattene**, **Vada via**, or **Se ne vada!** When bickering or disagreeing with someone, you can say "**Vai** in quel paese!" (*Go fly a kite!*), or you can get more to the point with "**Vai** all'inferno" or "al diavolo" (*Go to hell* or *To the devil!*). In my husband's hometown of Ravenna, the phrase "Ma **va** là!" means *O, forget about it!* or *Leave it alone!* You can find more uses for **andare** and its conjugation in the present tense in Chapter 3.

Capire (To Understand)

I can't remember taking part in a conversation in Italy where my companion or I didn't use the verb **capire** (*to understand*). Italians tend to use this verb more frequently than Americans; often, Italians conclude a sentence with "**capisci?**" (*do you understand*) or "**hai capito?**" (*did you understand?*). Italians also throw in the verb to create common insults: "Non **capisci** un fico secco!" (Literally: *You don't understand a dried fig*; Figuratively: *You don't understand a darn thing!*) And if you add "ne" or "ci" before the verb, you slightly change its meaning: "Non ne **capisco**" (*I don't understand it*) or "non ci **capisco** proprio" (*I just don't understand it*).

Dare (To Give)

Dare (*to give*) belongs in this list as much as the other verbs, due to its generous nature (and amount of uses)! **Dare** has a nice range of meaning, from "**Mi dai** una mano?" (*Will you give me a hand?*) to "**Dai!**" (*Come on! You're kidding!*) to the more common use — "**Dammi** un bacio!" (*Give me a kiss!*) You can find this verb in Chapter 3.

Dire (To Say or to Tell)

You hear the verb **dire** (*to say* or *to tell*) in many contexts. "**Dimmi!/Mi dica?**" (*Tell me!/ How can I help you?*) are two common ways a shopkeeper will greet you (although the second is the more formal and polite of the two and the one you're likely to hear if you don't know each other very well). The verb is bound to pop up in many types of dialogue. Here are some examples:

> **Andiamo** a Salerno . . . che ne **dici?** (*Let's go to Salerno . . . what do you say/what do you think about that?*)

> **Si dice** che Alessandro **sia innamorato** di Abbi. (*They say that Allessandro is in love with Abbi.*)

> **Stai dicendo** la verità? (*Are you telling the truth?*)

See Chapter 3 for the present tense conjugation of **dire.**

Fare (To Do or to Make . . .)

Most of the time in Italian, you can use the verb **fare** whenever you'd use the verbs *to do* and *to make* in English: "Sto **facendo** il compito" (*I'm doing my homework*) and "**Facciamo** l'amore!" (*Let's make love!*) are two examples. The verb **fare** means *to do* or *to make,* but it can also mean so many other things when combined with certain words or expressions (many of which you can find in Chapter 3). The combinations range from *packing your bag* (**fare** la valigia), to saying *the weather is nice* (**fa** bello), to saying that something or someone disgusts you (**fare** schifo), to saying that something hurts on your body: "**Mi fa** male la testa" (*My head hurts*) or "**Mi fanno** male i piedi" (*My feet hurt*). The possibilities go on and on.

Mangiare (To Eat)

The verb **mangiare** (*to eat*) expresses the essence of Italian life and of every traveller's experience in Italy! You can have only one acceptable answer to the following question: **Come si mangia** in Italia? (*How's the food in Italy?* Literally: *How does one eat in Italy?*) And that answer is "Benissimo!" (*Very well!*)

You can combine **mangiare** with interrogatives to ask plenty of questions:

Dove **si mangia?** (*Where are we eating?*)

Che cosa **avete mangiato?** (*What did you eat?*)

Quando **mangi?** (*When are you eating?*)

Con chi **mangiate?** (*Who are you eating with?*)

A che ora **si mangia?** (*What time are we eating?*)

And if you're ever at someone's house, and you hear your hosts say, "**Si mangia!**" or "A tavola! **Si mangia!**," you should go directly to the table because supper or dinner is ready and waiting!

Stare (To Be . . .)

The verb **stare** can mean *to be, to stay, to remain, to stop, to continue, to be well,* and so on. "**Stammi** bene" (*Take care/Be well*) is one common use of the verb, as is **stare** + per (*to be about to do something*): "**Stavo** per **telefonarti!**" (*I was just about to phone you!*) When you're wearing something nice, or when your hair looks good, you may hear someone say to you, "**Ti sta** bene (quel vestito)" (*That dress suits you*) or "**Ti stanno** bene i capelli così" (*Your hair looks good that way*).

You should also pay attention to other common uses of **stare**, such as "**Sto** bene, grazie, e Lei?" (*I'm well, thanks, and you?*) and "**Stai** lontano da mia figlia!" (*Stay away from my daughter!*) You can find a bundle of other uses in Chapter 3.

Volere (To Want)

You can use the verb **volere** (*to want*) by itself, as in "**Voglio** una nuova macchina" (*I want a new car*), or together with another verb, as in "**Voglio andare** in vacanza!" (*I want to go on vacation!*) Of course, using the present tense like I just have — **voglio** (*I want*) — sounds just as impolite as it does in English!

Always use the conditional **vorrei** (*I would like*) when declaring that you want something in a store and, more importantly, when asking your hostess or concierge for a service.

Oh, and here's one very polite thing you can say: "**Ti voglio** bene!" (*I love you!*)

Chapter 25

Ten Italian Verbs Most Frequently Mixed Up

. . . .

In This Chapter

▶ Noting connotative differences in verbs

▶ Separating a verb's meaning from what you think it should mean

▶ Having a good time (and talking about it the right way)

. . . .

*I*f you're an astute observer, you'll notice that I actually include more than ten verbs in this chapter. You get the excess because I'm presenting two verbs together in the sections that follow — that is, two verbs, battling head to head, that people studying Italian often mix up. Part of knowing Italian is being able to distinguish these verb couplets (many of which translate the same way in English) and being able to understand and use all the verbs individually. The sections that follow present the battles and show you the way.

Conoscere versus Sapere

Conoscere means *to be acquainted with, to know.* For example, you can **conoscere** a person or a city. **Sapere** means *to know any type of information or fact* or *how to do something* (**Sai ballare** il tango? *Do you know how to dance the tango?*). The differences between these two verbs are connotative.

Compare:

Conosci Matteo? (*Do you know Matteo?*)

versus

Sai quanti anni **ha** Matteo? (*Do you know how old Matteo is?*)

Here are a couple more examples:

Conosci Roma? (*Do you know Rome [Are you acquainted with Rome]?*)

versus

Sai dov'è Roma? (*Do you know where Rome is?*)

You use the expression "lo **so**" or "non lo **so**" to answer questions with **sapere** in them. Here are a couple examples:

Sai dove **abita** Liora? (*Do you know where Liora lives?*)

Sì, lo **so.** /No, non lo **so.** (*Yes, I know./No, I don't know.*)

The following tables show the conjugations of **sapere,** which is irregular in the present tense (as it is in the future; see Chapter 10), and **conoscere,** which you conjugate like a regular **-ere** verb (which you can find in Chapter 2).

sapere (*to know information or facts, to know how to do something*)	
io **so**	noi **sappiamo**
tu **sai**	voi **sapete**
lui/lei/Lei **sa**	loro **sanno**
Io **so** tutto di te! (*I know all about you!*)	

conoscere (*to be acquainted with, to know*)	
io conosc**o**	noi conosc**iamo**
tu conosc**i**	voi conosc**ete**
lui/lei/Lei conosc**e**	loro conosc**ono**
Io **conosco** tutti qui. (*I know everybody here.*)	

As if all that weren't enough, **sapere** and **conoscere** assume slightly different meanings in the present perfect tense (passato prossimo; see Chapter 14). **Sapere** in the passato prossimo means *to find out;* **conoscere** in the passato prossimo means *to meet* (as in to meet someone for the first time). Here are some examples:

Lei **ha saputo** che suo marito la **tradiva.** (*She found out her husband was betraying her.*)

Abbiamo saputo che **eravate** anche voi a Block Island! (*We found out that you all were on Block Island, too!*)

Ho conosciuto mio marito a Ravenna. (*I met my husband in Ravenna.*)

Quando **hai conosciuto** Marco? (*When did you meet Marco?*)

Giocare versus Suonare

The difference in the meaning of the verbs **giocare** and **suonare** is connotative. **Giocare** means *to play* a sport, cards, or chess, and **suonare** means *to play* an instrument. **Giocare,** however, is a **-care** verb (see Chapter 2 for info on what this means). Here's an example of each:

Giochiamo a calcio, e **suoniamo** il pianoforte. (*We play soccer, and we play the piano.*)

Vuoi giocare a scacchi stasera? **Mi dispiace,** ma non **posso; devo suonare** il violino. (*Would you like to play chess tonight? I'm sorry, but I can't; I have to play the violin.*)

Lavorare versus Funzionare

Both **lavorare** and **funzionare** mean *to work*, but **lavorare** refers to a person and **funzionare** refers to a mechanical object:

> Marco **lavora** oggi fino a tardi, anche se non **funziona** la sua macchina. (*Marco is working until late today, even though his car isn't working.*)

Fingere versus Pretendere

Fingere means *to pretend*, and **pretendere** means *to expect and/or demand*, even though it seems like the meanings should be switched. ***Note:*** You use the subjunctive with **pretendere** when the verb is in the main clause of a sentence (see Chapters 12 and 13). Here are some examples:

> Lui **finge** di non **conoscermi.** (*He's pretending not to know me.*)

> Cosa **pretendi?** È un idiota. (*What do you expect? He's a jerk.*)

> Io **pretendo** che i miei studenti **si comportino** bene. (*I expect/demand that my students behave well.*) ("**si comportino**" is in the present subjunctive.)

Prendere versus Avere

Prendere means *to take* or *to have*, especially when talking about *taking* transportation such as trains or cabs or *having* something to eat or drink:

> **Prendo** il treno delle 10:00. (*I'm taking the 10:00 train.*)

> Cosa **prendi** per colazione di solito? (*What do you have for breakfast, usually?*)

> Ieri sera **abbiamo preso** una granita di caffè meravigliosa. (*Yesterday evening we had a wonderful coffee granita.*)

Avere means *to have* and sometimes *to be* (see Chapter 4). What separates **avere** from **prendere** is that you never use **avere** when ordering food or when talking about what you had:

> **Ho** molti amici. (*I have many friends.*)

> **Avete** paura? (*Are you* (pl.) *afraid?*)

Andare in Bagno versus Fare il Bagno

Andare in bagno means *to go to the bathroom*, and **fare il bagno** means *to take a bath* or *to go for a swim*. Here are a few examples that show these verbs in action:

> Posso **andare in bagno?** (*May I go to the bathroom?*)

> **Ha fatto il bagno** la bambina? (*Did the baby have a bath?*)

> Non **fate il bagno?** (*Aren't you guys going to swim?*)

Essere d'accordo versus Andare d'accordo

Essere d'accordo means *to be in agreement about something*. A similar phrase, **andare d'accordo**, means *to get along well with each other*. Although getting along and agreeing may have similar uses in English, the following examples show that they have different uses, too:

> **Sei d'accordo** con me? (*Do you agree with me?*)
>
> Mia sorella ed io **andiamo d'accordo.** (*My sister and I get along well with each other.*)

Passare versus Spendere

The Italian language is beautiful because it separates the idea of *spending time* from the idea of *spending money*. In other words, Italian is one place where time doesn't equal money! Now, back to business. The verb **passare** means *to spend time*, and the verb **spendere** means *to spend money*. Here are a couple examples:

> Quando **siamo** in Italia, **passiamo** molto tempo al mare. (*When we're in Italy, we spend a lot of time at the beach.*)
>
> Quanto **hai speso** per il biglietto d'aereo? (*How much did you spend on your plane ticket?*)

Fermare versus Smettere di

Language that attempts to put a stop to someone or something is important in any language. In Italian, **fermare** means *to stop something* or *someone*, and **smettere di** means *to quit* or *to stop doing something*. I'll put a stop to this discussion and show you some examples:

> **Ho fermato** Gianni per strada per **parlargli.** (*I stopped Gianni on the street to talk to him.*)
>
> Quando **smetti di fumare?** (*When are you going to quit/stop smoking?*)

Smettila! is the tu (*you*) imperative of **smettere di** (see Chapter 5) and means *Cut it out!/Stop it!*

Divertirsi versus . . .

Yep. Only one verb here. **Divertirsi** has a few meanings: *to have a good time, to enjoy oneself,* and *to have fun*. But no matter how much I talk about this verb, many of my students just don't put it to use. They persist in literally translating "to have a good time" as "**avere** un buon tempo." Never do that! Here's the correct way to express your happiness:

> Quanto **ci siamo divertiti!** (*We had such a good time!/We had so much fun!*)
>
> Daniel **si diverte** a **sciare** con i suoi amici. (*Daniel has a good time skiing with his friends.*)

Part VI
Appendixes

The 5th Wave   By Rich Tennant

"My wife and I are taking the course together. I figure I only have to learn half as much, since she finishes all of my sentences anyway."

In this part . . .

One appendix provides a list of all the Italian/English verbs I use in this book (plus more); another provides an English/Italian list; and the third takes the top-ten greatest hits of irregular verbs and conjugates them in all their irregular forms.

Appendix A
Italian-to-English Glossary

The following is a list of about 540 common Italian verbs. There are many more, but if you memorize all the verbs in this appendix, you'll be well on your way to speaking Italian with ease and earning good grades. Many of these verbs are irregular or stem-changing (see Chapter 3). Here's a breakdown of some of the notation I use in this glossary:

- I provide you with irregular past participles in parentheses after the translation.

- -ire verbs that take the -isc are indicated.

- I indicate whether the verb (usually) takes **essere** (e.) in a compound tense (see Chapters 14 and 15); the ones without the "(e.)" generally take **avere**.

- Verb entries with "(like **verb**)" means that the verb is conjugated similarly to the one indicated, in all tenses. For example, the verb **benedire** (*to bless*) says "(like **dire**)," meaning that **benedire** has an irregular present tense conjugation **(io benedico)** and irregular past participle **(benedetto)** — just like **dire** after you add the **bene-** — as well as other similar irregular tenses.

abbandonare: *to abandon*

abbassare: *to lower, to pull down*

abbinare: *to match*

abbracciare: *to hug*

abbronzarsi (e.): *to get a tan*

abitare: *to live*

abituarsi (e.): *to get used to*

accarezzare: *to caress, to pet*

accellerare: *to accellerate*

accendere: *to light, to turn on* **(acceso)**

accettare: *to accept*

accludere: *to enclose* **(accluso)**

accomodare: *to fix something*

accomodàrsi (e.): *to make oneself at home, to make oneself comfortable, to take a seat*

accompagnare: *to accompany, to go with*

accontentarsi di (e.): *to be satisfied with*

accorgersi (e.): *to realize* **(accorto)**

adoperare: *to use*

adorare: *to adore*

adottare: *to adopt*

affidare: *to entrust*

affondare: *to sink*

affrontare: *to face or to deal with*

aggiungere: *to add* (like **giungere**)

aiutare: *to help*

affiggere: *to post up, to put up* (a poster) **(affisso)**

affliggere: *to afflict* **(afflitto)**

aggiustare: *to fix*

alienare: *to alienate*

allacciare: *to fasten*

allenare: *to train, to practice*

allevare: *to raise* (animals and children)

allontanarsi (e.): *to go away, to depart, to leave, to take off*

alzare: *to raise*

alzarsi (e.): *to get up*

amare: *to love*

ammettere: *to admit* (like **mettere**)

ammirare: *to admire*

ammobiliare: *to furnish*

analizzare: *to analyze*

andare (e.): *to go*

annegare: *to drown*

annoiare: *to bother*

annoiarsi (e.): *to be bored*

annusare: *to smell* (to smell something)

apparecchiare: *to set the table*

apparire: *to appear* (**apparso**)

appartenere: *to belong to* (like **tenere**)

appassionarsi (e.): *to be passionate about*

aprire: *to open* (**aperto**)

arrabbiarsi (e.): *to become angry*

arrivare (e.): *to arrive*

ascoltare: *to listen*

asciugare: *to dry*

aspettare: *to wait for*

aspettarsi (e.): *to expect*

assaggiare: *to taste*

assicurarsi (e.): *to make sure, to assure*

assistere: *to attend, to witness*

assomigliare: *to resemble*

assumere: *to hire* (**assunto**)

attaccare: *to stick, to paste, to attack, to plug in*

attendere: *to wait for* (**atteso**)

attrarre: *to attract* (**attratto**)

attraversare: *to cross* (a street, a bridge)

augurarsi (e.): *to hope*

avere: *to have*

avvertire: *to inform, to warn*

avvicinarsi (e.) *to go near*

avvisare: *to inform, to let know*

baciare: *to kiss*

ballare: *to dance*

benedire: *to bless* (like **dire**)

bere: *to drink* (**bevuto**)

biasimare: *to blame*

bloccare: *to block, to be stuck*

bollire: *to boil*

brillare: *to shine*

bruciare: *to burn*

buttare: *to throw, to fling, to throw something away*

cadere (e.): *to fall*

cambiarsi (e.): *to change one's clothes*

camminare: *to walk*

cancellare: *to erase, to cancel*

cantare: *to sing*

capire: *to understand*

capitare: *to happen, to come, to turn up*

cascare (e.): *to fall*

cavalcare: *to ride a horse*

cedere: *to cede*

chiacchierare: *to chatter*

chiamare: *to call*

chiamarsi (e.): *to be called*

chiarire (isc): *to make clearer, to clarify*

chiedere: *to ask for* (**chiesto**)

chiudere: *to close* (**chiuso**)

cogliere: *to pick, to grasp* (the meaning of something) (**colto**)

coinvolgere: *to involve* (**coinvolto**)

collaborare: *to collaborate*

colpire (isc): *to strike, to hit*

coltivare: *to cultivate, to grow*

cominciare: *to begin*

commettere: *to commit* (like **mettere**)

commuovere: *to move, to touch* (like **muovere**)

competere: *to compete*

complimentare: *to compliment*

comporre: *to compose* (like **porre**)

comportarsi (e.): *to behave*

comprare: *to buy*

comunicare: *to make known, to communicate, to tell*

concedere: *to concede, to award* (**concesso**)

concepire (isc): *to conceive*

concludere: *to conclude* (**concluso**)

condire (isc): *to dress* (a salad or a pasta dish)

condividere: *to share* (like **dividere**)

condurre: *to drive, to bring about* (**condotto**)

confondere: *to confuse* (**confuso**)

confondersi (e.): *to be confused* (like **confondere**)

conoscere: *to know* (**conosciuto**)

consegnare: *to hand over, to deliver*

consentire: *to agree*

consigliare: *to advise*

consistere: *to consist* (**consistito**)

consumare: *to consume, to wear down*

continuare: *to continue*

contribuire (isc): *to contribute*

controllare: *to check, to check up on, to verify*

convertire: *to convert*

convincere: *to convince* (like **vincere**)

convivere: *to live together, to cohabitate* (like **vivere**)

coprire: *to cover* (**coperto**)

correggere: *to correct* (**corretto**)

correre: *to run* (**corso**)

corrompere: *to corrupt* (**corrotto**)

costare: *to cost* (**costa, costano**)

costruire (isc): *to build*

crescere: *to grow, to raise something* (**cresciuto**)

cucire: *to sew*

cuocere: *to cook* (**cotto**)

curare: *to take care of*

dare: *to give* (**dato**)

decidere: *to decide* (**deciso**)

dedurre: *to deduce* (**dedotto**)

deludere: *to disappoint* (**deluso**)

desiderare: *to desire, to wish*

determinare: *to define, to determine, to fix* or *settle*

dichiarare: *to declare, to state*

difendere: *to defend* (**difeso**)

dimagrire (isc) (e.): *to lose weight*

dimenticare: *to forget*

dipendere: *to depend* (like **pendere**)

dipingere: *to paint* (**dipinto**)

diplomarsi (e.): *to graduate* (from high school)

dire: *to say, to tell* (**detto**)

dirigere: *to direct, to manage* (**diretto**)

discutere: *to discuss, to argue* (**discusso**)

disegnare: *to draw*

disperare: *to despair*

disperdere: *to disperse* (like **perdere**)

dispiacere: *to displease, to be sorry* (like **piacere**)

disporre: *to arrange, to set out* (like **porre**)

distrarre: *to distract* (**distratto**)

distribuire (isc): *to distribute*

distruggere: *to destroy* (**distrutto**)

diventare (e.): *to become*

divertirsi (e.): *to have fun, to enjoy oneself, to have a good time*

dormire: *to sleep*

dovere: *to have to, to need to*

dubitare: *to doubt*

durare (e.): *to last*

eccitare: *to arouse, to excite*

educare: *to educate, to train*

eleggere: *to elect* (**eletto**)

eliminare: *to eliminate*

emozionarsi (e.): *to be excited, to be stirred, to be touched, moved*

entrare (e.): *to enter*

esaminare: *to examine*

esaudire (isc): *to grant* (a wish)

esaurire: *to use up, to exhaust*

escludere: *to exclude* (**escluso**)

esibire (isc): *to exhibit*

esigere: *to demand* (**esatto**)

espandere (isc): *to expand* (**espanso**)

espellere: *to expel* (**espulso**)

esplodere: *to explode* (**esploso**)

esplorare: *to explore*

essere (e.): *to be* (**stato**)

estrarre: *to extract* (**estratto**)

esultare: *to exalt*

evitare: *to avoid*

evocare: *to evoke*

fallire (isc): *to fail*

fantasticare: *to dream up*

fare: *to do, to make* (**fatto**)

favorire (isc): *to favor, to* (do the) *honor, to try* (some food)

fermare: *to stop* (a car, a person)

fermarsi (e.): *to stop oneself*

festeggiare: *to celebrate*

fidarsi (e.): *to trust*

filmare: *to film*

finire (isc): *to end, to finish*

firmare: *to sign*

fissare: *to fasten, to stare, to obsess*

formare: *to form, to shape*

fornire (isc): *to provide, to supply*

fotografare: *to photograph*

fraintendere: *to misunderstand*
(like **intendere**)

frenare: *to brake, to curb*

frequentare: *to attend, to frequent*

friggere: *to fry* **(fritto)**

fuggire (e.): *to flee*

funzionare: *to work* (something mechanical)

galleggiare: *to float*

generare: *to generate*

gettare: *to throw*

giocare: *to play* (a sport, a game)

girovagare: *to wander* (the world)

giudicare: *to judge*

giungere: *to arrive, to reach, to get as far as*
(giunto)

giurare: *to take an oath, to swear*

godere: *to enjoy*

gonfiare: *to blow up*

gridare: *to yell, to shout*

guadagnare: *to earn*

guardare: *to look, to look at*

guidare: *to drive*

illudersi (e.): *to be under the illusion,*
to cherish the (false) *hope* **(illuso)**

illuminare: *to illuminate, to light*

illustrare: *to illustrate, to show*

imbarazzare: *to embarrass, to puzzle,*
to bewilder

imbarcare: *to board* (a boat or plane)

immaginarsi (e.): *to imagine, to guess*

immigrare: *to immigrate*

imparare: *to learn*

impazzire (isc) (e.): *to go crazy*

impedire (isc): *to impede*

impegnare: *to pledge to reserve something*

impegnarsi (e.): *to make a commitment,*
to work hard

improvvisare: *to improvise*

incartare: *to wrap*

inchinare: *to bow*

incoraggiare: *to encourage*

incrociare: *to cross* (your legs, your fingers)

individuare: *to individuate, to characterize*

indovinare: *to guess*

infliggere: *to inflict* **(inflitto)**

influenzare: *to influence*

informarsi (e.): *to enquire, to get information*
about

informarsi (e.): *to find out about something*

infrangere: *to shatter* (glass, a heart)
(infranto)

inginocchiare: *to kneel*

ingrandire (isc): *to enlarge*

ingrassare (e.): *to gain weight, to get fat*

innamorarsi (e.): *to fall in love*

inquinare: *to pollute*

insegnare: *to teach*

inserire (isc): *to insert*

insistere: *to insist* **(insistito)**

intendere: *to understand, to mean something* **(inteso)**

interessarsi di (e.): *to be interested in, to take an interest in*

interrogare: *to question, to interrogate*

intervenire (e.): *to intervene* (like **venire**)

intrattenere: *to entertain* (like **tenere**)

intrecciare: *to braid*

invitare: *to invite*

iscriversi (e.): *to enroll in* (like **scrivere**)

isolare: *to isolate*

istruire (isc): *to teach, to instruct*

lamentarsi di (e.): *to complain*

lanciare: *to throw, to launch*

lasciare: *to leave*

laurearsi (e.): *to graduate* (from college)

lavare: *to wash*

lavarsi (e.): *to wash oneself*

lavorare: *to work* (as in a job)

leccare: *to lick*

legare: *to tie*

leggere: *to read* **(letto)**

levigare: *to smooth, to polish* (marble), *to sand* (wood)

liberare: *to free*

licenziare: *to fire someone*

licenziarsi (e.): *to quit* (a job)

litigare: *to fight, to quarrel*

lodare: *to praise*

lottare: *to struggle, to fight*

lusingare: *to flatter*

maledire: *to curse* (like **dire**)

mancare: *to miss*

mandare: *to send*

mangiare: *to eat*

manifestare: *to show, to display*

mantenere: *to keep, to maintain* (like **tenere**)

mentire: *to lie*

meravigliarsi (e.): *to be surprised, to be amazed*

meritare: *to deserve*

mettere: *to put, to place* **(messo)**

mettersi (e.): *to put on* (like **mettere**)

migliorare: *to improve*

montare: *to mount, to assemble*

mordere: *to bite* **(morso)**

morire (e.): *to die* **(morto)**

muoversi (e.): *to move* **(mosso)**

nascere (e.): *to be born* **(nato)**

nascondere: *to hide* **(nascosto)**

negare: *to deny*

noleggiare: *to rent*

nuotare: *to swim*

obbedire (isc.): *to obey*

occuparsi di (e.): *to busy oneself with, to be engaged in* (with regard to a profession)

occorrere: *to need* **(occorso)**

offrire: *to treat, to offer* **(offerto)**

opporsi a (e.): *to oppose* (like **porre**)

opprimere: *to oppress* **(oppresso)**

ossessionarsi (e.): *to obsess*

ottenere: *to obtain* (like **tenere**)

pagare: *to pay, to pay for*

paragonare: *to compare*

pareggiare: *to tie* (a game score)

parere (e.): *to seem* (**parso**)

parcheggiare: *to park*

parlare: *to speak*

partecipare: *to participate*

partire (e.): *to leave, to depart*

passeggiare: *to go for a walk*

peggiorare: *to worsen*

pendere: *to lean* (**peso**)

penetrare: *to penetrate*

pensare: *to think*

pentire (e.): *to regret*

percepire (isc): *to perceive*

perdere: *to lose* (**perso, perduto**)

perdonare: *to forgive, to pardon*

permettere: *to allow* (like **mettere**)

permettersi: *to afford* (like **mettere**)

pescare: *to fish*

piacere (e.): *to like* (**piaciuto**)

piangere: *to cry* (**pianto**)

picchiare: *to hit*

piegare: *to fold*

piovere (e.): *to rain*

porre: *to put, to lay down, to pose* (a question) (**posto**)

potere: *to be able to*

praticare: *to practice*

preferire (isc): *to prefer*

pregare: *to pray, to beg*

prendere: *to take, to have* (**preso**)

prenotare: *to make a reservation*

preoccuparsi (e.): *to worry*

preparare: *to prepare*

prepararsi (e.): *to get ready*

prestare: *to lend*

presumere: *to presume, to imagine* (**presunto**)

pretendere: *to expect* (**preteso**)

privare: *to deprive*

produrre: *to produce* (**prodotto**)

proibire (isc): *to prohibit, to forbid*

promettere: *to promise* (like **mettere**)

proporre: *to propose* (like **porre**)

proteggere: *to protect* (**protetto**)

pubblicare: *to publish*

pulire (isc): *to clean*

pungere: *to sting* (**punto**)

punire (isc): *to punish*

puzzare: *to smell* (something smells)

raccogliere: *to gather, to pick, to pluck* (like **cogliere**)

raccontare: *to recount*

radersi (e.): *to shave* (**raso**)

raggiungere: *to reach, to meet* (like **giungere**)

ragionare: *to reason*

rallentare: *to slow down*

rassegnarsi (e.): *to resign oneself*

reagire (isc): *to react*

reggere: *to hold* (**retto**)

rendere: *to render, to make* (**reso**)

rendersi conto: *to realize* (like **rendere**)

resistere: *to resist* **(resistito)**

respingere: *to push away* (like **spingere**)

respirare: *to breathe*

restituire (isc): *to give back*

ricevere: *to receive*

richiedere: *to request* (like **chiedere**)

riciclare: *to recycle*

riconoscere: *to recognize* (like **conoscere**)

ricordare: *to remember*

riempire: *to fill*

ridere: *to laugh* **(riso)**

rientrare (e.): *to go, come back home*

rifugiare: *to take refuge*

rifiutare: *to refuse, to reject*

riflettere: *to reflect*

rilassarsi: *to relax*

rimanere (e.): *to remain, to stay* **(rimasto)**

ringraziare: *to thank*

ripetere: *to repeat*

risolvere: *to resolve* **(risolto)**

risparmiare: *to save*

rispondere: *to answer* **(risposto)**

ritenere: *to deem, to think* (like **tenere**)

ritirare (e.): *to withdraw*

ritornare (e.): *to return*

riuscire (e.): *to be able to, to succeed at doing something* (like **uscire**)

rivolgersi (e.): *to turn to someone (with a question, usually)* **(rivolto)**

rompere: *to break* **(rotto)**

salire (e.): *to go up, to get on*

saltare: *to jump*

salutare: *to greet*

salvare: *to save*

sanguinare: *to bleed*

sapere: *to know*

saziare: *to satiate*

sbagliare: *to make a mistake*

sbarcare: *to disembark*

scalare: *to climb*

scaldare: *to heat up*

scambiare: *to exchange something, to mistake something for something else*

scappare: *to run away*

scatenare: *to unleash, to give free reign to (to go wild)*

scattare: *to sprint, to snap a photo*

scavare: *to dig, to excavate*

scegliere: *to choose* **(scelto)**

scendere (e.): *to go down, to get off* **(sceso)**

scherzare: *to joke*

schiaffeggiare: *to slap*

sciare: *to ski*

sciogliere: *to melt* **(sciolto)**

scolpire (isc): *to sculpt*

scomparire: *to disappear* (like **apparire**)

sconfiggere: *to defeat* **(sconfitto)**

sconvolgere: *to upset* **(sconvolto)**

scoprire: *to uncover, to discover, to reveal* (like **coprire**)

scrivere: *to write* **(scritto)**

scusarsi (e.): *to apologize, to excuse oneself*

sdegnare: *to scorn*

sedersi (e.): *to sit down*

sedurre: *to seduce* (**sedotto**)

seguire: *to follow*

sembrare (e.): *to seem*

sentire: *to hear, to taste, to feel, to touch*

sentirsi (e.): *to feel* (well, poorly, happy)

seppellire (isc): *to bury* (**sepolto, seppellito**)

sequestrare: *to kidnap*

servire: *to serve*

sfidare: *to challenge*

sfruttare: *to exploit*

sistemare: *to arrange, to put something in order*

sistemarsi (e.): *to settle down*

smettere: *to quit* (doing something) (like **mettere**)

soffiare: *to blow*

soffrire: *to suffer* (like **offrire**)

sognare: *to dream*

sopportare: *to stand, to bear* (I can't stand him), *to support*

sopravvivere: *to survive* (like **vivere**)

sorridere: *to smile* (like **ridere**)

sorvegliare: *to watch closely, to supervise*

sostenere: *to support, to sustain, to maintain* (like **tenere**)

sparare: *to shoot*

sparecchiare: *to clear the table*

spaventare: *to frighten*

spazzolare: *to brush*

specchiarsi (e.): *to look at oneself in the mirror*

spedire (isc): *to send, to mail*

spegnere: *to turn off, to extinguish* (**spento**)

spendere: *to spend* (like **pendere**)

sperare: *to hope*

spettegolare: *to gossip*

spezzare: *to break apart*

spiare: *to spy, to see*

spiegare: *to explain*

spingere: *to push* (**spinto**)

spogliarsi (e.): *to get undressed*

sporcarsi (e.): *to get dirty*

sporgere: *to stick out, to hold out* (**sporto**)

sposarsi (e.): *to get married*

spostare: *to move something, to shift*

sprecare: *to waste*

sprezzare: *to despise, to scorn*

spruzzare: *to spray*

sputare: *to spit*

stabilire (isc): *to establish*

staccare: *to detach*

stampare: *to print* (from a printer)

stancare: *to tire*

stancarsi (e.): *to get tired*

stare (e.): *to stay*

starnutire (isc.): *to sneeze*

stendere: *to lay, to hang* (clothes on a line) (**steso**)

stracciare: *to tear up*

studiare: *to study*

stuprare: *to rape*

succedere (e.): *to happen* (**successo**)

succhiare: *to suck*

sudare: *to sweat*

suggerire (isc): *to suggest*

suonare: *to play an instrument*

superare: *to overcome*

svegliarsi (e.): *to wake up*

svitare: *to unscrew*

tacere: *to be quiet* **(taciuto)**

tagliare: *to cut*

telefonare: *to phone*

tenere: *to keep, to hold, to take*

tirare: *to throw (a ball)*

toccare: *to touch*

togliere: *to remove, to take away* **(tolto)**

torcere: *to twist, to wring* **(torto)**

tormentare: *to torment*

tornare (e.): *to return*

tossire (isc): *to cough*

tradire (isc): *to betray*

tradurre: *to translate* **(tradotto)**

trafiggere: *to pierce through, transfix* (like **sconfiggere**)

trascinare: *to drag*

trascorrere: *to spend time* **(correre)**

trascurare: *to neglect*

trasferirsi (isc) (e.): *to move (locations)*

traslocare: *to move houses*

trattare di: *to be about*

trattarsi di (e.): *to be a matter of*

truccarsi (e.): *to put on make up*

uccidere: *to kill* **(ucciso)**

urlare: *to shout, to scream*

usare: *to use*

uscire (e.): *to go out*

vedere: *to see* **(visto, veduto)**

vegliare: *to stay awake, to keep vigil*

vendere: *to sell*

venire (e.): *to come*

vergognarsi (e.): *to be ashamed, to be embarrassed*

vestirsi (e.): *to get dressed*

viaggiare: *to travel*

vincere: *to win* **(vinto)**

violare: *to violate*

violentare: *to rape*

visitare: *to visit*

vivere: *to live* **(vissuto)**

volare: *to fly*

volere: *to want*

voltarsi (e.): *to turn around*

zoppicare: *to limp*

Appendix B
English-to-Italian Glossary

●●●

*H*ere is a list of all of the verbs from Appendix A, except here they are in English first.

to abandon: **abbandonare**

to accelerate: **accellerare**

to accept: **accettare**

to accompany, to go with: **accompagnare**

to add: **aggiungere** (like **giungere**)

to admire: **ammirare**

to admit: **ammettere (ammesso)**

to adopt: **adottare**

to adore: **adorare**

to afflict: **affliggere (afflitto)**

to afford (e.): **permettersi** (like **mettere**)

to agree: **consentire**

to alienate: **alienare**

to allow: **permettere** (like **mettere**)

to analyze: **analizzare**

to answer: **rispondere**

to apologize, to excuse oneself (e.): **scusarsi**

to appear (e.): **apparire (apparso)**

to arrange, to put something in order: **sistemare**

to arrange, to set out: **disporre** (like **porre**)

to arrive (e.): **arrivare**

to arrive, to reach, to get as far as: **giungere (giunto)**

to ask for: **chiedere (chiesto)**

to attend, to frequent: **frequentare**

to attend, to witness: **assistere**

to attract: **attrarre (attratto)**

to avoid: **evitare**

to be (e.): **essere (stato)**

to be a matter of (e.): **trattarsi di**

to be able to, to succeed at doing something (e.): **riuscire** (like **uscire**)

to be able to: **potere**

to be about: **trattare di**

to be ashamed, to be embarrassed (e.): **vergognarsi**

to be bored (e.): **annoiarsi**

to be born (e.): **nascere (nato)**

to be called (e.): **chiamarsi**

to be confused (e.): **confondersi** (like **confondere**)

to be excited, to be stirred, to be touched, moved (e.): **emozionarsi**

to be interested in, to take an interest in (e.): **interessarsi di**

to be passionate about (e.): **appassionarsi**

to be quiet: **tacere (taciuto)**

to be satisfied with (e.): **accontentarsi di**

to be surprised, to be amazed (e.): **meravigliarsi**

to be under the illusion, to cherish the (false) *hope* (e.): **illudersi (illuso)**

to become angry (e.): **arrabbiarsi**

to become (e.): **diventare**

to begin: **cominciare**

to behave (e.): **comportarsi**

to belong to: **appartenere** (like **tenere**)

to betray: **tradire (isc)**

to bite: **mordere (morso)**

to blame: **biasimare**

to bleed: **sanguinare**

to bless: **benedire** (like **dire**)

to block, to be stuck: **bloccare**

to blow up: **gonfiare**

to blow: **soffiare**

to board (a boat or plane): **imbarcare**

to boil: **bollire**

to bother: **annoiare**

to bow: **inchinare**

to braid: **intrecciare**

to brake, to curb: **frenare**

to break: **rompere (rotto)**

to break apart: **spezzare**

to breathe: **respirare**

to brush: **spazzolare**

to build: **costruire (isc)**

to burn: **bruciare**

to bury: **seppellire (sepolto** and **seppellito)**

to busy oneself, to be engaged in (with regard to a profession) (e.): **occuparsi di**

to buy: **comprare**

to call: **chiamare**

to caress, to pet: **accarezzare**

to cede: **cedere**

to celebrate: **festeggiare**

to challenge: **sfidare**

to change ones clothes (e.): **cambiarsi**

to chatter: **chiacchierare**

to check, to check up on, to verify: **controllare**

to choose: **scegliere (scelto)**

to clean: **pulire (isc)**

to clear the table: **sparecchiare**

to climb: **scalare**

to close: **chiudere (chiuso)**

to collaborate: **collaborare**

to come (e.): **venire**

to commit: **commettere** (like **mettere**)

to compare: **paragonare**

to compete: **competere**

to complain (e.): **lamentarsi**

to compliment: **complimentare**

to compose: **comporre** (like **porre**)

to concede, to award: **concedere (concesso)**

to conceive: **concepire (isc)**

to conclude: **concludere (concluso)**

to confuse: **confondere (confuso)**

to consist: **consistere (consistito)**

to consume, to wear down: **consumare**

to continue: **continuare**

to contribute: **contribuire (isc)**

to convert: **convertire**

to convince: **convincere** (like **vincere**)

to cook: **cuocere (cotto)**

to correct: **correggere (correto)**

to corrupt: **corrompere (corrotto)**

to cost: **costare (costa, costano)**

to cough: **tossire (isc)**

to cover: **coprire (coperto)**

to cross (a street, a bridge): **attraversare**

to cross (your leg, your fingers): **incrociare**

to cry: **piangere (pianto)**

to cultivate, to grow: **coltivare**

to curse: **maledire** (like **dire**)

to cut: **tagliare**

to dance: **ballare**

to decide: **decidere (deciso)**

to declare, to state: **dichiarare**

to deduce: **dedurre (dedotto)**

to deem, to think: **ritenere**

to defeat: **sconfiggere (sconfitto)**

to defend: **difendere (difeso)**

to define, to determine, to fix or settle: **determinare**

to demand: **esigere (esatto)**

to deny: **negare**

to depend: **dipendere** (like **pendere**)

to deprive: **privare**

to deserve: **meritare**

to desire, to wish: **desiderare**

to despair: **disperare**

to despise, to scorn: **sprezzare**

to destroy: **distruggere (distrutto)**

to detach: **staccare**

to die (e.): **morire (morto)**

to dig, to excavate: **scavare**

to direct, to manage: **dirigere (diretto)**

to disappear: **scomparire** (like **apparire**)

to disappoint: **deludere (deluso)**

to discuss, to argue: **discutere (discusso)**

to disembark: **sbarcare**

to disperse: **disperdere** (like **perdere**)

to displease, to be sorry: **dispiacere** (like **piacere**)

to distract: **distrarre (distratto)**

to distribute: **distribuire (isc.)**

to do, to make: **fare (fatto)**

to doubt: **dubitare**

to drag: **trascinare**

to draw: **disegnare**

to dream up: **fantasticare**

to dream: **sognare**

to dress (a salad or a pasta dish, for example): **condire (isc.)**

to drink: **bere (bevuto)**

to drive, to bring about: **condurre (condotto)**

to drive: **guidare**

to drown: **annegare**

to dry: **asciugare**

to earn: **guadagnare**

to eat: **mangiare**

to educate, to train: **educare**

to elect: **eleggere (eletto)**

to eliminate: **eliminare**

to embarrass, to puzzle, to bewilder:
imbarazzare

to enclose: **accludere (accluso)**

to encourage: **incoraggiare**

to end, to finish: **finire (isc.)**

to enjoy: **godere**

to enlarge: **ingrandire (isc)**

to enquire, to get information about (e.):
informarsi

to enroll in (e.): **iscriversi (inscritto)**

to enter (e.): **entrare**

to entertain: **intrattenere**

to entrust: **affidare**

to erase, to cancel: **cancellare**

to establish: **stabilire (isc)**

to evoke: **evocare**

to exalt: **esulatare**

to examine: **esaminare**

*to exchange something, to mistake something
for something else:* **scambiare**

to excite: **eccitare**

to exclude: **escludere (escluso)**

to exhibit: **esibire (isc)**

to expand: **espandere (espanso)**

to expect: **pretendere (preteso)**

to expect (e.): **aspettarsi**

to expel: **espellere (espulso)**

to explain: **spiegare**

to explode: **esplodere (esploso)**

to exploit: **sfruttare**

to explore: **esplorare**

to extract: **estrarre (estratto)**

to face or deal with: **affrontare**

to fail: **fallire (isc)**

to fall (e.): **cascare**

to fall in love (e.): **innamorarsi**

to fall (e.): **cadere**

to fasten, to store, to obsess: **fissare**

to fasten: **allacciare**

to favor to (do the) *honor, to try* (some food):
favorire (isc.)

to feel (well, poorly, happy) (e.): **sentirsi**

to fight, to quarrel: **litigare**

to fill: **riempire**

to film: **filmare**

to find out about something (e.): **informarsi**

to fire someone: **licenziare**

to fish: **pescare**

to fix something: **accomodare**

to fix: **aggiustare**

to flatter: **lusingare**

to flee: **fuggire**

to float: **galleggiare**

to fly: **volare**

to fold: **piegare**

to follow: **seguire**

to forget: **dimenticare**

to forgive, to pardon: **perdonare**

to form, to shape: **formare**

to free: **liberare**

to frighten: **spaventare**

to fry: **friggere (fritto)**

to furnish: **ammobiliare**

to gain weight, to get fat (e.): **ingrassare**

to gather, to pick, to pluck: **raccogliere** (like **cogliere**)

to generate: **generare**

to get a tan (e.): **abbronzarsi**

to get dirty (e.): **sporcarsi**

to get dressed (e.): **vestirsi**

to get married (e.): **sposarsi**

to get ready (e.): **prepararsi**

to get tired (e.): **stancarsi**

to get undressed (e.): **spogliarsi**

to get up (e.): **alzarsi**

to get used to (e.): **abituarsi**

to give: **dare (dato)**

to give back: **restituire (isc)**

to go away, to depart, to leave, to take off (e.): **allontanarsi**

to go crazy (e.): **impazzire (isc)**

to go for a walk: **passeggiare**

to go near (e.): **avvicinarsi**

to go out (e.): **uscire**

to go up, to get on (e.): **salire**

to go (e.): **andare**

to go, come back home (e.): **rientrare**

to gossip: **spettegolare**

to graduate (from college) (e.): **laurearsi**

to graduate (from high school) (e.): **diplomarsi**

to grant (a wish): **esaudire (isc)**

to greet: **salutare**

to grow, to raise something (e.): **crescere (cresciuto)**

to guess: **indovinare**

to hand over, to deliver: **consegnare**

to happen (e.): **succedere (successo)**

to have fun, to enjoy oneself, to have a good time: (e.): **divertirsi**

to have to, to need to: **dovere**

to have: **avere**

to hear, to taste, to feel, to touch: **sentire**

to heat up: **scaldare**

to help: **aiutare**

to hide: **nascondere (nascosto)**

to hire: **assumere (assunto)**

to hit: **picchiare**

to hold: **reggere (retto)**

to hope (e.): **augurarsi**

to hope: **sperare**

to hug: **abbracciare**

to illuminate, to light: **illuminare**

to illustrate, to show: **illustrare**

to imagine, to guess (e.): **immaginarsi**

to immigrate: **immigrare**

to impede: **impedire (isc)**

to improve: **migliorare**

to improvise: **improvvisare**

to individuate, to characterize: **individuare**

to inflict: **infliggere (inflitto)**

to influence: **influenzare**

to inform, to let know: **avvisare**

to inform, to warn: **avvertire**

to insert: **inserire(isc)**

to insist: **insistere (insistito)**

to intervene (e.): **interrogare**

to invite: **invitare**

to involve: **coinvolgere (coinvolto)**

to isolate: **isolare**

to joke: **scherzare**

to judge: **giudicare**

to jump: **saltare**

to keep, to hold, to take: **tenere**

to keep, to maintain: **mantenere** (like **tenere**)

to kidnap: **sequestrare**

to kill: **uccidere (ucciso)**

to kiss: **baciare**

to kneel: **inginocchiare**

to know: **conoscere (conosciuto)**

to know: **sapere**

to last: **durare**

to laugh: **ridere (riso)**

to lay, to hang (clothes out on a line): **stendere (steso)**

to lean: **pendere (peso)**

to learn: **imparare**

to leave, to depart (e.): **partire**

to leave: **lasciare**

to lend: **prestare**

to lick: **leccare**

to lie: **mentire**

to light, to turn on: **accendere (acceso)**

to like (e.): **piacere (piaciuto)**

to limp: **zoppicare**

to listen: **ascoltare**

to live: **vivere (vissuto)**

to live together, to cohabitate: **convivere** (like **vivere**)

to live: **abitare**

to look at oneself in the mirror (e.): **specchiarsi**

to look, to look at: **guardare**

to lose: **perdere (perso** and **perduto)**

to lose weight (e.): **dimagrire (isc)**

to love: **amare**

to lower, to pull down: **abbassare**

to make a commitment, to work hard (e.): **impegnarsi**

to make a mistake: **sbagliare**

to make a reservation: **prenotare**

to make clearer, to clarify: **chiarire (isc)**

to make known, to communicate, to tell: **comunicare**

to make oneself at home, to make oneself comfortable, to take a seat (e.): **accomodarsi**

to make sure, to assure (e.): **assicurarsi**

to match: **abbinare**

to melt: **sciogliere (sciolto)**

to miss: **mancare**

to misunderstand: **fraintendere** (like **intendere**)

to mount, to assemble: **montare**

to move (locations) (e.): **trasferirsi (isc)**

to move (e.): **muoversi (mosso)**

to move houses: **traslocare**

to move something, to shift: **spostare**

to move, to touch: **commuovere** (like **muovere**)

to need: **occorrere (occorso)**

to neglect: **trascurare**

to obey: **ubbidire (isc), obbedire**

to obsess: **opprimere (oppresso)**

to obtain: **ottenere** (like **tenere**):

to open: **aprire (aperto)**

to oppose (e.): **opporsi a** (like **porre**)

to oppress: **opprimere (oppresso)**

to overcome: **superare**

to paint: **dipingere (dipinto)**

to park: **parcheggiare**

to participate: **partecipare**

to pay, to pay for: **pagare**

to penetrate: **penetrare**

to perceive: **percepire (isc.)**

to phone: **telefonare**

to photograph: **fotografare**

to pick, to grasp (the meaning of something): **cogliere (colto)**

to pierce through, transfix: **trafiggere** (like **sconfiggere**)

to play (a sport, a game): **giocare**

to play an instrument: **suonare**

to pledge to reserve something: **impegnare**

to pollute: **inquinare**

to post up, to put up (a poster): **affiggere (affisso)**

to practice: **praticare**

to praise: **lodare**

to pray, to beg: **pregare**

to prefer: **preferire (isc)**

to prepare: **preparare**

to presume, to imagine: **presumere (presunto)**

to print (from a printer): **stampare**

to produce: **produrre (prodotto)**

to prohibit, to forbid: **proibire (isc)**

to promise: **promettere** (like **mettere**)

to propose: **proporre** (like **porre**)

to protect: **proteggere (protetto)**

to provide, to supply: **fornire (isc)**

to publish: **pubblicare**

to punish: **punire (isc)**

to push: **spingere (spinto)**

to push away: **respingere** (like **spingere**)

to put on (e.): **mettersi** (like **mettere**)

to put on make up (e.): **truccarsi**

to put, to lay down, to pose: (a question) **porre (posto)**

to put, to place: **mettere (messo)**

to question, to interrogate: **interrogare**

to quit (a job) (e.): **licenziarsi**

to quit (doing something): **smettere** (like **mettere**)

to rain (e.): **piangere**

to raise (animals and children): **allevare**

to raise: **alzare**

to rape: **stuprare, violentare**

to reach, to meet: **raggiungere** (like **giungere**)

to react: **reagire (isc)**

to read: **leggere (letto)**

to realize (e.): **accorgersi (accorto)**

to realize (e.): **rendersi conto** (like **rendere**)

to reason: **ragionare**

to receive: **ricevere**

to recognize: **riconoscere** (like **conoscere**)

to recount: **raccontare**

to recycle: **riciclare**

to reflect: **riflettere**

to refuse, to reject: **rifutare**

to regret (e.): **pentire (isc)**

to relax (e.): **rilassarsi**

to remain, to stay (e.): **rimanere (rimasto)**

to remember: **ricordare**

to remove, to take away: **togliere (tolto)**

to render, to make (**reso**): **rendere**

to rent: **noleggiare**

to repeat: **ripetere**

to request: **richiedere** (like **chiedere**)

to resemble: **assomigliare**

to resign oneself (e.): **rassegnarsi**

to resist: **resistere (resistito)**

to resolve: **risolvere (risolto)**

to return (e.): **ritornare**

to return (e.): **tornare**

to ride a horse: **cavalcare**

to run: **correre (corso)**

to run away (e.): **scappare**

to satiate: **saziare**

to save: **risparmiare**

to save: **salvare**

to say, to tell: **dire (detto)**

to scorn: **sdegnare**

to sculpt: **scolpire (isc)**

to seduce: **sedurre (sedotto)**

to see: **vedere** (**visto** and **veduto**)

to see: **vedere**

to seem (e.): **sembrare**

to seem (e.): **parere (parso)**

to sell: **vendere**

to send, to mail: **spedire (isc)**

to send: **mandare**

to serve: **servire**

to set the table: **apparecchiare**

to settle down (e.): **sistemarsi**

to sew: **cucire**

to share: **condividere** (like **dividere**)

to shatter: (glass, a heart) **infrangere (infranto)**

to shave (e.): **radersi (raso)**

to shine: **brillare**

to shoot: **sparare**

to shout, to scream: **urlare**

to show, to display: **manifestare**

to sign: **firmare**

to sing: **cantare**

to sink: **affondare**

to sit down (e.): **sedersi**

to ski: **sciare**

to slap: **schiaffeggiare**

to sleep: **dormire**

to slow down: **rallentare**

to smell (something smells): **puzzare**

to smell (to smell something): **annusare**

to smile: **sorridere** (like **ridere**)

to smooth, to polish (marble), *to sand* (wood): **levigare**

to sneeze: **starnutire (isc.)**

to speak: **parlare**

to spend: **spendere (speso)**

to spend time: **trascorrere** (like **correre**)

to spit: **sputare**

to spray: **spruzzare**

to sprint, to snap a photo: **scattare**

to spy, to see: **spiare**

to stand, to bear (I cant stand him), *to support:* **sopportare**

to stay awake, to keep vigil: **vegliare**

to stay (e.): **stare**

to stick out, to hold out: **sporgere (sporto)**

to stick, to paste, to attack, to plug in: **attaccare**

to sting: **pungere (punto)**

to stop a (a car, a person): **fermare**

to stop oneself (e.): **fermarsi**

to strike, to hit: **colpire (isc)**

to struggle, to fight: **lottare**

to study: **studiare**

to suck: **succhiare**

to suffer: **soffrire** (like **offrire**)

to suggest: **suggerire (isc)**

to support, to sustain, to maintain: **sostenere** (like **tenere**)

to survive: **sopravvivere** (like **vivere**)

to sweat: **sudare**

to swim: **nuotare**

to take care of: **curare**

to take an oath, to swear: **giurare**

to take refuge: **rifugiare**

to take, to have: **prendere (preso)**

to taste: **assaggiare**

to teach, to instruct: **istruire (isc.)**

to teach: **insegnare**

to tear up: **stracciare**

to thank: **ringraziare**

to think: **pensare**

to treat, to offer: **offrire (offerto)**

to throw (a ball): **tirare**

to throw, to fling, to throw something away: **buttare**

to throw, to launch: **lanciare**

to throw: **gettare**

to tie (a game score): **pareggiare**

to tie: **legare**

to tire: **stancare**

to torment: **tormentare**

to touch: **toccare**

to train, to practice: **allenare**

to translate: **tradurre (tradotto)**

to travel: **viaggiare**

to trust (e.): **fidarsi**

to turn around (e.): **voltarsi**

to turn off, to extinguish: **spegnere (spento)**

to turn to someone (with a question usually) (e.): **rovolgersi (rivolto)** *to turn up* (to happen) *to come*: **capitare**

to twist, to wring: **torcere (torto)**

to uncover, to discover, to reveal: **scoprire** (like **coprire**)

to understand, to mean something: **intendere (inteso)**

to understand: **capire**

to unleash, to give free reign to (to go wild) (e.): **scatenare**

to unscrew: **svitare**

to upset: **sconvolgere (sconvolto)**

to use up, to exhaust: **esaurire**

to use: **adoperare**

to use: **usare**

to violate: **violare**

to visit: **visitare**

to wait for: **attendere (atteso)**

to wait for: **aspettare**

to wake up (e.): **svegliarsi**

to walk: **camminare**

to wander: **girovagare**

to want: **volere**

to wash oneself (e.): **lavarsi**

to wash: **lavare**

to waste: **sprecare**

to watch closely, to supervise: **sorvegliare**

to win: **vincere (vinto)**

to withdraw (e.): **ritirarsi**

to work (as in a job): **lavorare**

to work (something mechanical): **funzionare**

to worry (e.): **preoccuparsi**

to worsen: **peggiorare**

to wrap: **incartare**

to write: **scrivere (scritto)**

to yell, to shout: **gridare**

Appendix C

Ten Common Irregular Verbs

··

Here are 10 very common verbs with irregular forms in one or more tenses. If the verb is regular in that particular tense, I simply note that fact. I also note whether a verb is transitive (t.) or intransitive (int.)

Avere (to have)

Present participle: avuto **Gerund:** avendo

Present indicative: ho, hai, ha, abbiamo, avete, hanno

Present perfect: (t.) ho avuto

Past absolute: ebbi, avesti, ebbe, avemmo, aveste, ebbero

Imperfect: Regular

Future: avrò, avrai, avrà, avremo, avrete, avranno

Conditional: avrei, avresti, avrebbe, avremmo, avreste, avrebbero

Imperative: (tu) abbi, (Lei) abbia, (voi) abbiate, (Loro) abbiano

Present subjunctive: abbia, abbiamo, abbiate, abbiano

Imperfect subjunctive: Regular

Dare (to give)

Present participle: dato **Gerund:** dando

Present indicative: do, dai, dà, diamo, date, danno

Present perfect: (t.) ho dato

Past absolute: diedi, desti, diede, demmo, deste, diedero

Imperfect: davo, davi, dava, davamo, davate, davano

Future: darò, darai, darà, daremo, darete, daranno

Conditional: darei, daresti, darebbe, daremmo, dareste, darebbero

Imperative: (tu) dai/da', (Lei) dia, (voi) date, (Loro) diano

Present subjunctive: dia, diamo, diate, diano

Imperfect subjunctive: dessi, dessi, desse, dessimo, deste, dessero

Dire (to say)

Present participle: detto **Gerund:** dicendo

Present indicative: dico, dici, dice, diciamo, dite, dicono

Present perfect: (t.) ho detto

Past absolute: dissi, dicesti, disse, dicemmo, diceste, dissero

Imperfect: dicevo, dicevi, diceva, dicevamo, dicevate, dicevano

Future: dirò, dirai, dirà, diremo, direte, diranno

Conditional: direi, diresti, direbbe, diremmo, direste, direbbero

Imperative: (tu) di', (Lei) dica, (voi) dite, (Loro) dicano

Present subjunctive: dica, diciamo, diciate, dicano

Imperfect subjunctive: dicessi, dicessi, dicesse, dicessimo, diceste, dicessero

Dovere (should)

Present participle: dovuto **Gerund:** dovendo

Present indicative: devo, devi, deve, dobbiamo, dovete, devono

Present perfect: (t.) ho dovuto aspettare (int.) sono dovuta tornare a casa

Past absolute: Regular and irregular. Irregular: dovetti, dovesti, dovette, dovemmo, doveste, dovettero

Imperfect: Regular

Future: dovrò, dovrai, dovrà, dovremo, dovrete, dovranno

Conditional: dovrei, dovresti, dovrebbe, dovremmo, dovreste, dovrebbero

Imperative: Regular

Present subjunctive: debba, dobbiamo, dobbiate, debbano

Imperfect subjunctive: Regular

Essere (to be)

Present participle: stato/a/i/e **Gerund:** essendo

Present indicative: sono, sei, è, siamo, siete, sono

Present perfect: (int.) sono stata/o/i/e

Past absolute: fui, fosti, fu, fummo, foste, furono

Imperfect: ero, eri, era, eravamo, eravate, erano

Future: sarò, sarai, sarà, saremo, sarete, saranno

Conditional: sarei, saresti, sarebbe, saremmo, sareste, sarebbero

Imperative: (tu) sii, (Lei) sia, (voi) siate, (Loro) siano

Present subjunctive: sia, siamo, siate, siano

Imperfect subjunctive: fossi, fossi, fosse, fossimo, foste, fossero

Fare (to do)

Present participle: fatto **Gerund:** facendo

Present indicative: faccio, fai, fa, facciamo, fate, fanno

Present perfect: (t.) ho fatto

Past absolute: feci, facesti, fece, facemmo, faceste, fecero

Imperfect: facevo, facevi, faceva, facevamo, facevate, facevano

Future: farò, farai, farà, faremo, farete, faranno

Conditional: farei, faresti, farebbe, faremmo, fareste, farebbero

Imperative: (tu) fai/ fa', (Lei) faccia, (voi) fate, (Loro) facciano

Present subjunctive: faccia, facciamo, facciate, facciano

Imperfect subjunctive: facessi, facessi, facesse, facessimo, faceste, facessero

Potere (to be able)

Present participle: potuto **Gerund:** potendo

Present indicative: posso, puoi, può, possiamo, potete, possono

Present perfect: (t.) non ho potuto mangiare (int.) non sono potuta venire

Past absolute: Regular

Imperfect: Regular

Future: potrò, potrai, potrà, potremo, potrete, potranno

Conditional: potrei, potresti, potrebbe, potremmo, potreste, potrebbero

Imperative: N/A.

Present subjunctive: possa, possiamo, possiate, possano

Imperfect subjunctive: Regular

Sapere (to know)

Present participle: saputo **Gerund:** sapendo

Present indicative: so, sai, sa, sappiamo, sapete, sanno

Present perfect: (t.) ho saputo

Past absolute: seppi, sapesti, seppe, sapemmo, sapeste, seppero

Imperfect: Regular

Future: saprò, saprai, saprà, sapremo, saprete, sapranno

Conditional: saprei, sapresti, saprebbe, sapremmo, sapreste, saprebbero

Imperative: (tu) sappi, (Lei) sappia, (voi) sappiate, (Loro) sappiano

Present subjunctive: sappia, sappiamo, sappiate, sappiano

Imperfect subjunctive: Regular

Stare (to stay)
Present participle: stato/a/i/e **Gerund:** stando

Present indicative: sto, stai, sta, stiamo, state, stanno

Present perfect: (int) sono stato/a/i/e

Past absolute: stetti, stesti, stette, stemmo, steste, stettero

Imperfect: stavo, stavi, stava, stavamo, stavate, stavano

Future: starò, starai, starà, staremo, starete, staranno

Conditional: starei, staresti, starebbe, staremmo, stareste, starebbero

Imperative: (tu) stai/sta', (Lei) stia, (voi) state, (Loro) stiano

Present subjunctive: stia, stiamo, stiate, stiano

Imperfect subjunctive: stessi, stessi, stesse, stessimo, steste, stessero

Volere (to want)
Present participle: voluto **Gerund:** volendo

Present indicative: voglio, vuoi, vuole, vogliamo, volete, vogliono

Present perfect: (t.) ho voluto studiare (int.) sono voluta partire

Past absolute: volli, volesti, volle, volemmo, voleste, vollero

Imperfect: Regular

Future: vorrò, vorrai, vorrà, vorremo, vorrete, vorranno

Conditional: vorrei, vorresti, vorrebbe, vorremmo, vorreste, vorrebbero

Imperative: (tu) vogli, (Lei) voglia, (voi) vogliate, (Lei) vogliano

Present subjunctive: voglia, vogliamo, vogliate, vogliano

Imperfect subjunctive: Regular

Index

• R •

• S •

• T •

• U •

• V •

• W •

• Y •